MW00489333

——RANCHO LOS ALAMITOS——
EVER CHANGING, ALWAYS THE SAME

RANCHO LOS ALAMITOS
EVER CHANGING, ALWAYS THE SAME

Claudia Jurmain, David Lavender, and Larry L. Meyer

Foreword by Kevin Starr

Heyday, Berkeley, California
Rancho Los Alamitos Foundation, Long Beach, California

©2011 by Rancho Los Alamitos Foundation

All rights reserved. No portion of this work may be reproduced or transmitted in any form or by any means, electronic or mechanical, including photocopying and recording, or by any information storage or retrieval system, without permission in writing from Heyday.

Library of Congress Cataloging-in-Publication Data

Jurmain, Claudia K.
  Rancho Los Alamitos : ever changing, always the same / Claudia Jurmain, David Lavender, and Larry L. Meyer.
    p. cm.
  Includes bibliographical references and index.
  ISBN 978-1-59714-148-2 (pbk. : alk. paper) -- ISBN 978-1-59714-149-9 (hardcover : alk. paper)
  1. Rancho Los Alamitos (Long Beach, Calif.)--History. 2. Ranch life--California--Long Beach--History. 3. Long Beach (Calif.)--History. 4. Long Beach (Calif.)--Social life and customs. 5. Social change--California--Long Beach--History. I. Lavender, David Sievert, 1910-2003. II. Meyer, Larry L., 1933- III. Title.
  F869.L7J87 2011
  979.4'93--dc22
                        2010040732

Cover Art: The Old Garden, 1928. Tradition has it that Abel Stearns and Arcadia Bandini Stearns planted the pepper tree.
        Photograph by Albert E. Cawood.
Opposite title page: Geranium Walk, 1928. Photograph by Albert E. Cawood.
Book Design: Lorraine Rath

Orders, inquiries, and correspondence should be addressed to:
        Heyday
        P. O. Box 9145, Berkeley, CA 94709
        (510) 549-3564, Fax (510) 549-1889
        www.heydaybooks.com

Printed in Hong Kong by Global Interprint

10 9 8 7 6 5 4 3 2 1

For Marian Burton and Loretta Berner

CONTENTS

FOREWORD

Kevin Starr

RANCHO LOS ALAMITOS is a place soaked through in time and history. While dependent upon each other, time and history are nevertheless distinct from each other. Extending backwards in calendar time to its founding in 1790, Rancho Los Alamitos, as presented in this elegant book, is the product of a history embracing every decade from the late eighteenth century of Alta California of New Spain to the headlong American present of Long Beach, California. Indeed, were we only to have the story of Rancho Los Alamitos at hand, we might still be able to reconstruct the outlines and successive phases of this region's history from the immemorial era of the Tongva village Povuu'ngna on the Rancho site; to the mission and rancho era itself, as expressed in the land disputes between Rancho Los Alamitos and Mission San Gabriel Arcángel; to the brief but busy Mexican era of Don Abel Stearns and his Californio wife, Arcadia Bandini; to the Gold Rush itself, which first brought the Flints, Bixbys, and in turn the Hathaways from Maine to California and proved so profitable to the cattle business of the Rancho; to the rise of California as a corporate-capitalist entity in the 1870s, as expressed in the decade-long ownership of the Rancho as an investment by San Francisco–based financier Michael Reese; to the Americanization of Southern California during the loving stewardship of the Rancho by John and Susan Bixby in the boom of the 1880s; and, finally, to the long and creative tenure of Fred and Florence Bixby into the mid-twentieth century, which saw the rise of Southern California to global status as a center of commerce and culture.

Such is the perspective of history, perceived as linear development, process, dialectic, cause and effect. This linear history, moreover, is not only connected to place but is the result of place as well. From this perspective, the time frame of Rancho Los Alamitos is as cosmic and immemorial as the planet itself and hence pushes time back into the eons. The very earth of Rancho Los Alamitos and its artesian wells emerged in planetary time and offered Hispanic, Yankee, Basque, Belgian, and Japanese vaqueros, shepherds, and farmers a place and support system in which to herd cattle and sheep, to grow wheat and sugar beets, to plant pepper trees, jacaranda, cacti, and flowers around a ranch house whose adobe walls were taken from the very ground itself. From this perspective, the history of Rancho Los Alamitos constitutes a creative interaction between human time and stewardship, as expressed in animal husbandry and agriculture, and the goodness of nature when treated over time with proper regard. Here, then, is a Rancho Los Alamitos time sequence—of water, earth, weather, earthquake, and cleansing fire—as chthonic and linear as the planet itself.

But there is also Povuu'ngna time to take into consideration. Evident on the Rancho site are layers of midden left behind by thousands of years of feasting by the Tongva people on the abundant shellfish available from the nearby ocean. As a settlement, Povuu'ngna was once the very epicenter of a long-lasting Tongva ascendancy extending across thirty square miles of the Los Angeles plain as far as the foothills of the Santa Monica and San Gabriel mountains, proceeding out to sea to Catalina Island, traveled to by seagoing canoe, extending north into the coastal mountains of Malibu and sweeping south down the beaches and coastal valleys. Povuu'ngna time was and remains mythic: connected, that is, to the story of creation, the chieftainship of Ouiot and the handing down of law by the man-god Chinigchinich, who gave his people their beliefs, laws, and ceremonies and then ascended into the heavens, a narrative that evangelizing Franciscan missionaries found rather easy to recast into Christian terms.

For the surviving Gabrielino-Tongva people of the region, however, Povuu'ngna is more than a sum total of archaeological evidence, anthropological speculation, even the mythic history so lovingly recorded by the Franciscan missionary Gerónimo Boscana, as important as that record might be. Povuu'ngna is the living present, proof to the Gabrielino-Tongva people that they continue to exist. Povuu'ngna is a sacred place surviving in memory, imagination, and, yes, in real-time experience itself. Perceived through Gabrielino-Tongva eyes, Povuu'ngna is as real as the campus of California State University, Long Beach, or the crowded acres of suburban housing pressing in upon the miraculously preserved Rancho site. Perceived in the alembic of Povuu'ngna and Gabrielino-Tongva time—recurrent, cyclical, interactive, and ever present—Rancho Los Alamitos, as place and as the history presented in the text, photographs, and archival material of this book, becomes, as the subtitle of this history indicates, ever changing, always the same.

Thanks to Povuu'ngna, visitors to Rancho Los Alamitos as well as readers of this book have an opportunity to experience an omnipresent and interactive encounter with Southern California past, present, and future. Each aspect of the Rancho and each detail of the human story connected to it emerge as part of an omnipresent whole. The adobe walls of the ranch house can thus be analyzed from the perspective of architectural history—a one-story adobe, extended in the Mexican era with a new wing improved through the woodcraft of New England, covered with patterned wallpaper, paintings, and portraits in the Victorian period, modernized by skylight, plumbing, and electricity in the early decades of the twentieth century. But this surviving residence also reverberates with the living dreams, the hopes, triumphs, and travails of the men and women whose lives were lived within its walls. True, they expressed their linear time in the ranch house across successive eras, but for us today, empowered by Povuu'ngna time, the record of their lives can speak cumulatively of that search for a better life, a better way of living, that is at the core of the Southern California experience. Had the ranch house not been so adaptive to and receptive of the hopes of successive generations, it would have long since been demolished or, in an earlier era, left to be eroded by the fierce rains of the region back into the earth from which it came. The comfortable improvements made by Don Abel Stearns for his wife suggest the festive social life of Old California surviving into the first decades of the American era. John W. Bixby's great Red Barn was lost to fire in 1947, but photographs and descriptions of its three-story-high magnificence—its soaring interior spaces, the elegance of its lofts and stalls served by a network of catwalks, the light that slanted cathedral-like through its windows, its noble exterior lines and proportions—continue to testify to that pursuit of modern and efficient agriculture characteristic of Southern California in the late nineteenth century, when a generation of highly formed and aspiring New Englanders and Midwesterners turned to the land in search of livelihood and a better way of life. John and Susan Bixby's love of education is manifest in the grand parlor bookcase, no doubt crafted by John, filled with classics and volumes of California history in the Works of Hubert Howe Bancroft, still testifying to the late nineteenth-century belief that life on the land did not have to mean a repudiation of culture. Far from it: each ranch house was to become in and of itself a center of civility. In later years, Florence Bixby would embellish the family's growing library with Native American baskets, placed alongside her cherished English and American books, as if to suggest some subliminal sense of connection and continuity. The pepper trees planted by Susan and John W. Bixby and the Rose Garden, Jacaranda Walk, and Cypress Patio established by Florence Bixby in the 1920s continue to emanate hope for the transformation of Southern California into a neo-Mediterranean littoral through architecture and landscape design. Attached to this neo-Mediterranean dream was the hope—introduced

by Charles Dudley Warner in *Our Italy* (1891) and continuing through a course of commentary in the decades to follow—that American life in Southern California would shed some of the hard edges of the industrial East and agricultural Midwest and achieve a polish and graciousness reflective of Italy and Mediterranean culture.

Povuu'ngna time, Gabrielino-Tongva time, encourages us to recover and fuse into a living present all those peoples who derived their livelihood from the Rancho across the decades: the vaqueros riding after longhorn cattle on a thousand hills, the sheep shearers, Mexican and Basque, who arrived on the Rancho at shearing time, their thick black hair swathed in red bandanas, looking—so Sarah Bixby Smith would later remember them in *Adobe Days* (1925)—like bravos in an Italian opera, divesting each sheep of its winter wool in record time, then sitting down to abundant meals at long tables or in the cool of the evening lingering over cigarettes and coffee, laughter and talk, guitar music, some singing of songs from long ago. Equally important, if slightly less flamboyant, are the Chinese workers who sustained the agriculture of California through the 1870s, men condemned, through the exclusion by federal law of further immigration, to live without families, knowing that if they returned to China to marry they would most likely not be allowed back into the U.S., and so growing old immersed in solitude and hard work. Present in this workers' company as well are the hardscrabble hired hands of the American era—lean, sinewy men, with their faces lined beyond their years, gaps in their teeth, limbs twisted from broken bones not properly set, and other marks of life on a rugged frontier. Belgian tenant farmers succeeded these frontier types at the turn of the century and in the early 1900s: Flemish speakers with little English, family people, their children attending a local school founded by Florence Bixby on their behalf, paying a quarter of their crop for tenancy, figures from Van Gogh, or so it seemed, as they sat behind their horses atop a wagon piled high with rounded beets whose tops and stalks they had sliced away in one quick motion with a knife as they pulled each beet from the earth, leaving what they had cut away on the ground for cattle feed.

Starting in the 1890s and continuing steadily down through the first two decades of the twentieth century, immigration from Mexico into Southern California had resumed and this was evident in the Mexican families rejoining the Rancho workforce, settling into comfortable, self-respecting housing built for them by Fred Bixby, gracious people, hard-working, resilient, reestablishing some of the ambience of Old California and forecasting demographic developments to come. They too sent their children to the one-room schoolhouse established by the Bixbys and weathered the Depression through their housing and employment. Thriving in their outdoor life, dining on the abundant vegetables and dairy products of the Ranch, their children grew to American maturity, went off to war in the early 1940s, and returned to lay down the next sequence of the Mexican-American story. The Mexican families were joined by Japanese lease farmers, the last to arrive, Issei from Japan, and in time their American-born Nisei offspring, conspicuously industrious and self-respecting people arriving at Florence and Fred Bixby's annual Christmas party, the Issei in their colorful kimonos, their children probably dressed like the other American kids.

This was in so many ways a feudal lifestyle, paternalistic but benign, and so it would later seem so out of kilter with the larger patterns of twentieth-century American society as prefigured in the industrial sugar beet factory near the ranch and so evident, as time went on, in the rise of Long Beach, the oil derricks sprouting atop Signal Hill like dragons' teeth, the development of the harbor as a military naval base and commercial port, the rise of suburbia, and the transformation of nearby Los Angeles into a national metropolis. Yes, there was something old-fashioned about these working people, these tenant farmers carrying on their way of life in sub-tenant circumstances, however benevolent. Yet in later years their children and grandchildren—Belgian-, Mexican-, and Japanese-American alike—would remember this era as good times, decent times, however old-fashioned. Times, it was true, were changing, as evidenced in the automobiles and trucks beginning to appear in Rancho photographs by the teens. This sense of change, in fact, kept Fred Bixby in the business of breeding great Shire horses long after trucks and tractors had replaced these noble animals in the daily work of the Ranch. Like the Shires, Rancho Los Alamitos was by the 1920s, certainly by the 1930s, increasingly revealing itself to be an institution from an earlier era.

Still, Fred and Florence Bixby held on, albeit with their income now enhanced through divergent investments in oil, real estate, and other corporate interests. And while it is true that Fred and Florence Bixby raised their three daughters and two sons as privileged members of a solidly emergent upper middle class, they also demanded that their offspring acquire the skills and do the work of basic ranching. After all, that is how they had begun their life on the Rancho in 1898, two college graduates, refined and thoroughly modern, yet returning to the land like characters out of a novel by Jack London, determined to prolong and to make meaningful a lifestyle praised by London in a number of his novels and by Frank Norris in *The Octopus* (1901). And so while the children themselves, like their parents, were polished by social life in Los Angeles—clubs, dances, parties—and were sent off to college, Vassar and UCLA, they were also taught to ride, rope, brand, and herd in the style of the vaqueros and cowboys who had preceded them. And nowhere was this more true than in the case of the three Bixby sisters, Katharine, Florence, and Deborah, taught to ride in childhood, to work roundups and branding in adolescence, and in later life always to remember the 522-mile Trip with Father they took by horseback in 1916 down from San Francisco to the Rancho, sleeping by night in the outdoors, sometimes on hard granite, the sound of waves crashing on the nearby shore lulling them to sleep, with Katharine keeping a pistol at the ready in case of unwelcome visitors or some other untoward event. Likewise did the great public auction barbecues given by Fred and Florence Bixby in the 1920s and 1930s signal the desire of the Bixbys to preserve something of the exuberant joy of life of Old California, as an entire region now both remembered and mythologized the past.

All these good times could not preclude the inevitable tragedies of life. In May 1887 John W. Bixby, seemingly in the best of health, succumbed within days to appendicitis, dying at age thirty-nine. His wife, Susan, wore widow's weeds for the rest of her life. John's grandson and namesake, John T. Bixby, son of Fred and Florence, was killed in an automobile accident at the age of twenty-three and was mourned by parents, sisters, and surviving brother for the rest of their lives. Through the prism of Povuu'ngna, however, and in the alembic of Tongva time, these two Bixbys, so tragically lost, can be recovered in memory—which in Tongva time is also a recovery beyond mere memory—as they were

in happier times: John W., arriving in Southern California in 1871 with thirty dollars in his pocket and hoping to find, like his cousins, a better life and, like them as well, finding it married to a Hathaway sister from Maine, bringing his bride, after much work and saving, to the hilltop adobe ranch house that he had just now leased, the one built by Juan José Nieto in the early nineteenth century and enlarged by Don Abel Stearns, which John and Susan in the short time that would be allotted to them of life at the Ranch of the Little Cottonwoods would transform into a civil and productive place; and the second John, John T., lost at an even earlier time of life but now recovered in Tongva time as he stands on the beach with his brother and sisters and cousins sometime in the 1920s, a muscular and sunburnt Southern California boy, smiling into a future without limits.

Povuu'ngna time, Tongva time, refuses to allow any moment, any detail, of Rancho Los Alamitos to be lost. It all remains part of the present, just as the land and sky and hills, however circumscribed by modernity, remain the same. Rancho Los Alamitos, the Ranch of the Little Cottonwoods, has been reduced to 7.5 acres, but so has the Tongva domain centered on Povuu'ngna been reduced as well: in linear time, perhaps, but not in the time of Povuu'ngna and the Tongva people. And perhaps not in our time as well. For if only in memory, we too can be with José Manuel Perez Nieto as he rode the hills near the Pacific in 1784 and dreamt of becoming a lord of land and cattle. We too can once again hear the music and laughter of a Stearns-Bandini fiesta. Even now, it is spring and the sheepherders are arriving. Even now, the children of tenant farmers are walking, books in hand, to their schoolhouse. One of Fred Bixby's great Shires is standing in majestic repose. How could a mechanical engine ever prevail against such a noble animal? It is now 1898 and a youthful bride, Florence Bixby, is accompanying her husband from Berkeley to their new life as ranchers in the Southland. Fifty years later, in linear time, the couple, surrounded by over one thousand friends and family members, cuts an anniversary cake against a backdrop of pepper, palm, and cypress trees. All around them are at once the expectant silence of 1784 and the talk and laughter of 1948 and the sounds of Los Angeles County in the near distance. And in the company of Florence and Fred Bixby on that anniversary day are those who in their own way have before them tasted similar joys and known similar sorrows, centuries or decades ago in linear time and in the time to come in a place called Rancho Los Alamitos, Long Beach, Los Angeles County, Povuu'ngna.

PREFACE

RANCHO LOS ALAMITOS, located in Long Beach, California, is a small part of the original three-hundred-thousand-acre Los Coyotes land concession awarded to a Spanish soldier in 1790 for his service on the Gaspar de Portolá expedition. The roots of human habitation here go back even farther, though: the land once contained the ancestral village of Povuu'ngna within its boundaries, the place of origin of the native Tongva people of this region. This book will explore in detail the waves of owners, inhabitants, and eras that have washed over the land and how the place has affected its people. It relates the history of Southern California and Rancho Los Alamitos up to the 1950s through rich detail and intriguing characters. In 1968 the children of the last private owners of the Rancho deeded the 7.5 remaining acres to the City of Long Beach. Since then, in a public-private joint venture with the city, Rancho Los Alamitos Foundation has assumed all responsibility for the administration, preservation, and restoration of the site, carefully developing its educational potential.

The origin of *Rancho Los Alamitos: Ever Changing, Always the Same* dates back to 1986, the year Rancho Los Alamitos Foundation developed a comprehensive master plan to guide its now successfully completed effort to preserve, restore, and interpret the historic Ranch House, barns, gardens, and cultural landscape of the Rancho. In addition, the master plan called for a new on-site Education Center.

As part of this early process, David Lavender, the award-winning author of nearly forty books on western history, agreed to write the story of Rancho Los Alamitos in the context of the history and ecology of Southern California. Albeit brief, his engaging twenty-eight-page work chronicled the successive owners of the Rancho and loosely related their times to regional, state, and national events. In keeping with his signature style, David Lavender's lively prose grasped the distinct personality of the twentieth-century working ranch within the Southern California region. But apart from owner-centric references to the ranch hands and tenant farmer families at Alamitos, his historical narrative gave only passing reference to the presence and contributions of people who lived and worked at the Rancho. And although his chronological account began with Povuu'ngna, his history of the Tongva people ended in the past.

In the mid-1990s Rancho Los Alamitos Foundation asked Larry Meyer, a writer and professor of journalism at California State University, Long Beach, and coauthor of *Long Beach: Fortune's Harbor* (1983), to add complementary detail to the Lavender piece. Meyer's adroit contribution more than doubled the length of the original piece as he fleshed out the historical context, discussing the feats and tribulations of Alamitos owner Abel Stearns and including more information about the early Tongva people, the Spanish-Mexican and American eras, and the Long Beach environs. The core of the content, however, revolved around the owners, and despite the general context, isolated details about the Rancho operation and family lifestyle did not suggest greater patterns. The unpublished Lavender-Meyer manuscript was reserved for in-house purposes and further review.

Ten years ago the new collections management database for the Rancho Los Alamitos Archives took usable form, and with that accomplishment research to develop the new permanent exhibition for the planned Education Center began. In no time the solution to completing the Lavender-Meyer manuscript became obvious: the collections housed in the Rancho archives contained the perspective it lacked. The diversity of material within offered the voice of owner and worker alike, and the story they told together suggested how Rancho Los Alamitos was both part of, and apart from, the ongoing California experience.

Several of the collections were revealing and pertinent. Translations of the Spanish-Mexican *espedientes* (legal records) dating from 1784 documented Manuel Nieto's successive requests for land, his dispute with Mission San Gabriel, and his disparaging view of the native community, as well as the subsequent division of Los Coyotes, the formation of Rancho Los Alamitos, and the power struggle to gain land and water.

Entries found in the John Bixby ranch ledgers dating from 1872 disclosed the heretofore unknown names of diverse workers at the ranch, such as Ah-Fan Chinaman, Augustine Old Basque, John Italian, Black Frenchman, Captain Raphael, and the "Japaneese," as well as Sandy Kansas and Tom Elliot Texas herder.

The Rancho's oral history collection contains over one hundred and thirty interviews with the ranch hands, farmers, and Bixby family members who lived at Alamitos during the early twentieth century. Family members and descendants of the Mexican ranch workers, the Belgian tenant farmers, and the Japanese lease farmers offer compelling testimonials to a place they still called home. Additional interviews with Katharine and "Sister," daughters of the last private owners of the Rancho, Fred and Florence Bixby, also evoke the functional and emotional ties of the extended family which underwrote daily life at the ranch. Finally, recent interviews with members of the Tongva community document the continuing story of the descendants of Povuu'ngna and their belief that the ground at Alamitos is sacred.

Over twenty-four hundred historic photos and maps illustrate the changing landscape of Rancho Los Alamitos, the historic structures and gardens, the ranch and farming economy, and the array of faces and activities at Alamitos from the 1880s through the mid-twentieth century. Nineteenth- and twentieth-century correspondence, personal family diaries, newspapers, and ephemera measure the everyday rhythm and overriding concerns of the Rancho that bound the place to the economy and politics of the region, state, and nation during peace and war, in good times and bad. Issues of immigration and labor, environmental policy and scarce water, urban development and fleeting open space are also reflected in the collections.

The revision of the Lavender-Meyer manuscript prompted by these discoveries in the archives culminated in the publication of *Rancho Los Alamitos: Ever Changing, Always the Same*. For the most part, the work in hand reflects the chapter sequence and style of the earlier manuscript. Chapter one, "Povuu'ngna" has been for most purposes rewritten, and the ongoing story of the native Tongva people has been woven in throughout the book, as it is throughout the history of the Rancho. The remaining five chapters were edited and revised, and substantive material was added as follows: when possible, primary quotes from the archival collections were introduced to reflect the cultural diversity of worker and owner alike and give them voice; illustrative archival material (ledger entries, correspondence, diaries, photos, etc.) was assembled and grouped to show how Rancho Los Alamitos and its owners and workers fared in relation to the greater California experience; text was added to reflect recent scholarship and thought placing the Rancho within the context of historical patterns and emerging policies pertaining to economics and technology, culture and ethnicity, labor, the environment, water, land, development, and open space; running quotes

from *Adobe Days* by Sarah Bixby Smith were paired with archival material to include her astute personal observations; and finally, a new introduction brings the significance of the historic landscape together with the documented record to suggest the continuing legacy of Povuu'ngna and Rancho Los Alamitos.

The result is *Rancho Los Alamitos: Ever Changing, Always the Same*, a book which takes its title from the Education Center's exhibition as well as the Rancho's timeless quality. A publication in its own right, the work serves also as a companion to the exhibition, moreover representing the ongoing commitment of Rancho Los Alamitos Foundation to creative scholarship, education, and this exceptional place.

Claudia K. Jurmain
January 2010

ACKNOWLEDGMENTS

All the authors of this volume have, in their own time, acknowledged a debt of gratitude to Rancho Los Alamitos Foundation staff and volunteers who have established and maintained the Rancho's archives. Today this book rests on the incalculable accomplishments and expertise of David Lavender and Larry Meyer, as well as ongoing Foundation staff and volunteers. In the beginning Executive Director Pamela Seager and Curator Pamela Young Lee established the Rancho archives and increased its collections, to the lasting benefit of history. Margaret Monti, the current Archivist, made the difficult transition from paper to computer-based collection management, preserving the archival collection and enabling its use. In recent days, she has been an essential partner in preparing the complex array of selected archival graphics and photos for this publication. Steve Iverson, Historical Curator at Rancho Los Alamitos, graciously assisted in the search for images, as did Paul Spitzzeri, Collections Manager at the Workman and Temple Family Homestead Museum. In addition, Dr. Craig Hendricks read and offered comments on the Lavender-Meyer manuscript.

The valued oral history collection at Rancho Los Alamitos reflects decades of dedicated volunteer effort. In tandem, Marian Burton and Beverly Miller tracked down ranch workers, tenant farmers, and their families through succeeding generations. They interviewed all and transcribed their words from tape for the record. Without this extraordinary effort the story of Rancho Los Alamitos could not have been told.

Loretta Berner, another early volunteer, accomplished an unthinkable task: she collected the translated documents from the Spanish-Mexican era pertaining to Rancho Los Alamitos that were housed in state and federal archives in Washington and California and in private institutions. Her analysis of the difficult material ultimately led to her own manuscript, "Los Dos Ranchos" in which she fully documented the early history of Rancho Los Alamitos and Los Cerritos. Now diseased, Loretta Berner left behind work that is essential to the Rancho story.

A special debt is owed to three individuals for their scholarship. William McCawley's *The First Angelinos: The Gabrielino Indians of Los Angeles* (1996) provided the basis for the revision of the first chapter. A coauthor of *O, My Ancestor: Recognition and Renewal for the Gabrielino-Tongva People of the Los Angeles Area* (2009), McCawley has, in recent research and writing, contributed to the telling of the ongoing, contemporary story of the Tongva. Pamela

Young Lee's curatorial documentation of the Rancho's Native American collection from the late nineteenth and early twentieth centuries provided essential, site-specific detail which connects to Native American history in general. Finally, Kevin Starr's multivolume, exhaustive series exploring the California Dream in all its variations is the staggering accomplishment which underpins much of *Rancho Los Alamitos: Ever Changing, Always the Same*. Throughout the process of developing this book, we have relied on and returned to his essential work and, as always, marveled at its breadth. His foreword to this volume is most appreciated in many ways.

The vision for *Rancho Los Alamitos: Ever Changing, Always the Same* has been maintained and supported by Pamela Seager, executive director of the Rancho. She has with unerring excellence preserved, restored, and transformed the historic landscape of Rancho Los Alamitos for tomorrow's use in keeping with the institutional backing of the Rancho Los Alamitos Foundation Board of Trustees. Preston Hotchkis, board chairman and grandson of Fred and Florence Bixby, deserves special mention. At the time the Foundation was founded, he mandated that Rancho Los Alamitos must interpret the larger Southern California experience rather than take the more conventional, popular path of following his family's story alone. It was a far-reaching vision that has sustained the completion of this publication, and it revealed early on the rare insight which has always marked the Bixby family legacy at Rancho Los Alamitos.

Funding for the Rancho Los Alamitos Foundation Master Plan, including the David Lavender and Lavender-Meyer manuscripts, was received from the following generous sources: Peter Bedford, Bedford Properties, Bixby Ranch Company, The Hotchkis Foundation, The Janeway Foundation, John D. Lusk, Lusk Companies, Albert C. Martin & Associates, Peck Jones Company, Nathan Shapell, Shapell Industries, Inc., Standard Pacific Corporation, and Wells Fargo Bank & Realty Finance.

The specific development and publication of *Rancho Los Alamitos: Ever Changing, Always the Same* has been made possible through additional contributions from Mary Alice Braly, The Janeway Foundation, and The Earl B. and Lorraine Miller Foundation under the direction of Walter Florie, who has consistently supported the Rancho's effort to tell a story which speaks to the education of tomorrow's children.

Without doubt, Malcolm Margolin, publisher of Heyday, made this book possible, understanding the value within and agreeing to work with Rancho Los Alamitos for a second time, much to our delight. Gayle Wattawa, our editor at Heyday, transformed the intent into substantive style. This book bears her mark, her words, and her talent throughout. I cannot thank her enough. Thanks also to Jeannine Gendar for her careful editing.

I wish to acknowledge the effort of designer Margi Denton, who very early on developed a format for the work, which began the process leading to Lorraine Rath's inspired book design. My longtime colleague William S. Wells, designer of the Education Center at Rancho Los Alamitos, and his wife, writer/designer Linda Allison, reviewed much of the primary source material contained in this book as we developed the Education Center exhibition. Years of thanks go to Bill and Linda for their patient interest in this project, their creative insight, and their valued friendship.

Always and foremost I thank my family. Their story is the history that still compels me to think about other people and places, because in our past the journey has often led to California.

INTRODUCTION

Claudia Jurmain

> The growing habits of the place persist; it is alive.
> Each time I go back I find some new thing.
> —Sarah Bixby Smith, *Adobe Days*

A WEB OF TANGLED FREEWAYS snares its victims daily. Shiny office towers reach out to commerce across the globe and rampant growth below. In the twenty-first century Southern California is an impossibly intertwined network. Solid concrete and steel; receding rivers, trees, and plants; and tiny fiber-optic cables strung together by corporate deals defy the possibility that any landscape within this constantly changing realm could have flourished, even survived on its own terms, for centuries. Yet the place called Rancho Los Alamitos has retained a certain resilient identity.

How so? Today Rancho Los Alamitos is tucked away in a modern gated community and is for the most part obscured by the overbuilt environment that now dwarfs the prominent hilltop setting of past days. But the surviving 7.5-acre site is twice listed on the National Register of Historic Places—once for the historical evolution of its cultural and natural landscape, and once for its significance as the ancestral village of Povuu'ngna. Although the scant shell midden visible in the Jacaranda Walk is the only surface evidence of the village's early existence, Povuu'ngna remains the spiritual home of its native descendants, a belief heard in the words of Cindi Alvitre, a contemporary Tongva. "I don't see Long Beach, Cal State Long Beach, Rancho Los Alamitos...," she says. "I see Povuu'ngna."[1]

There is more. The old adobe built during the Spanish-Mexican era is now hidden within the sprawling Ranch House that evolved around its crumbling walls. The simple line of California pepper trees that first divided the raw open space of the 1880s and separated the small home on the hilltop from the vast fields below would eventually be embedded in the more sophisticated landscape design of the early twentieth century; lush greenery soon enveloped the residential hilltop, as cultivated gardens grew in quiet contrast to the nearby working barns of the noisy, dusty ranch. Today these layers of time, intent, and changing values are preserved in the historic landscape of Rancho Los Alamitos.

The restored Ranch House and barns and the gracious grounds and gardens of the Alamitos hilltop easily point to the former owners of the Rancho and its regional context, but the historical ledgers, personal diaries, letters, oral histories, and photographs found in the Rancho archives are witness to the presence and contributions of others who lived and worked at the Rancho over time. When seen together, the preserved site and related archives fully reveal the combination of nature and culture which has defined the lasting character of this exceptional place.

Located on sacred ground and under temperate skies, Rancho Los Alamitos is rich in essential resources. Without fail, this place has filled the needs of successive generations, offering a sacred place of origin; thirst-quenching water; land on which to hunt and gather, graze, grow, and build; oil to ease hard times; and in today's urban setting, historic open space—which in many ways is a microcosm of the Southern California experience.

Intertwined through history, nature and culture are one on the Alamitos landscape. Since the time of Povuu'ngna, the diverse attributes of each have recombined to meet difficult circumstances with new opportunities supporting both change and stability. In the process Rancho Los Alamitos has survived the unexpected and altered and adapted to new ways, but never has the place failed to offer hope and the possibility of home.

Today the site is a refreshing oasis offering an alternative perspective on life within a culture driven by new technology. For as always, the ongoing story of the place connects to its locale, to the Southern California region and the state—its people, predicaments, and its possibilities. But it tells its own unique tale as well.

The resilience of Rancho Los Alamitos comes from the depth of its diversity, its ready well of renewal, but its legacy echoes the enduring meaning of Povuu'ngna. This is a place of new beginnings, a place of value—ever changing and always the same.

ONE

POVUU'NGNA

A COPIOUS SPRING SURROUNDED BY A GROVE of cottonwoods once emerged brightly from the lower slope of the hill of Rancho Los Alamitos. As the water flowed across the sloughs, ponds, and marshlands of Alamitos Bay toward the coastal beaches two miles away and Pacific blue beyond, it stirred into greenness coarse grasses and rushes. At the source of this renewing spring stood a village.

This was Povuu'ngna, the sacred place of origin of the Tongva people, whose ancestral land spread over present-day Los Angeles County and a portion of Orange County, out to the islands of Santa Catalina, San Clemente, and San Nicolas.[1] Here the deity Chinigchinich revealed his truths and taught the first people how to survive, and the Tongva gathered from far and wide at the village for customary greetings, trade, and the ceremonies required to ensure the future of the world.[2] The ways of the Tongva influenced the traditional practices of neighboring tribes throughout Southern California.[3] Today Povuu'ngna is the cherished home of the Tongva community, a place of beginnings and an ongoing pilgrimage site where people honor the ancestors and their ways and find meaning for the future.

Sometime around 1822, Father Gerónimo Boscana, a Spanish missionary and an "ethnographer" long before there were such curiously defined people, was the first to record the extensive customs and beliefs of the Tongva, in his oft-cited work *Chinigchinich*. In the writings of Father Boscana, Povuu'ngna is the only village mentioned in two surviving versions of the Tongva creation story. One story comes from the inland Tongva; the other, as related by Boscana and told here, is from the coastal and island people[4]:

"An invisible and all-powerful being called Nocuma made the world, the sea, and all that is therein contained, such as animals, trees, plants, and fishes. In its form it was spherical, and rested upon his hands. But, being continually in motion, he resolved to secure the world by placing in its center a black rock called Tosaut,

Facing page: "The Creation of Man," by Jean Goodwin, from *Chinigchinich*, by Father Gerónimo Boscana. In one telling of the creation story, Chinigchinich creates man and woman from clay found at the borders of a lake. The Tongva people today are their descendants.

Ernie Salas, a Tongva elder and spiritual leader within his community, standing in the Jacaranda Walk.

and it remained firm and secure as at the present time...Nocuma, having created all the things contained in the world...created the first Indian, out of the earth and called him Ejoni. Afterwards he created woman and gave her the name of Aé. Many years after...one of their descendants...had a son, and they gave him the name of Ouiot....Out of the confines of a *ranchería*, called Pubuna [Povuu'ngna], came the monster, Ouiot. At that time, all the inhabitants were at peace...but Ouiot, being of a fierce disposition, a warrior, ambitious and haughty, soon managed to gain a supremacy over many of the towns adjoining that where he originated...he gradually exposed his ferocity, and persecuted many of his vassals, treating them cruelly, and some he put to death.

"Having suffered so much from Ouiot, they determined to rid themselves of the tyrant...A consultation was held by the elders, and it was decided that he should receive his death by means of poison...One of them was entrusted with its execution...After his death they sent off couriers to all the towns and settlements which Ouiot had governed, summoning the people to the interment of their grand captain. In a few days, so great a

collection had assembled that the city or town of Pubuna could not contain them and they were obliged to encamp in the outskirts...The funeral pile was made, the deceased placed upon it, the pile was fired, and...they danced and sang songs of rejoicing.

"...These ceremonies concluded, and before the return of the people to their different places of abode, a council was called to regulate the collecting of grain or seeds of the fields, and flesh to eat, for up to this time they had fed upon a kind of clay. While conferring...there appeared to them one, called Attajen...but they knew not from whence he came...Accordingly he selected from the multitude a few of the elders, and endowed them with the power to cause the rain to fall, to make grain, and others to make animals...such power was to descend to their ancestors.

"Many years, and perhaps ages, having expired since the death of Ouiot, there appeared in the same town of Pubuna, one called Ouiamont... Ouiamont did not appear, like Ouiot, as a warrior, but as a god. To him they were to offer presents. And this was the god,

Cindi Alvitre singing and dancing in the Jacaranda Walk at Rancho Los Alamitos, 2006. Ty Milford Photography

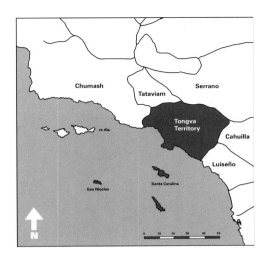

Tongva territory and neighboring Indian groups: Tongva territory covered fifteen hundred square miles, most of Los Angeles and Orange counties today, in addition to Santa Catalina, San Clemente, San Nicolas, and Santa Barbara islands. Map by William McCawley, drawing by William S. Wells, 2009

POVUU'NGNA'S SITUATION

Before the coming of the Spanish in the eighteenth century, Povuu'ngna was one of fifty or so villages scattered over the Los Angeles Basin and the ocean islands; each usually supported a population of between fifty and one hundred and fifty people, and a few sustained several hundred people.[7] The hilltop of Povuu'ngna was a coastal landmark drawing together earth and sky, ocean and land.[8] In more precise contemporary terms, Povuu'ngna is

Chinigchinich, so feared, venerated, and respected by the Indians, who taught first in the town of Pubuna."[5]

In the tradition of great ancestral teachings, the story of creation at Povuu'ngna is both the explanation of existence and a moral imperative that comes with stern warnings about responsibility and accountability, as well as the consequences of power and abuse. As Cindi Alvitre, a Tongva leader and scholar, puts it, "Here is where the dreams of the ancestors emerged."[6]

located in the city of Long Beach, about two miles north of the Pacific shore and a half-mile inland from Alamitos Bay. The ancestral village proper included the hilltop of today's Rancho Los Alamitos, which rises sixty-five feet above sea level; the surrounding private residential community; and the historic ranch land below the hill known today as California State University, Long Beach.

To say that the spiritual and cultural center of Tongva territory was well situated is an enormous understatement. The Los Angeles Basin's border on the west and south is the Pacific Ocean. The high, rugged San Gabriel Mountains form a barrier in the north; deserts and more mountains block any easy outlet to the east. Most of the time the mountains shut out the

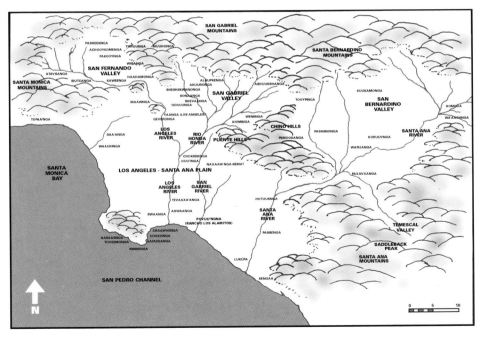

Tongva villages on the mainland. Map by William McCawley, drawing by William S. Wells, 2009

"The Brother Came unto the Sister," by Jean Goodwin, from *Chinigchinich*, by Father Gerónimo Boscana. The creation story of the Tongva people who lived inland differs from that of the coastal people. In the inland tradition, before the existing world was created there were two, the heaven (darkness) above and the earth below. The coming together of brother and sister created the earth as we know it.

intense summer heat of the interior valleys and the deserts. (Today they also hold in smog.) The air over the basin is further tempered by fog and mist drifting inland from the sea. With few exceptions rainfall occurs only between late October and early April and averages about fifteen inches a year. Skimpy though the total is, it was enough, in pre-cement days, to spread a brilliant verdure, streaked with orange fire of poppies, across the land from the beaches to the hilltops. But not too little to inconvenience humans in long sequences of crystal winter days.

This is not to say that paradise is perpetual, rather somewhat fragile and fleeting. Each spring and fall, the occasional collapse of masses of high-pressure air over the Great Basin east of the Sierra Nevada pushes roaring Santa Ana winds across the San Gabriel Mountains—winds that fan brush fires into dreaded infernos and parch the Los Angeles lowlands to such an

extent that they have been accused of everything from increasing asthma to causing crimes of passion. Rare winter downpours have created such rampaging floods that rivers have changed their courses and, more recently, have led worried local planners and engineers to excavate and line the water channels with concrete. But, at least so far, the balmy days always return to seduce humans into continuing their affair with the nature of this place.

Historian William McCawley once drew a circle around the land base of the Tongva people, curious about its physical epicenter: "The top of the circle brushes the mountains along the northern boundary, the ones the Spanish called the Sierra Madre, while the bottom sweeps over the long, narrow form of San Clemente Island. Only the distant outpost of San Nicolas Island, sixty miles out to sea, falls outside the line. Near the center of the circle, where the coastline curves inward and then turns south beneath the jutting nose of the Palos Verdes Peninsula, you will find the village of Povuu'ngna."[9]

Within Povuu'ngna's thirty-square-mile territory, there were no less than seven habitats in which to forage, hunt, fish, and collect whatever supplies and materials were needed to construct homes and make tools, utensils, and clothes.[10] Ocean, salt- and fresh-water marshes, riparian woodlands, and grass-and-herblands came together at Povuu'ngna. A benign climate with almost frost-free growing seasons, together with a fecund detrital soil washed out of the mountains during past eons, fostered an exuberant plant life on which unnumbered deer, rabbits, and ground squirrels feasted, as did clouds of migratory waterfowl that settled in wetlands formed where spring water and streams mingled with tidal inlets.

The Tongva had options in this well-endowed and resilient landscape—a rare luxury in any time. A case in point: the Tongva knew that the people living along the Colorado River were raising corn and other crops in

Kimberly Morales Johnson at Mission San Gabriel, 2006. Ty Milford Photography

river-flooded lowlands,[11] but the people of Povuu'ngna and other bands throughout the region preferred hunting and gathering to more sedentary farming. Why? Perhaps tradition, perhaps the long summer dry seasons which made farming too unpredictable, even with irrigation.[12] Maybe they already had enough food, something that tells us much about the topography, ecology, and climate of the Los Angeles Basin, as well as the prehistoric Tongva's management of their natural resources.[13]

From their advantageous location, the Tongva at Povuu'ngna took huge numbers of shellfish from nearby coastal waters and tidal inlets, and the resulting middens accumulated on the east of the village hilltop. Like the Chumash, their neighbors farther north, they built plank canoes and ventured as far as Santa Catalina Island, sometimes spearing marine mammals or large fish along the way. The life of the Tongva who lived inland was not as easy or comfortable, and their creation story speaks to a different geography.[14]

In addition to their ocean bounty, the Povuu'ngna villagers (and other Tongva) survived on and sometimes feasted on land-based plants and animals. They collected basketfuls of seeds during the harvest season, then stored and managed the harvest for future use. When the time came, they ground the seed into flour with mortars and pestles made from stone and either baked the meal into cakes or boiled it into mush. Acorns gathered from wild oaks that grew in folds of the hills were the mainstay.[15] The bitter tannic acid in the nuts was leached out in an ingenious process devised so long ago that no one recalls its origins.

Lest our glimpses into Tongva culture and practices seem mired in the distant past, Kimberly Morales Johnson, a modern-day Tongva, reminds us that "the books in schools say the Indians 'used to' do this and that. No, we still do. We still eat traditional foods; we still gather plants. When [people are] taught 'that is what they used to do,' then they just assume we're gone."[16] The same could be said of Povuu'ngna.

THE VILLAGE OF POVUU'NGNA

Historical, anthropological, and archaeological evidence indicates that the village of Povuu'ngna was on and around the site of the Rancho Los Alamitos hilltop today.[17] Father Boscana first mentioned the location of the village in his early writings; in 1852, over a century later, Hugo Reid published a series of letters about the Tongva in the *Los Angeles Star* newspaper. Reid, a Scottish cattle rancher, had come to California in 1832 and married a Tongva woman named Victoria, the respected daughter of a chief from the San Gabriel region and a land grant owner in her own right.[18] Relying on information provided by Victoria and her Tongva family, Reid described the culture of the Tongva people and the implications of early California statehood, also documenting the location of several Tongva villages, including Povuu'ngna.[19]

By the early twentieth century the name and location of Povuu'ngna were not common knowledge. New permanent structures and uses had

Rancho Los Alamitos hilltop and Ranch House, 2008. *Cristina Klenz Photography*

is covered with shell debris—the remains of the rancheria of Puvú." Among those he interviewed from the native community, José de los Santos Juncos (Tongva) and José de la Gracia Cruz (Ajachemem, the people native to parts of Orange and San Diego counties) "equated this village and spring, and the ranch house on the hill upslope...to the Spanish name Los Alamitos."[20]

Contemporary archaeological investigations have determined that the midden of Povuu'ngna—the deep, dense shell deposits which indicate the early and oldest area of habitation—extends from the front lawn of the Ranch House today east to the Jacaranda Walk, where it is most densely visible, and beyond.[21] Today the sprawling Ranch House dominates the top of the hill at Rancho Los Alamitos, but during the time of Povuu'ngna, as many as twenty-five to fifty houses stood about the village environs. From his study of the landscape, William McCawley surmises that the village chief and his council may have lived in the hilltop area where the tennis court and Jacaranda Walk are today; families of leadership, power, and wealth probably assumed the prerogatives and pleasures of high ground and proximity to water. Before the water table dropped, other inviting springs may have existed throughout the village, each surrounded by a small cluster of homes. At least ten archaeological sites have been identified at neighboring California State University, Long Beach.[22]

Tongva homes were efficient and sometimes large, from twelve to fifty feet in diameter. They were dome-shaped, made from bent willows covered with plaited mats of brush and grass which were sometimes chinked with mud to guarantee a watertight and warm home. Since Povuu'ngna was near the coast, the villagers may have used whale ribs instead of wooden posts, or preferred sea lion hides to mats for cover.[23]

The people of Povuu'ngna filled their homes with necessities and creature comforts: tule mats, soft rugs and blankets made of rabbit, sea otter, and bear

redefined the hilltop and the area below. On top of the hill, very near the Ranch House, stood the big red barn which loomed over all, dwarfing the stallion barn behind, the nearby cow barn and blacksmith shop, and the outlying feed shed, granaries, and other working barns. Sundry livestock corrals filled the spaces in between while fields of barley, beans, alfalfa, and sugar beets as well as pastures below the hill yielded feed for the cattle and horses. The busy, if not bucolic scene gave proof to the land's latest incarnation and owner—it was now the Fred Bixby Ranch at Los Alamitos.

But for those who looked, and for those who remembered the village, evidence of Povuu'ngna still remained in plain view. In the early 1900s Smithsonian anthropologist John Peabody Harrington observed that "due east of the... Bixby [ranch] house and downslope from it...in the alfalfa field...the ground

hides.[24] On the coldest mornings, a cloak of rabbit fur might feel good; otherwise the men and children wore nothing except yucca fiber sandals for traveling on rough terrain. The women wore simple skirts consisting of a front and back flap made of plant material or animal skins, often decorated with beads or fringe. Men and women adorned themselves with elaborate regalia for ceremonies. They decorated themselves with tattoos, body painting, and flowers. They wore necklaces, bracelets, and earrings made of shell, feathers, and stone beads.[25]

Work was the path to esteem and recognition in the village hierarchy. Successful hunters, fine craftsmen, skilled basket weavers and homemakers all garnered prestige within the community.[26]

Few outsiders crossed the deserts or mountains to live among the California Indians. But the resource-rich, year-round village of Povuu'ngna always attracted people. In less hospitable seasons, when Povuu'ngna or another Tongva village became too crowded

Craig Torres, a contemporary Tongva, reflects at the altar at the Povuu'ngna site at California State University, Long Beach, 2006. Ty Milford Photography

The Jacaranda Walk at Rancho Los Alamitos, 2008. The surface shell in the walkway reveals the kitchen midden of Povuu'ngna. Cristina Klenz Photography

and this caused a strain on the resources, families would divide—probably amicably, for the most part—and one group would leave to form a new village and family line.[27]

A PLACE OF GATHERING

In cultural traditions around the world, the act of naming distinguishes individual identity, and for better or worse brands character. Povuu'ngna was no exception. In the early twentieth century, during his interview with anthropologist J. P. Harrington, a Tongva named José Zalvidea stated that the name

"The Sun Ascends to the Sky," by Jean Goodwin, from *Chínigchinich*, by Father Gerónimo Boscana. For the Tongva people then and now, the winter solstice continues to be a time of great celebration and ceremony, since the rise of the sun and the return of longer days signal warmth, beauty, and bounty.

Povuu'ngna meant *en la bola*: "in the sphere" or "circle." "There must have been a *bola* of stone, maybe, there," he thought. Possibly. But *en la bola* also means "in the crowd," a translation which more likely suits the scene at the trading village of Povuu'ngna.[28]

From coastal, inland, and island villages, people came to Povuu'ngna to socialize, trade, and witness the sacred ceremonies conducted on the prominent hilltop, where sweeping views surrounded the natural stage in all directions. South past the cottonwoods lay the open ocean and Catalina Island; further west the Palos Verdes Peninsula jutted out from the coast. Beyond the plains and valleys to the north were the great San Gabriel Mountains, and to the east over the low wetlands rose Saddleback Mountain and the Santa Ana Mountains.[29] Nature's extraordinary vista surely created a powerful backdrop for song and dance at Povuu'ngna.

Lengthy, intricate dances accompanied by commemorative "travel songs" explained a family lineage's migration to their home and verified their claim to land. Other dances and songs marked passages of life.[30] Political rituals, such as the acknowledgment of a new village chief, upheld the social hierarchy. Religious occasions celebrated the fall acorn and seed harvests, memorialized the dead, and marked the summer and winter solstices. Ceremonial and practical, the ritual gatherings regulated the economy and food distribution through trade and reinforced cultural customs and beliefs.[31]

In 1542 the expedition of Juan Rodríguez Cabrillo would land at Santa Catalina, marking the Tongva's first contact with the Spanish outsiders.[32] In time the land of Povuu'ngna would be taken from its native people. In centuries to come, this same land would support ranching, farming, and development; give up oil; and offer open green space in crowded urban times. These changes and patterns, and the opportunities and spirit that drove them, are part of the compelling history of a place called Povuu'ngna by some, and Rancho Los Alamitos by others.

But first, the newcomers.

"Panes Flees to the Hills and Chinigchinich Transforms Her," by Jean Goodwin, from *Chínigchinich*, by Father Gerónimo Boscana. In the traditional belief of the Tongva, a young girl named Panes ran away to the mountains. When she by chance met Chinigchinich, he transformed her into a bird. The annual bird feast celebrating Panes and the white-headed eagle is the most honored of all Tongva feasts.

TWO

BROWN ROBES AND LEATHERJACKETS

A NEW ORDER AND A NEW RELIGION CAME from the south. Franciscans led by Padre Junípero Serra arrived at San Diego Bay in 1769 after a weary trek from Mexico. From there a segment of the newcomers under the command of Gaspar de Portolá marched northwest through the upper reaches of the Los Angeles Basin (fording the Santa Ana river fifteen miles east of Povuu'ngna) on their way to explore lands as far north as the future San Francisco. They liked the basin, and the native people in the region often fed and guided the expedition in exchange for strings of the multicolored beads they prized.[1]

In 1771 San Gabriel Mission was founded, the fourth in a chain of twenty-one missions that ultimately reached the northern shores of San Francisco Bay and went on to Sonoma. The Spanish Crown's motive for this expansion out of Mexico was the need to block any Russian advance from Alaska or English incursions from the sea. Since Spanish colonists were reluctant to settle on the distant frontier, the government in Madrid hoped to repeat in California a strategy developed in other remote lands they had colonized. The native population would be transformed, largely through missionary activity, into loyal Catholic subjects capable of strengthening Spanish claims. Politics aside, the missionaries' quest was one of religious fervor, with the aim of saving souls for Christ.[2]

For the Tongva people and the villagers of Povuu'ngna, the founding of Mission San Gabriel in 1771 was an irreversible, even cataclysmic, turning point in history. (Originally located approximately twenty miles north of Povuu'ngna, the mission was moved to its present location in San Gabriel a few years later.[3]) The Spanish named the native people (and mountains) of the immediate region "Gabrielino" after the nearby mission, but the mission's population of about seventeen hundred also included people from the Serrano, Kitanemuk, Cahuilla, and other tribes, who spoke different languages.[4] On the day the converts entered the

Facing page: Painting of Mission San Gabriel by Ferdinand Deppe, 1832. In the lower right corner is a traditional Gabrielino-Tongva home; the rows of adobe buildings to the left of the mission were occupied by the Christian Indians. Courtesy of Santa Barbara Mission Archive Library

mission, they became neophyte Christians—no longer "gentiles," "pagan," or "wild Indians."[5] By 1773, sixty-three Tongva had been baptized at San Gabriel.[6] Between 1785 and 1805, thirty-two villagers from Povuu'ngna were baptized at the mission; two more were baptized at the San Juan Capistrano Mission.[7]

The tenets of the new religious faith, their rigid enforcement, and the daily routine imposed on the native converts devastated the traditional beliefs and mores of familial village life they had been accustomed to. The regimen of planting and harvesting the fields, herding and tending cattle, learning new trades, weaving cloth, and washing European-style clothes was a world apart from the choices dictated by nature and the free movement the men and women had known as they hunted, fished, or gathered plant materials for food and other practical uses in their village homes.[8] Even in times of bounty, the repetitive mission diet of corn and grain soup was no substitute for the nutritional assortment found in traditional fare.[9]

When the last recorded baptism of a Tongva from the village of Povuu'ngna took place, in 1805,[10] the once populous area around Povuu'ngna was likely deserted. An epidemic of measles had swept through Santa Catalina and Santa Cruz islands, as well as the upper California missions, between 1803 and 1806. Coastal villages were likely also infected,[11] and this forced villagers from Povuu'ngna to join other tribes or enter Mission San Gabriel's compounds, where families were torn asunder in new ways.

In keeping with the tenets of Catholicism (and in this case Western culture), Christian Indians were allowed only one wife, regardless of their standing in the village hierarchy. Divorce was forbidden, as were infanticide and homosexuality. Throughout the missions the physical arrangement of living and work quarters reinforced the Church's moral precepts regarding extra-marital sex and birth control.[12] Single women, widows, and girls eight years and older were taken from their families to stay in the *monjerío,* the complex of workshops, patios, and crowded sleeping rooms which housed the fifty to one hundred young women who were locked in nightly under the watchful eye of a guard. Unmarried men were sometimes subject to the same arrangements.[13]

Moreover, the reality of intimidating, coercive discipline[14] underlay the moral precepts and regimen of the mission. The priests were assisted in this task by a *mayordomo,* who oversaw all daily business with the help of the Indian *alcaldes* and *regídores* responsible for supervising the baptized Indians and, in turn, doling out harsh corporal punishments.[15] One early account claimed the *alcaldes* at Mission San Gabriel were "appointed annually by the Padre, and chosen from among the very laziest of the community."[16] However, recent studies have shown that the men who assisted the *mayordomo* were often former leaders within the villages; the priests knew that their traditional roles and position of authority still commanded the respect of the mission population.[17]

Once Indians converted, their choices diminished—as did their life expectancy—since converts could not abandon the mission or its religious indoctrination.[18] Twice daily the converts recited the catechism and memorized doctrines of the priests' faith, although many continued to combine the new religion with traditional beliefs.[19] For example, throughout California crosses were decorated in the sacred tradition of Indian prayer poles.[20] But perhaps the Tongva at San Gabriel who did not perish from diseases brought by the whites learned more than they wanted to know about another god who, they were told, had also risen heavenward without leaving a material trace behind to watch over his people from above.

Some converts resisted by continuing customary practices—gathering acorns and collecting food plants, hunting game and fowl, and fishing to supplement their paltry mission diet[21] as absenteeism rose in the mission workforce.[22] Others openly resisted the coercive, disease-ridden environment through organized sporadic violence. Between 1771 and 1810, the Tongva attacked Mission San Gabriel five times. Tongva who ran from the mission were tracked down and severely punished, but the numbers alone tell the compelling story: more than 8 percent of the mission Tongva had fled by 1817.[23]

Today the Tongva community views the era with emotion and considered opinion, as contemporary scholarship continues to uncover and emphasize the overwhelming toll of the missions on the Indians. Nonetheless, although some families never entered the mission, many (especially in older generations) see it as a place of origin: as Craig Torres notes, his mother "connects to the San Gabriel Mission because that's all she knew." He continues, "It is sacred to her generation. For me and my generation it's different because of what I know, but I still consider it a very important place in our history. I don't like to speak about it negatively. Acknowledging what happened is very important, because it's part of our healing." Janice Ramos, a descendant of mission Indians, adds, "As negative as the missions were in so many ways, they allowed my great-great-great-grandmother to survive. They gave her the skills to survive in the world. They gave her the ability to speak the language, so she could tell you some of the stories, and translate. As negative as it was, it was still a meeting place where we were together."[24]

Craig Torres at Rancho Los Alamitos, 2006. Craig is using clapper sticks, a traditional Tongva percussion instrument. Striking the sticks against his palm, he marks the beat for Tongva songs and dance. Ty Milford Photography

The Tongva, now an urban-based native people without formal recognition from the federal government, remain rooted in their ancestral land, though much knowledge of many of their ancestors' rituals and customs has been lost or destroyed.

My mom connects to the San Gabriel Mission because that's all she knew. It is sacred to her generation. For me and my generation it's different because of what I know, but I still consider it a very important place in our history. I don't like to speak about it negatively. —*Craig Torres, Tongva*

Janice Ramos in the Jacaranda Walk at Rancho Los Alamitos, 2006. Her great-great-great-grand-mother Narcisa Rosemyre was baptized at Mission San Gabriel in 1844. Ty Milford Photography

As negative as the missions were in so many ways, they allowed my great-great-great-grandmother to survive. They gave her the skills to survive in the world. They gave her the ability to speak the language, so she could tell you some of the stories, and translate. As negative as it was, it was still a meeting place where we were together.—*Janice Ramos, Tongva*

The Morales family at Mission San Gabriel, 2006. Left to right: Andrew Morales; Anthony Morales, tribal chair of the Gabrieleno/Tongva Tribal Council of San Gabriel; Vivian Morales Barthelemy; Art Morales; Kimberly Morales Johnson). Ty Milford Photography

A SOLDIER'S REWARD

José Manuel Pérez Nieto (Manuel Nieto) was one of the tough leather-jacketed soldiers who had marched north with Portolá and Pedro Fages in 1769. He remained in California, still a soldier, as part of the garrison stationed at the San Diego presidio. Because troopers often were given guard duty at the missions, he almost certainly stayed at San Gabriel for indeterminate lengths of time. The region appealed to him. At San Diego, where his military duties were light, he began raising horses and cattle on the side. There was one drawback, though. The country around San Diego was hilly and often fogbound.

The Los Angeles Basin, by contrast, provided wide, flat reaches of sunnier lands. Another attraction was the little town, or pueblo, of Los Angeles, established on September 4, 1781, by a mixed group of forty-four colonists—two Spaniards, nine Christian Indians from Mexico, two blacks, eight mulattos, one mestizo (of mixed Spanish and Indian blood), and their wives and children. Such a center might someday grow into a market for livestock.[25]

Taken overall, the area seemed an agreeable place for one wishing to retire from military service, perhaps the first example of this persuasive element of California's appeal.

With the help of someone who could write (he could not), Nieto applied to his former commander, Pedro Fages, recently appointed governor of California. Nieto asked for permission to graze "bovine stock" and horses at a place called La Zanja. Earnestly

To the Señor Governor,

Señor, I, Manuel Perez Nieto, a soldier of the Royal Presidio of San Diego...say, that I have my stock, horses and cattle at the Royal Presidio of San Diego, and that they have much increased, and that I have no place to put them, having no place assigned to me. I pray Your Honor to be pleased to assign me a place which is about three leagues distant from the Mission San Gabriel, on the Road to the Royal Presidio of San Carlos of Monterey, which place is called La Zanja.... This will not prejudice anyone living at the Mission of San Gabriel and less the inhabitants of the Pueblo of Los Angeles. I earnestly pray Your Honor to be pleased to grant my petition.

Manuel Nieto to Governor Pedro Fages, Spanish-Mexican Land Grant Records, Espediente No. 103

November 20, 1784

Dear Sir,

I hereby communicate to you that on my passage to the Pueblo de la Reina de Los Angeles, the commissioner there, Victor Feliz, showed me the crops of the residents and the adjoining farmers which all together amount to 1800 fanegas [bushels].

They have finished their houses, places of safety, town house, and they are building their church, all of adobe and with platforms and sufficient extent and neatness; all of which together with the cornfields and the perseverance with which he has devoted himself to cultivation, moves me to communicate to you because I judge from that indication that he deserves your superior consideration.

The resident Francisco Sinova who has served some time as Superintendent on the Mission of San Antonio, asked me to settle in said Pueblo with his family and I have granted it him, as also Manuel Butron in the Pueblo of San Jose.

The cattle are increasing in such a manner that it being necessary, for several, to give them some extension of land, they have asked me for some sitios [places], which I have granted provisionally, such as to Juan José Domínguez, who was a soldier in the Presidio of San Diego, and has at this moment 4 herd of mares and about 200 head of cattle on the river below San Gabriel, to Manuel Nieto for a similar cause that of La Zanja on the highway from said Mission along by the oak trees, and to the sons of the widow Ignacio Carrillo that on the deep creek contiguous to the foregoing on, under the orders that they are to take care to alternately surround it continually without using subterfuges and to give the Indians or the cattle of the Mission and Pueblo of the light-maiz.

Governor Pedro Fages to his superiors in Mexico, from records of U.S. Land Commission Case 404, Abel Stearns claimant for the place Los Alamitos

(In 1852 Abel Stearns, future owner of Rancho Los Alamitos, filed a claim with the U.S. Land Commission to prove his title to the rancho. The submitted document and other records in Case 404 offer detailed information about the rancho during the Spanish-Mexican era.)

he promised not to harm "anyone living at the Mission of San Gabriel, and less the inhabitants of the Pueblo of Los Angeles." Fages granted the petition on October 21, 1784.[26]

Nieto was not the first veteran to benefit from Fages's generosity with the king's land, though only about twenty private land-use permits were given in all to loyal ex-soldiers of the king.[27] Preceding him by a few months was old soldier Juan José Domínguez, who brought his herds of cattle and horses from San Diego to Rancho San Pedro, a vast expanse of land immediately west of the future Nieto spread.[28] After Domínguez got his grant, Corporal José María Verdugo, stationed at Mission San Gabriel, asked the governor for some choice land he coveted just to the northwest of the mission and close to the three-year-old pueblo of Los Angeles. Fages granted Verdugo more than thirty-six thousand acres of what is now Glendale and Burbank for his Rancho San Rafael on October 20, 1784.[29] All were given the right to use the land under the following conditions: they would build a stone house; they would stock their rancho with at least two thousand cattle; they would hire vaqueros to prevent cattle from wandering; and they would not

San Gabriel

October 21st, 1784

I concede to the petitioner the permission to place his cattle and horses on the place of La Zanja, provided he does not prejudice the Mission of San Gabriel or the Pueblo of Los Angeles, nor the Indians in the neighborhood, the persons taking care of the same being required to spend their nights in the Pueblo.

Governor Pedro Fages, Spanish-Mexican Land Grant Records, Espediente No. 103

impact the nearby mission or pueblo.[30] Before long Nieto would discover the full meaning of this last stipulation.

Nieto's first request was answered the following day with a concession of land for grazing rights known as "La Zanja de Zacamutin," subsequently described rather vaguely in a letter by Fages as being "on the High Road (El Camino Real) from said Mission (San Gabriel), towards the Encino (oak tree)." In his petition, Nieto describes the Zanja property as being "about three leagues distant from the Mission of San Gabriel, on the road to the Royal Presidio of San Carlos of Monterey."[31]

In 1790 Nieto wrote to his former commander again, requesting additional land, "in view of the fact that some difficulties have occurred in relation to stock on account of the small extent of the tract of the land I occupy, since it is close to the watering places of the Pueblo and the Mission San Gabriel; and if it should be the will of God that the stock of the same should increase."[32] Nieto's choice? "Wherefore, I pray your Honor to be pleased to grant another place which is the place of the Encino, which will be sufficient for the stock that God may be pleased to give me." Fages did not give Nieto what he asked for, but directed him to proceed with his stock to the place of Los Coyotes, since at present there were "some difficulties in the way of giving the place of the Encino."[33] (Los Encinos was once the thriving Tongva village of Siutanga. Its natural springs provided year-round freshwater and thermal pools. Located in the San Fernando Valley, the village disappeared when the San Fernando Mission was completed in 1797.[34])

Nieto moved his family and herds to the three-hundred-thousand-acre tract of Los Coyotes, whose distant boundaries were "the river San Gabriel, the river Santa Ana, the main road leading from San Diego along the hills to San Gabriel and the seacoast." He appears to have abandoned the Zanja land in favor of his new land grant, for in 1794 Nieto's brother in arms and neighboring ranchero, José María Verdugo, petitioned for and received the land of La Zanja de Zacamutin from the newly appointed Governor Diego de Borica.[35]

The priests at San Gabriel objected to the Nieto transaction (as padres at other missions did in similar cases), charging that Nieto was encroaching on land needed for cultivation to feed what the priests hoped would be the mission's growing Indian population. In the early days of the mission, many Tongva had been lured by the promise of food,[36] and indeed the harvests at Missions San Gabriel, San Carlos, San Luis Obispo, and San Antonio in 1774 were, for the most part, ample, and the missions exchanged goods and food to offset shortfalls. (The mission padres sometimes had to resort to other, and in their view less desirable, ways of supplementing the food supply in less bountiful years: in 1795 a poor harvest caused Mission San Gabriel to send half of its Indian community to the mountains to forage and hunt for food, and place the other half on rations until the wheat was harvested.[37]) By 1805, nineteen missions and twenty thousand Indians would raise almost sixty thousand fanegas (one fanega is 1.58 bushels) of wheat, corn, barley, and beans—a thirty-fold increase in thirty years. By 1810, the missions controlled the fledgling economy of California.[38]

Responding to mounting pressure, Nieto, who had retired from the army in 1795, complained bitterly to Fages's successor: "I find myself harassed in such a way on the part of the mission that I appeal to your Worship's powerful protection."[39] In 1796, the dispute was settled. Governor Borica determined that Nieto could retain the land he had under cultivation, but the remainder was to be used by the mission to feed the Indians. This left Nieto and his heirs with 167,000 acres—*más o menos* (more or less)—still the largest land permit or grant awarded by either Spain or Mexico in California.[40]

To the Señor Governor

I, Manuel Nieto, a soldier in the Presidio of San Diego, respectfully represent to Your Honor, that my stock having considerably increased...the predecessor of Your Honor thought proper to give me permission to place my stock on the place called Los Coyotes....No one had a right to disturb me in said place; neither the mission nor an individual....With this assurance I proceeded to build a house, and spent a considerable amount in making the water ditches, for the purpose of irrigating the land, by which means I have caused it to produce reasonable crops during the last two years. Now, Sir, I am so much persecuted by the Mission.... They are continually endeavoring to force me to abandon the place to the Indians, who have no right to the land. It appears to me that since the place is not within the limits of the Mission, and seeing that I have made the same productive is the reason why the Fathers desire to take the same from me....The Mission sowed the ground that I have plowed at my own expense...without regard to the fact, that I have conducted the water to said land, the Fathers tell me not to take one drop....I only ask Your Honor to give me such protection as You ever give as the Father of the Poor, judging this case with integrity.

Manuel Nieto to Governor Diego de Borica, n.d.,
Spanish-Mexican Land Grant Records, Espediente No. 104

Monterey

May 14, 1796

Without prejudice in any manner to the rights claimed in this Espediente by the Mission San Gabriel and Manuel Nieto and to the end that the land in question may be cultivated, I have determined that Nieto shall retain the land that he has cultivated and the remainder shall be used by the Mission San Gabriel; and that this may have its due effect, let a copy of this decree be sent to the Commandant of Santa Barbara; that the same may be sent to the Reverend Father Minister and to Manuel Nieto; the lands measured at once to be enclosed in order to avoid difficulties.

Governor Diego de Borica, Spanish-Mexican Land Grant Records, Espediente No. 103

Though Nieto had to change the location of his headquarters ranch several times, he kept his grazing rights. In time he settled permanently, with his wife and four children, in a compound at a site between Los Angeles and present-day Whittier known as "Los Nietos" since so many relatives joined the family there.[41] Located in the area of Los Coyotes which would become Rancho Santa Gertrudes, Nieto's residential compound was both a supply center and a travelers' rest on the way from the southern missions to Los Angeles. Povuu'ngna lay farther south, in the area of Los Coyotes called Los Alamitos, but former dwellers at the village likely were among those who served the Nieto family as house servants and field hands, as cowhands and planters and pickers and makers of domestic implements—for a sharecropper's portion of the herding and harvesting proceeds.

Nieto's early losing battle with Mission San Gabriel demonstrates the powerful influence of the religious institution. The long-standing, bitter competition between the missionaries and rancheros over land and labor waged on. From the priests' perspective the mission model was profitable, wildly successful, and straightforward: if the Indians would become Christians and work to build the mission into a prosperous community, the missionaries would protect them and hold their lands in trust until they were able to manage them on their own.[42] Mission San Gabriel, for example, held about 1.5 million acres in trust[43]

My name is Felipe Talmantes, my age is about eighty five....I knew Manuel Nieto upwards of fifty years ago. I was in his employ, I lived with him about two years. I knew the boundaries of his rancho: they were the River Santa Ana, the River San Gabriel, the old Main Road and the Sea Coast....Nieto was a soldier and was an old man when he retired from the service. I believe the land was given him by the King.

Felipe Talmantes, testimony submitted for U.S. Land Commission Case 404,
Abel Stearns claimant for the place Los Alamitos

and quickly became the most prosperous of all missions.[44] By 1834 its enviable assets included 163,578 vines and 2,333 fruit trees in addition to 12,908 head of cattle (plus 4,443 cattle loaned), 2,938 horses, and 6,548 sheep.[45]

Semi-captive mission labor upheld the phenomenal success of the missions, an arrangement made possible, according to one scholar, by the Indians' "need for food and community life" and the "Spaniards' willingness to make them work and remain at the mission."[46] They were neither slaves nor indentured servants,[47] but the baptized Indians were not free to cast off their newly acquired identity and obligations as mission Indians.

However, finding that they could get Spanish goods without converting to Christianity, quite a few unconverted Tongva and other native peoples slipped out of the mission's reach and instead gave up their freedom by working for the pueblos, ranchos, and presidios for payment in kind.[48] Through the mid-1830s "domesticated heathens," as the census of the time described the unconverted Indians, provided most of the labor on the ranchos and in Los Angeles.[49]

In the early years Indians planted and harvested wheat for the settlers of Los Angeles in exchange for one-third of one-half the crop. They cultivated corn, kidney beans, lentils, and garbanzo beans and worked as vaqueros, muleteers, and domestic servants.[50] "The Indian for his labor," wrote Father Señan in 1796, "is given his meals and a blanket,"[51] as well as clothing and beads.[52] But the missionaries saw the opportunity as well and contracted their skilled Indian labor to the pueblo, presidios, and ranchos, withholding the payment they believed was sufficiently offset by room, board, and clothing.

The missionaries railed against indolent rancheros who paid for Indian labor and didn't mind when the workers left the ranchos after harvest: "In the town and on the ranchos...both men and women who are pagans assist in the work of the fields. Also they are employed as cooks, water carriers and in other domestic occupations. This is one of the most potent causes why the people who are called *gente de razón* ["people of reason," referring here to rancheros] are given so much to idleness," stated one missionary report on the condition of the Indians at San Gabriel.[53] Another missionary complained that rancheros "prefer to hold in hand a deck of cards rather than a hoe or plow."[54] And yet the rancheros coveted the enormous landholdings held in trust for the Indians they depended upon to work their land.[55]

Manuel Nieto died in 1804 the wealthiest man in California, owner of a large horse herd and between fifteen thousand and twenty thousand "black" cattle (cattle fit for slaughter)—all acquired at little or no cost.[56] Such is a piece of the fantasy turned real that ever since has clung to the word "California."

The vast landholdings passed undivided to Nieto's widow and children.[57] Their workers hauled wheat and other produce to the pueblo in ox-drawn carts, and while looking over their herds, one or another of them undoubtedly rode across the gentle hills of Los Alamitos—and perhaps stopped on occasion for a drink of cool water at tree-shaded Povuu'ngna, although no one knows when the village disappeared. Statements made years later say that Nieto's oldest son, Juan José, built a small adobe near the Povuu'ngna spring on the section of land called Alamitos, perhaps sometime between 1804 and 1833. The original adobe—perhaps meant to shelter vaqueros and their mounts—may be the core of the Rancho Los Alamitos Ranch House seen today on the hilltop of Povuu'ngna.[58]

NEW MASTERS, OLD PROBLEMS

In 1821, rather to the surprise and disgust of most conservative Californios, rebellious Mexico, fueled by the liberal idealism of the American and French Revolutions, won independence from Spain.[59] Mexican independence meant that the poor and neglected Spanish province was now the poor and neglected property of a bunch of zealous reformers. In 1824 the federal government of Mexico abolished the *casta* system (at one point, no fewer than fifty-six race-based categories of people existed, along with intricate rules about how they should interact in work and in marriage),[60] and two years later all Indians were made full and equal citizens under the law. In 1829 slavery was abolished.[61]

Concerned Californios were determined to assert a regional identity apart from Mexico by controlling the answers to questions affecting their immediate future: What was the role of the Franciscans now that the Indians were to be emancipated? Who would own the land held in trust by the missions for the Indians? Who would control the mission labor force? On July 25, 1826, Governor José María Echeandía issued a "Decree of Emancipation in Favor of the Neophytes" which granted Indians the right to leave their mission under certain conditions and restricted Franciscan authority over those who remained. Slowly over the next several years, men and women throughout the missions petitioned for emancipation.[62]

The residents of Alta California had reasons to take heart. Mexico opened ports that Spain had tried to keep closed to foreign trade, though the new nation meant to monitor that trade closely and collect duties that would compensate the policing agents. Commerce did not flourish overnight. In 1829 the only California port open to arriving foreign vessels was

Monterey, though "coasting-trade" stops were allowed at San Francisco and Santa Barbara. Yet trade with California's rancheros for their limited wares did increase. English merchants were the first to take advantage of the new openness, but they were quickly joined and surpassed in number by acquisitive Yankees. Both took on cargoes of cowhides, which could be turned into leather shoes and belting for agitating factory machines in New England and the British Isles, and tallow, for the making of soap and candles used by miners in Peru. Skins stripped from the lean, tough cattle that roamed the grassy land were at once worth as much as two dollars each. Payment was made mostly in the form of manufactured household utensils, foods, and luxury items more dazzling than the isolated Californios had seen or been accustomed to.[63]

To attract customers to their floating stores, the early traders sent Spanish-speaking agents on horseback visits to the principal missions and ranchos in the coastal section of Southern California. Gathering as many eager people around him as he could, the representative showed them lists of the merchandise his ship carried and announced the dates when the vessel would arrive at certain spots. The landing generally designated for Mission San Gabriel and the neighboring ranches was the shallow bay at San Pedro. On the appointed day, lines of wooden-wheeled carts creaked toward the rendezvous, laden with hides and skin containers filled with tallow. Potential customers were carried by sailors through the surf to waiting dories and rowed to the ship, where a display room was set up: axes, saws, kettles, elegant chairs, coffee, sugar, white flour, linen shirts, silk slippers, costume jewelry, fringed shawls, mirrors, fine china, and silver table settings. No doubt members of the Nieto family were among the shoppers.

To get a jump on competitors, Yankee and English hide-buying companies began stationing agents in California. These men were wise to ingratiate themselves with prospective customers. In order to own land and do business, many embraced Mexican citizenship, became Catholics, learned Spanish, and—often wooing the daughters of their best clients—married into prominent Mexican families. The new entrepreneurs even made loans against the day the companies' ships would call at the natural harbors along the coast.

Despite Mexican liberalization of trade, few Californios found it fair or just, as administered. Under Spain's mercantile system, colonies had been required to send raw materials home and buy finished commercial goods exclusively from their political masters; smuggling understandably became an honorable and necessary pastime in California, going back to the otter pelt trading of the late eighteenth and early nineteenth centuries. Though trade under Mexican rule was more relaxed, the government assumed that the cost of civil government and military garrisons should be paid for by duties collected, and smuggling became—if anything—even more rife.

RANCH OF THE LITTLE COTTONWOODS

It wasn't long before the rancheros had more to celebrate than Mexico's open trade policy and the fresh supply of goods. In 1824 the new government passed a Colonization Act, followed by a *Reglamento* in 1828 making it easier to obtain land grants, thus increasing immigration to the Mexican frontier. Unlike the Spanish land-use permits, the Mexican land grants conferred title.[64] The existing Spanish claims were recognized as well under the new land policies, though not without complication, since the informality and lack of documentation concerning the early Spanish land permits caused much confusion about rights and boundaries.

The Manuel Nieto family was a prime example. In March 1827, Juan

To the Superior Political Chief

I apply to Your Honor to be pleased to grant me the possession of the place named Los Alamitos, towards the south. On the said Rancho there is a zanja [water ditch] of permanent water; it is however, without timber except a few alamos [poplars] at the point where I intend to make a settlement....The land is in part irrigable, and it is adaptable to sowing.

Patricio Ontiveras, Pueblo of Los Angeles, March 8, 1833, Spanish-Mexican Land Grant Records, Espediente No. 57

(In his statement Patricio Ontiveras indicates that there is water at Rancho Los Alamitos, or Ranch of the Little Cottonwoods; the name of the rancho already suggested this fact, since cottonwoods generally grow near water.)

José Nieto, Manuel Nieto's eldest son, asked José Figueroa, Commandant General and Superior Political Chief of the Territory, to confirm his family's title to the land corresponding to the Spanish land-use permit given to his father.[65] By this time some members of the Nieto family had been pursuing the matter for years in an effort to divide the inheritance and forestall recent claims to the land. On July 26, 1833, after a series of complicated events, the acting representative of Juan José wrote to Figueroa, now the newly appointed governor, to request that title to Los Coyotes be given to the children of Manuel Nieto; a search of the archives had proven the legality of their father's claim. He further requested that Los Coyotes be divided and distributed among the heirs and included a map showing the agreed-upon split, asking that Figueroa issue a corresponding title to each heir.[66]

To complicate matters further, in March 1833 Juan Patricio Ontiveras, a retired soldier from the presidio company at San Diego and former majordomo of Mission San Juan Capistrano, had also petitioned Governor Figueroa for possession of a portion of the Nieto land known as Los Alamitos.

There is some irony in the fact that Ontiveras's family was already living, cultivating, and grazing stock on Nieto land at the invitation of Juan José Nieto. But Ontiveras coveted land south of where the Nieto family had built its compound.[67] Implying that Alamitos was vacant, he went on to say that "on said rancho there is a ditch of permanent water; it is, however, without timber, excepting a few cottonwoods at the point where I intend to make my settlement." He promised to stock the Alamitos with cattle, build "respectable" dwellings, cultivate the land, and plant a vineyard if the governor was so generous as to grant his request.[68]

Ontiveras's brief understatement alluded to the significance of freshwater in a semi-arid land—and moreover the value of Rancho Los Alamitos, the "Ranch of the Little Cottonwoods." Because cottonwoods flourish on the banks of watercourses, as they did at the springs of Povuu'ngna, the descriptive name of the rancho hinted that there was sufficient water there to sustain cattle and crops.

Monterey, March 29th, 1833

Let the Ayuntamiento of the pueblo of Los Angeles report if the land petitioned for hearing pertains to any individual corporation of Pueblo, or if it is considered as vacant.

Governor José Figueroa, Spanish-Mexican Land Grant Records, Espediente No. 57

Pueblo of Los Angeles, June 21st, 1833

The land petitioned for by the citizen Ontiveras is one of the accumulations of the Rancho Santa Gertrudes belonging to Juan José Nieto....It is considered vacant since there is only found upon it some wild cattle and horses, belonging to different owners, the smallest portions of them belonging to the said Nieto.

José Antonio Carrillo, Vincent Moraga, town council (ayuntamiento) report to the governor, Spanish-Mexican Land Grant Records, Espediente No. 57

To the Superior Political Chief

I, the Citizen, Juan José Nieto, a resident of the Rancho of Santa Gertrudes; with due respect, represent to Your Honor, in answer to the foregoing order; that the land of Alamitos asked for by Patricio Ontiveras, within the foregoing petition, is included within the land claimed by myself, and of which I have had peaceable possession from time immemorial: and that it is manifest that the right I have to the same is unquestionable, and this the Ayuntamiento do not deny, notwithstanding their opinion that the same must be considered vacant, since there is very little stock upon the same owned by myself, which statement proves my right to the same, since it is an admission, however weak, that the land is not vacant, and consequently not denounceable; and too, there are heirs, who besides the right of inheritance, have that of possession, which they have enjoyed for more than twenty-nine years.

Juan José Nieto, as attorney, Lucián Grijalba, Pueblo of Los Angeles, September 15, 1833, Spanish-Mexican Land Grant Records, Espediente No. 57

(The Spanish land concessions only conferred the right to live on, use, and work the land. Later, Mexican land grants gave title. Spanish grantees were required to build a house of stone (adobe), graze at least one thousand head of cattle, and have enough vaqueros to keep stock from straying on neighboring lands. According to attorney Lucián Grijalba, the Nieto family had met these criteria and enjoyed "the right of inheritance.")

Governor Figueroa required Ontiveras to provide a *diseño*, or map, of the desirable tract and ordered that the matter be investigated by the *ayuntamiento* (town council) of the pueblo of Los Angeles. The *ayuntamiento* reported that the "land petitioned for by the citizen Ontiveras is one of the accumulations of the rancho...belonging to Don Juan José Nieto"; that "it is considered vacant since there is only found upon it some wild cattle and horses, belonging to different owners, the smallest portions of them belonging to the said Nieto."[69] Somewhat compromising of the *ayuntamiento's* claim that the Nieto land was vacant, the diseño submitted as an addendum to the petition shows a casa in the approximate location of today's Ranch House.

To The Superior Political Chief

I, the Citizen, Lucián Grijalba, a native of the State of Sonora, and a resident of this Territory, with ample power from Juan José Nieto, whose rights I represent to Your Honor....[represent] That in the Year 1784, the possession of the land shown upon the map herewith presented, was granted by the Señor Governor Don Pedro Fages, to Don Manuel Nieto....I pray Your Honor, if it should not be inconvenient to do so, that a separate title be issued to each one of the portion belonging to him, as the same is marked out on the map, in the following manner. The place of Santa Gertrudes, for Doña Josefa Cota and her children, as the widow of the late Antonio María Nieto; The place of Bolsa, for Doña Caterina Ruiz, and her children, as the widow of the late José Antonio Nieto. The place of los Serritos for Doña María Manuela Nieto; and the remainder, comprehending the places of named Coyotes, Alamitos, Palo Alto & etc. for Don Juan José Nieto, who as head of the family, has made this division for the benefit of the owners; and in order to avoid all cause of dispute, I earnestly pray that possession be given to each one of the part belonging to him.

Lucián Grijalba, San Diego, July 26, 1833, Spanish-Mexican Land Grant Records, Espediente No. 103

San Diego, July 27th, 1833

In view of the foregoing petition, and of the notorious peaceful possession by Manuel Nieto and his heirs of the land marked out on the map, which possession has never been disturbed, and in view of the Espediente in which is found the concession of the land made by Governor Don Pedro Fages, to the said Nieto, and with all other matters necessary to be considered in entire conformity with the laws and Regulations...Don José Nieto is declared owner in property of the places named Coyotes, Alamitos and Palo Alto: Doña Manuel Nieto owner of Los Cerritos, Doña Josefa Cota, widow of Don Antonio María Nieto, owner of the Santa Gertrudes, and Doña Caterina Ruiz, widow of Don José Antonio Nieto, owner of the place of Las Bolsas. Let the corresponding titles issue, and let the judicial possession be given, as asked.

José Fígueroa, Augustín V. Zamorano, Spanish-Mexican Land Grant Records, Espediente No. 103

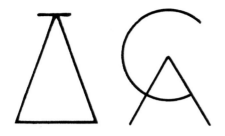

Left: Rancho Los Alamitos brand used by
Juan José Nieto
Right: Rancho Los Alamitos brand used by
Governor José Figueroa

Juan José vigorously disputed Ontiveras's petition, saying the presence of Nieto cattle verified current occupancy and use.[70] He offered an alternative tract of land, and this proposal was accepted. However, the matter of boundaries would not be fully resolved until 1837, in part due to another dispute over "the scarcity of water, which is required for the stock," as Nieto would state.[71] While it dragged on, the Ontiveras challenge clouded the title to the land that the Nieto family had considered theirs for nearly half a century and threatened their most valuable asset—water. With the help of a recently arrived Yankee immigrant named Abel Stearns, who acted as a surveyor for the Nieto family, Juan José obtained Governor Figueroa's permission to formally divide Los Coyotes on July 27, 1833, one day after the formal request.

Its 165,000 acres were divided into five large ranchos and one smaller ranch, or *sitio*. The widow of Antonio María Pérez Nieto, the youngest son of Manuel Nieto, received the old family homestead, Rancho Santa Gertrudes. Rancho Los Cerritos was given to Manuel Nieto's only surviving daughter, María Manuela Antonia. The widow of José Antonio Nieto got Rancho Las Bolsas. And Manuel Nieto's eldest son, Juan José himself, received Rancho Los Coyotes, Rancho Los Alamitos, and the small *sitio* called Palo Alto, located in the hills to the northeast of the old Nieto home site at Santa Gertrudes.[72]

In the Pueblo of Los Angeles on the 30th June 1834, before me the constitutional Alcalde and Judge of the 1st Instance, acting as delegate Judge for want of a Notary Public, appeared Juan José Nieto, native and resident of Rancho Santa Gertrudes...who stated...he sells and gives over in real sale...unto Brigadier General D. José Figueroa, domiciled in Monterey...the tract of land known by the name of Los Alamitos situated on the sea shore...and comprising 6 leagues.

It borders Northerly on Los Coyotes, Southerly on the sea, Easterly on Las Bolsas and Westerly on Los Serritos. It was granted by the Government to the settler Manuel Nieto, said concession having been confirmed unto the grantor on the 25th of July in the year 1833 last....He sells it...for 500 dollars.

—*José Pérez, Man. Arraga, Vicente Moraga, from records of U.S. Land Commission Case 404, Abel Stearns, claimant for the place Rancho Los Alamitos*

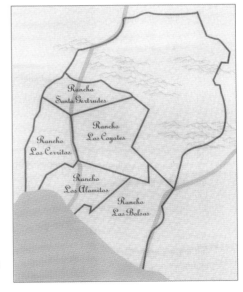

The divisions of Los Coyotes over time:
1790: The Spanish Crown grants Manuel Nieto the right to use the 300,000-acre tract.
1796: Manuel Nieto's holdings are reduced to 167,000 acres after Mission San Gabriel is granted the upper portion of land.
1833: Los Coyotes is divided into five great ranches and distributed among Nieto's heirs.

My name is José Castro, I am forty-five years of age and I reside in Monterey. I was acquainted with him (José Figueroa). He is now dead, and died in 1835 in Monterey. He made a will in Monterey. I was present at this death....I know it (Alamitos) and have known it since I knew anything. Juan José Nieto was the first occupant, he sold to José Figueroa about 1835 or 34....He [Juan José Nieto] occupied it ever since I was twelve years of age, he had on it about eight or nine thousand head of cattle. He had on it three or four large houses, one very large corral and another smaller one, some of the land enclosed and under cultivation....Immediately after José Figueroa bought it, he had it occupied by his mayordomo and his servants, and had other houses built on it, corrals, and put stock on it, and cultivated a portion of the land. I think he occupied it in this way about one year....After his death it was occupied by the same mayordomo under the charge and direction of the administrator, Francisco Figueroa his brother, lived on it himself....The stock put there by Governor Figueroa which consisted of about one thousand head, is the lowest number I ever knew it to be at one time. The reason why Governor Figueroa did not reside in this place was that he was Governor and his duties required him to reside elsewhere.

José Castro, February 27, 1854, testimony for U.S. Land Commission Case 404, Abel Stearns, claimant for the place Rancho Los Alamitos

On June 30, 1834, while the Ontiveras petition was still unsettled, Juan José Nieto, having already received his share of the distribution, sold the 28,500-acre Rancho Los Alamitos to the very Governor Figueroa who had confirmed its ownership. The price? A paltry five hundred dollars—less than two cents an acre. Although Nieto claimed he had made inquiries and could not get a better offer, a deal had been cut; Figueroa was being royally paid for his quick consent to the division of the original Los Coyotes property.[73]

Upon acquiring Los Alamitos, Figueroa formed a partnership with Nicolás Gutiérrez and Roberto Prado called *La Compañía Agricultural* with

the intent of stocking and operating the ranch. Apparently the company built quarters there for a majordomo and vaqueros, but the sudden death of Governor Figueroa in 1835 dissolved the enterprise. His brother Francisco Figueroa became administrator of the estate and manager of the ranch, at which he resided, according to one source.[74] The tedious process of settling his brother's estate would drag out for eight years—at the end of which Rancho Los Alamitos would come into the possession of perhaps the most picturesque and influential figure in California's rancho era. This new owner would soon discover that the legal intrigue and matters of title surrounding the "Ranch of the Little Cottonwoods" had not been put to rest.

MISSIONS' END

Alta California's political instability under Mexico derived from several factors, not the least of which was that the anticolonial new nation had a fractious and neglected colony of its own to deal with. Anticlericalism and the new reformist government's determination to make more land available to more people for settlement merged into policy in Alta California under Mexico's brief rule. Under Spain, California's twenty-one missions held enormous blocks of lands in trust for the Indians they were seeking to convert to Catholicism while at the same time teaching them to be self-reliant Spanish subjects. The status and rights of the Indians changed with Mexican independence: in 1826, the reformist Mexican government granted citizenship to the Indians, but it didn't acknowledge their claim to ancestral lands held in trust by the missions. The government wanted as much mission land as possible made available to non-Indian settlers (from Mexico)—an agenda which would be thwarted by the Californios who already lived near mission land.[75]

In 1833 the Mexican National Congress passed legislation to secularize the missions in Baja and Alta California but omitted any mention of Indians or the distribution of land.[76] The next year Governor José Figueroa, soon to be owner of Rancho Los Alamitos, defined the terms of secularization in Alta California.

Under these drawn out, complicated terms, the missions' common land and some property was reserved for the Indians, and they could claim shares of the land upon secularization (parish priests retained rights to churches and living quarters).[77] Any remaining mission land or property was to revert to the pueblo and the public domain. Mission San Gabriel was placed in the hands of an incompetent, corrupt, civilian administration. It quickly fell into debt, and living conditions deteriorated. In protest, one hundred and forty Tongva from the community delivered a petition of grievance to Governor Pío Pico in 1846 requesting that the mission be converted into a pueblo and its lands distributed to them. Their petition was denied in less than a month.[78]

The Tongva were still entitled to apply for shares of mission land as individuals, and a few benefited, though to petition they had to be recommended by the mission administrators or officials.[79] We don't know if any land grants were given to people from Povuu'ngna, and in any case the land around the village was private rancho land, therefore not the mission's to return.

Anthony Morales, today the tribal chair of the Gabrieleno/Tongva Tribal Council of San Gabriel, recalls that one of his ancestors was a mission *capítan* (men chosen by the missionaries from prominent families to keep order and protect mission property) and that others were "very active in the mission." "When the missions were told by the Mexican government they had to allot some of the land back to the local Indian

Anthony Morales, tribal chair, Gabrieleno/Tongva Tribal Council, San Gabriel, 2006. Ty Milford Photography

people, not everybody got land. We were pretty fortunate," he says, "I'm thinking because of our involvement."[80]

Most often, however, the Mexican governors granted the former mission lands to non-Indian settlers. The Indians who lived in villages and settlements located within these new land grants were denied title to property, in spite of the fact that their right to occupy and use the land was, at least in theory, protected under Mexican law. Some villagers sought ownership of the land as legally promised; some succeeded, but it was usually a fruitless effort. California Indians were Mexican citizens, and slavery had been abolished, but, in reality, Indians were being forced to work on public lands without pay.

The mission system had ended, but its economic practices continued. In effect, the Californios now controlled the land and the labor. But not for long: though distant and relatively hard to get to from the Valley of Mexico, the golden land's-end of North America lay right in the path of aggressive overland expansion.

When the mission systems were breaking up, and the Mexican government was taking over, our family was given a land grant.... When the missions were told by the Mexican government they had to allot some of the land back to the local Indian people, not everybody got land. We were pretty fortunate—I'm thinking because of our involvement [with Mission San Gabriel]. We were here where the community was, and we were the original people here.

—Anthony Morales, tribal chair, Gabrieleno/Tongva Tribal Council of San Gabriel, 2006

THREE

THE CATTLE ON THE GOLDEN HILLS

WHEN THE OLD WORLD AND MONARCHY embodied in Spain yielded to New World energies and the republican ideas of an independent Mexico, California was forced to confront a half-century of change and instability. In passing the Colonization Act in 1824 and the supplementary *Reglamento* in 1828, the Mexican government meant to promote agricultural development and encourage settlement on lands at home and in the far-flung and sparsely populated territories it had inherited from Spain. The result was an acquisitive frenzy, and the issuing of hundreds of land grants after the secularization of the missions quickened the pace of settlement in California. The frantic land-rush momentum carried over into the uneasy days just prior to the American invasion.[1]

In keeping with its reformist policies, the Mexican government restricted the amount of land an individual colonist could claim (depending on whether the land was irrigable, was dependent on rainfall, or had water in place for cattle), but it was uncommonly generous in welcoming law-abiding foreigners as settlers. Because Mexican citizens were to get preferential treatment, aliens who felt slighted could theoretically even the playing field and better their landholding chances by the not-difficult act of becoming Mexican citizens.

A surprising number of *norteamericanos*—especially Yankees, already renowned for their acquisitive drive, discipline, and entrepreneurial acumen—took the United States of Mexico up on its offer. South and west they came in the 1820s, converting to Catholicism, applying for citizenship, eager to open all doors where they heard opportunity's slightest tap. One of that number was destined to own the Ranch of the Little Cottonwoods and leave his long and lasting mark on the history of California.

Facing page: Abel Stearns. Reproduced by permission of The Huntington Library, San Marino, California

ENTER THE ABLE DON

Homely Abel Stearns, Massachusetts-born in 1798 and orphaned at age twelve, renounced poverty early by following New England tradition and going to sea. Voyages to China, the East Indies, the West Indies, and the coast of South America taught him the trade of trade, and a trader he would be for the rest of his long life. After landing at Vera Cruz in 1826, Stearns obtained a passport that allowed him to travel in Mexico. He became a Catholic, applied for citizenship, passed the days as a merchant, and in August 1828 petitioned the Mexican government for a land grant in Alta California, where he hoped to establish a colony. [2]

Such quick progress for a business on the move slowed to a frustrating crawl after Stearns stepped off the schooner *Dorotea* and set foot in Monterey on July 28, 1829. Welcome to chaotic California! His documents ready and in order, Stearns immediately petitioned Governor Echeandía for his land grant. [3] The governor did not even notify Mexico of Stearns's arrival or his request for a few months. A busy man, Echeandía had arrived in 1825 with orders to gradually secularize the missions, and two years later he announced the forthcoming emancipation of Indians at some missions to great uproar. [4] Echeandía also found himself occupied with putting down a rebellion of mostly presidio soldiers from Monterey and San Francisco who were unhappy about not being paid or fed.

Early in 1830, Stearns pressed his case again, asking for a grant of land on the Sacramento River. More delays followed until October of that year, when Echeandía decreed that Stearns and a partner be granted twenty square leagues on the San Joaquin—not the Sacramento—River. Now for final approval by the Supreme Government in Mexico. Stearns was pleased. Land at last! [5]

Unfortunately for the ambitious Yankee, a change of governments in Mexico moved the liberals out and the conservatives in, and in California supplanted Echeandía with Manuel Victoria, a conservative soldier at odds with republican sympathies, especially secularization, [6] and suspicious of foreigners. He had a special, pre-formed hatred of Stearns, whom he had been led to believe was not only a *norteamericano* but a ringleader of the liberal troublemakers. His assumption was probably incorrect, since the cautious Stearns always favored the pursuit of business over the rights of people. Perhaps more warranted was Victoria's belief that Stearns was a threat to Mexico who would bring his land-hungry fellow countrymen in the east into California—to the dire detriment of Mexico. When Stearns met with the governor in the summer of 1831 to press his land claim, he not only met refusal but was ordered to leave the territory for Mexico, where, he was told, the papers regarding his case had gone before him. His protests and written arguments to no effect, Stearns departed Monterey in the summer of 1831 bound for his adopted homeland, but the brigantine *Catalina* got temporarily sidetracked on other business and he was put off in San Diego to await its return. [7]

September 1847

I received from Don Antonio y Ignacio, the total 83 hides for the account of Don Abel Stearns. Eight of the same were sent to San Pedro with the Carreta of Abila whose 8 hides Don Alejandro gave a receipt—the 75 hides were freighted by carts from the ranch.

Abel Stearns

Stearns did not wait for his deportation. Instead he joined a band of prominent Californios in a revolt against Victoria's ten-month rule. This had been heating up across the territory but came to a boil in San Diego.[8] The rebels described the tactless Victoria as a despot, a lawbreaker, and unfit for office. An armed skirmish near the Pueblo of Los Angeles resulted in the governor's defeat and painful wounding, not to mention the death of the missionaries' last hope.[9] Echeandía, whom the rebels restored to the governorship, asked Stearns to head a fundraising drive for Victoria's passage back to Mexico.[10] Stearns did, but it was a hollow vengeance for the able Yankee. His petition for land could not be found in Alta California; the papers were presumed lost, probably forever, in the archives of Mexico. For the time being, Abel Stearns shelved his plans to be a landholder in favor of making money...or better, accumulating wealth, since goods, not specie, were the stuff of commerce in the neglected territory.

Restless as ever, Stearns went to Los Angeles, where he hired out as a bill collector and a sales agent, and before 1833 was even half over he was operating a thriving retail store in the flourishing pueblo. With times right for commerce he added a second outlet in deserted San Pedro, where he built a combination warehouse, retail store, and residence close to arriving vessels.[11] Quickly he became Southern California's ultimate middleman, collector of hides and tallow from the missions and ranchos, dispenser of finished wares brought by ships that no longer had to waste pricey sailing days while their crews drummed through the hinterlands buying and selling.[12] Put another way, by holding the hides, Stearns enabled his customers to kill their animals at their convenience and to buy goods from time to time against the stored hides, rather than indulging in one annual orgy of slaying and spending.[13]

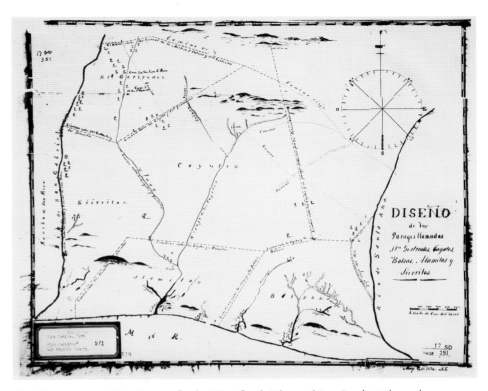

Abel Stearns surveyed Los Coyotes for the Nieto family. The resulting 1834 *diseño* shows the subsequent division of the 167,000-acre property into five ranchos. Stearns's initials appear in the lower right corner. Courtesy of The Bancroft Library, University of California, Berkeley

As possessor of such a lucrative monopoly, Stearns prospered. When people needed money, they came to Stearns, and in no time several influential Californios were in his debt—debts Stearns would later collect in land.[14] Enterprising to a fault, Stearns also hired himself out to do land surveys. One such *diseño* was done in 1834 for the Nieto family in breaking up Los Coyotes;[15] it is safe to surmise the spread caught his acquisitive eye.

Built in 1842, "El Palacio" was the residence of Abel Stearns and Arcadia Bandini Stearns and for years the social center of Los Angeles. Courtesy of the California Historical Society

later, after Los Angeles was named a city and (temporarily at least) the capital of Alta California, Stearns served the *ayuntamiento* in the office of treasurer. He was also named, on January 2, 1836, a member of the vigilante Committee for Public Order and subsequently protested—at least verbally—the summary execution of two murderers.

There is a dark side to Don Abel's story as well. Success, not to mention monopoly, generates envy. More than once Stearns was accused of smuggling, as well as buying hides—"California bank notes," as the American traders called them—on the sly from rustlers peddling them at the going rate of two dollars apiece. Though he fought the charges (and his guilt or innocence has never been conclusively proven), he lost property through official confiscation.[17]

Alta California was a rough and violent country then, made more so by Mexico's practice of deporting criminals to that distant frontier—a practice strongly opposed by law-abiding Californios,[18] who wished to distinguish themselves from lower-class undesirables from Mexico by aligning themselves with Yankees like Stearns.[19] Stearns was painfully exposed to that reality one September night in 1835, when a drunken saloon keeper from Kentucky named William Day, angry over the purchase of a cask of less-than-vintage brandy, knifed Stearns in his pueblo store, slashing his hand, shoulder, and face and nearly severing his tongue. Stearns survived, thanks to the nearness of a skilled doctor, but with a nasty facial scar and a permanent speech impediment.[20]

In December 1834 he purchased a lot in the pueblo for 150 pesos; shortly thereafter he began construction on the imposing Palacio de Don Abel, the spacious home that was to be the center of the good life in Los Angeles for years to come. His palace was almost surely built by skilled Indian laborers who had come to the pueblo after secularization. In 1830 the census taker recorded 127 "Domesticated Heathens" in the pueblo, noting that "all the heathens of the neighborhood who come here and work with whites, are treated well and live a civilized and quiet life." By 1844, 650 Indians lived in town, and over 400 of them came from the southern missions of San Diego, San Luis Rey, and San Juan Capistrano.[16] The influx of inexpensive but skilled labor far exceeded demand, allowing Abel Stearns to build a palace.

With wealth and status came civic obligations for the New England native. At the end of 1835, he was elected *síndico* (the equivalent of business and legal counsel) to the *ayuntamiento* (town council). A few months

The same month of the attack, Governor Figueroa died, leaving a vacancy that was filled in May of the following year by short-term Governor Mariano Chico, who came with Abel Stearns at the top of his list of enemies. Indeed, Chico vented his rage on the subversive Stearns at their first meeting and actually threatened to hang him for plotting revolution. A few days later Chico reduced the sentence to deportation.[21]

Again, it was the resilient don who had the last horse laugh, when Chico was sent packing by the Californios after an inglorious term of three months in office. Mexico's attempt to succeed Chico with Carlos Carrillo as provisional governor almost provoked a civil war. The powerful Committee of Six, led by Abel Stearns, gave Carrillo a no-confidence vote and backed native-born Juan Bautista Alvarado, who would hold the post from 1838 through 1842.[22]

YANKEE DONS

An economic slump hit the hide trade hard in the late 1830s and lasted into the early 1840s. Even the well-heeled man-about-pueblo Abel Stearns was hurting...or so he complained to Governor Alvarado in an August 1839 letter. He might just have to go into ranching, he said, to make ends meet.

As early as February 1840 Stearns approached Francisco Figueroa, brother of the late governor and administrator of the ailing *La Compañía Agricultural,* about purchasing Rancho Los Alamitos; according to one source, Francisco had taken up residence at the ranch as its manager. Figueroa's asking price of nine thousand pesos, the amount of the outfit's outstanding debt, seemed too high to Stearns. He did ride out to the ranch with a friend, a Yankee merchant named Jonathan (Don Juan) Temple, to inspect

the land he had surveyed for Juan José Nieto seven years back. They found three adobe houses with rush roofs, several hundred head of livestock, and odds and ends of ranching equipment.[23] Ever careful and shrewd, Stearns decided he was best served by waiting—for the legal snarls to be untangled and the price to drop.

Needs of the heart, not the purse next occupied Don Abel's considerable energies. In 1841, when he was forty-three, Stearns married fourteen-year-old Arcadia Bandini, one of the five daughters of the prominent Californio Juan Bandini, an influential politico with whom Stearns had done business since the 1830s.[24] Stearns was familiar with many of the old Californios: the previous year he had thrown a party at his home for the elite in celebration of *El Grito de Dolores* (the day Padre Hidalgo declared independence from Spain). But nearby in the public plaza, another celebration for the holiday was underway, this one attended by the majority of the Mexican population. Symbolic of the growing division between Mexican and

Arcadia Bandini Stearns. In 1841, fourteen-year-old Arcadia Bandini, the daughter of Juan Bandini, a prominent Californio, married forty-three-year-old Abel Stearns. After Stearns's death in 1871 she married Colonel Robert S. Baker. By all accounts both were prosperous unions. Reproduced by permission of The Huntington Library, San Marino, California

I have been to examine the ranch of the Alamitos, and with Señor Temple we have had a conference with Don Francisco Figueroa who had fixed the [price] of the ranch at 9 thousand pesos, the value placed upon it, so we are informed by the former owners. According to your list of large and small cattle and the horses here, calculating the current prices, the value will not run much above 4,000 pesos.

—Abel Stearns, to José Antonio Aguire (The Huntington Library, San Marino, California, Abel Stearns Papers)

In the city of Los Angeles in the department of both Californias on the 12th day of July, 1842 before me Manuel Dominquez, 1st Justice of the Peace... appeared Don Francisco Figueroa who...has presented...a letter dated 15th of July 1840....The heirs of the deceased General Don José Figueroa, his successors...sell and give over in real sale...unto Don Abel Stearns domiciled in this city...the land known by the name of Los Alamitos, comprising six square leagues, situated on the sea shore within the limits of this new municipality... its boundaries being northerly on Los Coyotes, southerly on the sea, easterly on Las Bolsas and westerly on Los Serritos, the deceased General having bought the land of Juan José Nieto...for the consideration of one thousand five hundred dollars....For the lands and the appurtenances thereto, Don Abel Stearns will make the payment in this form—First he will deliver to Don Antonio Aguire the sum of 2050 dollars 7 shillings in suet and hides; the suet at 12 shillings and the hides at 2 dollars each brought to San Pedro—half...reckoned from the day he is possessed of the estate and the other half in the course of the year of 1843—Likewise will pay to Don Eulogio Celis the sum of 1483 in suet and hides, the suet at 12 shillings and the hides at 2 dollars each brought to San Pedro, but this payment shall be in the space of two years....The delivery of Los Alamitos ...shall be in August or September next.

I attest it, Manuel Dominquez

U.S. Land Commission Hearing Case 404, Abel Stearns claimant for the place named Los Alamitos

Californio, as well as the alignment of Californio and Yankee, these parties signaled troubled times to come.[25] Little did Juan Bandini know that he would end his impoverished days supported by his Yankee son-in-law.[26]

Arcadia Bandini was famed throughout Southern California for her budding beauty, while Stearns already owned the descriptive name *Cara de Caballo* ("Horseface") among the populace. Those who snickered at this April-October match perhaps knew that Don Abel shaved three years off his age in the nuptial papers and further requested of Padre Narciso Durán that, "wishing to avoid the ridicule that the disparity in years might excite in the idle young...I beg of Your Reverence to please exempt me from the three banns [announcements]." Padre Durán did, with a fine of twelve dollars per bann, and on June 22, 1841, at Mission San Gabriel, the ceremony was performed.[27]

In what for all appearances may have been a good and happy marriage, Don Abel and Doña Arcadia settled into the elegant town home El Palacio, close to where Stearns in 1858 would erect a complex of commercial buildings to be known as the Arcadia Block.[28] Romantic tradition says that in order to provide his young wife with a cool summer house, and perhaps an escape from the raucous pueblo, Stearns made his move to acquire the sea-facing rancho of *los alamitos*, with its glorious golden stands of mustard.

The deed of sale, dated 12 July 1842, called for Stearns to pay $1,500 for the six square leagues of land, $279 for the miscellaneous items on the grounds, including a large iron pot and four pairs of shearing scissors, and the $4,155 balance for the animals in place. We get a glimpse at uses of the land and the value of various stock in the following breakout: 240 horses at $549, 100 hogs at $146, nearly 1,000 sheep at $997, and 900 cattle at $2,463. Cattle indeed was king.

An inventory taken before the sale also described three buildings: "One house of adobe, with two apartments covered with pitch and others without roofs and with two opposite doors. One more house of adobe with three apartments covered by rushes and with one door placed therein. One other house of adobe with two apartments covered by rushes and with one door."[29]

We don't precisely know how Stearns developed his new ranch, or exactly what he did to the structures, but we can assuredly say one thing: just as the first Spanish newcomers left their imprint on the landscape of Povuu'ngna by building adobe structures and introducing livestock, Stearns, with his New England sensibilities, would do the same.

We can reasonably assume that he repaired the largest and least deteriorated of the adobes described in the inventory. He was probably the one to plant the first "exotics" (non-natives) on the landscape. And likely the new rancher used the roomiest and most comfortable building as headquarters for his operation, as well as a cool escape for himself and his young bride when the heat and smells of Los Angeles became too much.

Around 1845 he added a north wing to the old adobe to house his vaqueros. His addition was divided into nine bays with one window and one door in each bay, with a wood floor and ceiling topped by a gabled roof. Wood, a rare commodity in the semi-arid terrain, had to be brought from afar, perhaps shipped through his own trading depot in San Pedro.[30]

How much time Don Abel and Arcadia spent near the little cottonwoods watered by the nourishing spring of Povuu'ngna can only be guessed, but family lore says that they used some of that water to plant a new California pepper tree (*Schinus molle*) on the near north side of the Ranch House, probably for shade. The mission fathers, knowledgeable horticulturalists,

The north wing of the Los Alamitos Ranch House, ca. 1880. Abel Stearns built an addition with gabled roof and wood siding and floors onto the old adobe on the hilltop. The addition reflected Stearns's New England background and a new cultural mix.

introduced the drought-tolerant species to the region early on, knowing that the tree would do well in its new semi-arid environment.[31] If tradition holds true, Stearns's pepper tree was the first exotic plant to be nourished by the springs of Povuu'ngna.

After 1844 there was another good reason to leave raucous Los Angeles for the ranch. Don Abel had a new and kindred neighbor on the mustard coast, none other than his friend and occasional business partner Don Juan Temple. Jonathan Temple had likewise become a Mexican citizen and a Catholic, come to California, and entered the retail trade, and he had married Rafaela Benecia Cota of Santa Barbara, a second cousin to the Nietos who had inherited Rancho Los Cerritos.[32]

In December 1843 Temple bought, for $3,025, this twenty-seven-thousand-acre Ranch of the "Little Hills" that characterized the otherwise

Jonathan Temple with his wife, Rafaela Cota, and son-in-law Gregorio de Ajuria. Courtesy of the Workman and Temple Family Homestead Museum, City of Industry, California

Rancho Los Cerritos, the home of Yankee Don Juan Temple, as it appeared in the 1870s

broad plain reaching back from the coast of present-day Long Beach. On this choice oceanfront property that formed a bracket of sorts along the western side and northwestern tip of Los Alamitos, on a hill that sloped toward the San Gabriel River, the Temples built a two-story, Monterey-style home in 1844. (The style was named for a type of structure developed in that town by Thomas Oliver Larkin. A fellow New England Yankee trader and a friend of Abel Stearns, Larkin acted for many years as the American consul in Mexican California and as a secret agent for the United States in the years leading up to the Mexican-American War.[33])

The Temple residence was graced by a redwood verandah supported by slender posts; single-story wings ran U-like to the rear. The gentleman rancher imported bricks around the Horn for foundations and water-proofed the plank roof with asphalt carted south from the La Brea tar pits, where the Los Angeles County Museum of Art/Page Museum would take form more than a century later. To soften the rectangular severity of the place, Don Juan and Rafaela oversaw the planting of lush and extensive gardens.[34]

What a splendid place for picnics, barbecues, dances, and neighborly get-togethers! While Abel and Arcadia spent most of their time in Los Angeles and left the running of Los Alamitos to majordomos, the Temples resided at their ranch and received visitors with the hospitality the age was known for. Rides to the beach, dances, and high-stakes horse races beloved by both the native and naturalized Californios spiced the days. Annually the caballeros staged a match race of their best, since in all ways horses symbolized the "gentility of the Californio elites."[35] One famous encounter pitted a stallion belonging to Abel Stearns against Jonathan Temple's famous El Besarero for a prize of one thousand head of cattle. The course lay along the

The gardens at Rancho Los Cerritos, ca. 1870s. Courtesy Rancho Los Cerritos Historic Site, Long Beach, California

unfenced boundary of the two ranches from the base of Signal Hill, highest in the region (365 feet above sea level) to the bluffs above the shore and back, a total of eight miles. Temple's long, rangy bay won the match race. Victors and losers celebrated together at Los Cerritos over several broached casks of wine and brandy and an entire barbecued ox. Of such times are romantic myths begun.[36]

THE CRISIS YEARS

Meanwhile, back from the ranch, Stearns, along with all his fellow Californios—naturalized or not—entered turbulent times. After the October 1842 premature raising of the American flag over Monterey by Commodore Thomas ap Catesby Jones (commander of the United States Navy's Pacific Squadron), it became clear that not only did Mexico lack the resources to govern Alta California, it lacked the means to protect its territory from an expanding American power. Certainly

the Californios wanted no part of Mexico, which continued to export mostly inept governors and the harvest of its jails to plague the people of the distant northwest. A last straw came in the company of Governor Manuel Micheltorena, who arrived in Alta California in 1842 with empty pockets and an army of three hundred unpaid and unfed fresh recruits from Mexico's prisons, who looted the local bounty.[37]

The season was ripe for change. While a few Californios favored an independent nation, sager heads knew it would be too weak to last long, before a major player in the imperial game picked it from the vine. France had an interest and a small following of intriguers in place. England was the greater threat and had its supporters, including Micheltorena. He thought his country's position was hopeless and suggested ceding California to Britain for debts owed and to keep it from being overrun by North Americans. Last, but certainly not least, was the United States, drawn by Manifest Destiny's call, with a sizable fifth column in the vast rich land that counted its non-Indian population at roughly fifteen thousand.[38]

Point man for the plotters was Thomas O. Larkin, an open advocate of U.S. annexation of California, who communicated regularly by letter with Stearns during the crisis years of 1845 and 1846. In February 1845, Governor Micheltorena quickly surrendered to a Californian force headed by Juan Bautista Alvarado and José Castro in the bloodless battle of Cahuenga, apparently relieved that he and his despised troops could get back to Mexico alive. More instability followed, with Pío Pico assuming the governorship and residing in the capital, Los Angeles, but José Castro, the recognized military commander, residing in Monterey and thus controlling the custom house and the revenue. An internecine war between north and south loomed even as the North Americans made their move.[39]

In October 1845, Larkin was appointed President James Polk's confidential agent, charged with doing everything he could to see that neither France nor England laid claim to California. Larkin tried to recruit Stearns as his active agent in the south but could only count him as a willing correspondent. Though Stearns had been drawn reluctantly back into the political fray, he kept a certain distance from Larkin, resolutely staying in the center of the competing parties and interests; after all, business—specifically Stearns's business—came first for this practical and respected man. Evidence of Stearns's reputation as a trustworthy man of the center can be deduced from the action of Governor Pío Pico.[40] An unyielding foe of North Americans, when he headed north from Los Angeles in mid-June of 1846 with troops and the intent of removing General Castro from his command, Pico appointed Stearns to what amounted to the position of acting governor in Pico's absence.

That internecine squabble never came to pass. Word arrived that a group of American settlers had revolted and declared a "California Republic" under a Bear Flag; moreover, the flamboyant American officer John Charles Frémont, with some sixty men, had joined them to remove "military despotism" from California. On July 7, Commodore John D. Sloat, commander of the U.S. Pacific Squadron, hoisted the Stars and Stripes over Monterey. The United States was at war with Mexico (declared on May 13, 1846), and the tottering, faction-ridden, orphaned territory was about to fall to the Americans. Following several months of resistance in Southern California, the Capitulation of Cahuenga on January 13, 1847, ended the immediate opposition to the American occupation.[41] A few days later, under military rule, acting governor John Charles Frémont appointed Abel Stearns to a three-man committee to assess damage claims by civilians in the brief and not very bloody conquest. Stearns obliged.

NEW DIVIDING LINES

A few days before the Treaty of Guadalupe Hidalgo was concluded on February 2, 1848, ceding California to the United States, gold was found at Sutter's Mill, in the foothills of the Sierra Nevada. In short order the remote province of Mexico was catapulted into the likes of a nation-state[42] as the population of California exploded—from about 26,000 non-natives to 264,435 according to the census of 1852. For the most part, the Gold Rush was a Northern California phenomenon, albeit with some far-reaching implications for Southern California.

The treaty, along with the Gold Rush, ushered in dark times for Californios and natives. New ways of thinking would soon solidify into law, and Californios would suffer irretrievable losses of land, property, and stature. And the American takeover, with the assumed privileges of conquest, would reduce the state's native population by 80 percent during the coming decade.[43] Put simply and powerfully by Tongva descendant Anthony Morales in a 2006 interview, "They [the Americans] wanted to exterminate us. They wanted us gone."[44]

Under the treaty's terms, non-Indian Mexican citizens were recognized as American citizens, their right to land in theory protected, though the validity of land grants made by the Mexican government was left open to interpretation.[45] In the case of California Indians, the treaty was painfully clear: Indians were not considered U.S. citizens, and they had no rights to their land.[46] Perhaps this was a moot point: after all, Indians were recognized as Mexican citizens with land rights under the Mexican government, but nevertheless most legal title to their ancestral land had been taken away.

On September 1, 1849, delegates to the constitutional convention gathered in Monterey in anticipation of statehood, and of the forty-eight delegates, eleven were from the less populated Southern California districts.[47] Their work and resulting constitution reflected the reality of California's populace (both Spanish and English were made official languages) as well as the intent of the Treaty of Guadalupe Hidalgo (the rights of Mexican citizens were protected). The antislavery section of the constitution passed locally without issue, with delegates opting for the high ground in the great national debate, though the provision almost derailed California's quest for statehood until a compromise was reached between the Northern and Southern factions in Congress: California would be a free state, but the newly organized territories of Utah and New Mexico would not prohibit slavery.[48]

Abel Stearns played his civic part in these profound political changes. He served as one of the delegates to the 1849 convention and also as one of Southern California's few representatives in the legislature, which despite the antislavery clause in the state constitution, passed in 1850 "An Act for the Government and Protection of Indians." Putting aside morality for economic interests, the new law addressed an old concern of the Californios,

legalizing the indentured servitude of Indians and thereby guaranteeing the supply of inexpensive labor.[49]

But the injustices didn't end there for the state's native population. That same year Congress authorized three Indian agents (commissioners) to negotiate a series of treaties with California tribes in an effort to remove them from their ancestral lands to less desirable inland areas away from the white population.[50] The resulting eighteen treaties affected 7,488,000 acres of land and 139 tribes or bands of native peoples.[51] The Tongva people of the Los Angeles Basin were not recognized in the process. Nor, as it turned out, were any of the 139 tribes. In 1852 Congress failed to ratify any of the treaties. (Meager financial restitution for these lands would finally be made by the U.S. government in the twentieth century, and this restitution did include the Tongva.)[52]

In addition to legalizing indentured servitude, the 1850 Act for the Government and Protection of Indians stated that sheriffs and local authorities were to mark the boundaries of land occupied and used by Indians and protect them from encroachment by non-Indian settlers. A marginal effort would safeguard some Indian land in Southern California through the 1850s and early 1860s,[53] but as time went on, land was often taken through threat, fraud, or deceit.

Abel Stearns understood the practical implications and repercussions of federal and state policy better than most. In 1851 both Californios and Yankees feared that a rebellion led by Cupeño leader Antonio Garra (who lived on the Warner Ranch in San Diego County) would unite all the tribes west of the Colorado River. Garra's rumored intention was to force all Americans (but not Mexicans) from his homeland. In November, the Los Angeles Court of Session appointed five commissioners, including

The Indian Laborers and servants are "domesticated;" mix with us daily and hourly; and...appear to be a necessary part of the domestic economy. They are almost the only house or farm servants we have....The common pay of Indian farm hands is from eight to ten dollars per month; and one dollar per day the highest in town—but few pay so much.

—*Benjamin D. Wilson Report, 1852*

Abel Stearns, to procure arms, horses, and equipment and raise a force to confront the Indians. Within days two hundred men were outfitted to go. The immediate crisis ended—though not the lingering fear of revolt—with Antonio Garra's capture and execution in December.[54]

As a result, in 1852 Superintendent of Indian Affairs Edward F. Beale commissioned a report by Benjamin D. Wilson which described the living conditions of Indians in Southern California and recommended that a reservation be established. Located about sixty miles north of Los Angeles, the Sebastian Military Reserve, also known as the Tejon Reservation, was the first voluntary Indian reservation established in the state. Few Tongva chose to go, perhaps fearing the loss of what little land still belonged to them. In ten years' time, the Tejon Reservation was converted into Beale's private rancho.[55]

A WORKING RANCH

Even Abel Stearns, this most knowledgeable and opportunistic of Californios, could not have guessed the changes instantly in store for him and his rancher friends on their acquired land. Most fortunes in Gold Rush California were not made by the miners, but by those who served the miners, especially in Southern California. Stearns stands tall in that number. He had his own homegrown gold—yellow mustard mixed with sere wild grasses that rippled in the afternoon's onshore breeze like a golden extension of the sea. (Seeds of mustard, native to Mediterranean regions, had crossed to Mexico and were then brought up from San Blas. In California's receptive soils, where almost everything grows, if you can find the water to irrigate with, the mustard spread like a chaparral fire across the ranchos.) In places the golden-flowered stalks soared higher than the head of a rider on horseback. Cattle hid in the green-gold mist of its shade, and Abel Stearns and his neighbors held at least one rodeo a year—usually in late spring—to round up their cattle in what were known as "runs through the mustard."[56]

Meanwhile, hardworking miners up north were hungry. Why trifle with suet and skins when beef on the hoof brought forty dollars a head down south—an eight- to ten-fold increase over hide-peddling days—and sold for fifty and sixty dollars, even seventy-five a head in San Francisco?[57] So Stearns and his fellow dons of the "cow counties" entered a seven-year boom, driving their herds north for sale. How profitable it was!

In 1851 John Charles Frémont, self-promoting hero of the Mexican-American War, now one of California's first two senators and five years off from being a nascent Republican Party's first candidate for the presidency, offered

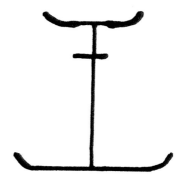

Abel Stearns's Alamitos brand

Stearns $300,000 for Los Alamitos and its 10,000 cattle, 1,100 sheep, and 700 horses.[58] It was Frémont who first expressed the hope for a new Mediterranean ideal on California's West Coast, suggests historian Kevin Starr.[59] Is it possible that he felt this potential on the hilltop of Rancho Los Alamitos, with its cool breezes and the refreshing springs of Povuu'ngna below? A more practical Stearns declined. His stock was on the rise.

Not that the Gold Rush didn't bring its share of problems to the Southland. With wages soaring in the mining camps, labor headed north. It should be noted here that Stearns ran several hundred head of sheep that required shearing, and he had developed a passion for breeding fine horses. Portions of the rancho were planted to corn and other vegetables that fed the necessary workforce of vaqueros, shepherds, common laborers, and their families. The great majority of these were Native Americans who were paid in goods. When the vaqueros began to head north, those left behind thought it a good time to ask for a raise, from one dollar a day to two (three if the vaquero owned his own horse). But Charles Brinley, the tough majordomo who ran Los Alamitos for Don Abel during the 1850s, refused. He instead hired "all the Indians of three years old and upwards" in the neighborhood, or at least as many as he could, and then still needed more.[60] He summed up the solution in a message he sent to his boss on August 30, 1852: "I wish you would deputize someone to attend the auction that usually takes place on Mondays and buy me five or six Indians."[61]

His words referred to the practice of using involuntary Indian labor, which had continued from the Spanish-Mexican era and had been legalized by the new state in the aforementioned Act for the Government and Protection of Indians. Any Indian found loitering, strolling about, or near public places selling liquor could be arrested by anyone and tried by a justice

My name is José Justo Morillo, my age is fifty-seven years and I reside in the county of Los Angeles. I knew the rancho called Alamitos….When I first knew the land in 1834, it was occupied by José Figueroa. He had a house on it in which he had a mayor domo and people living, had corrals and a stock of horses and cattle. There were two houses on the land and he cultivated some of the land. I was Mayor Domo of Figueroa and I remained there until the possession was delivered to Abel Stearns. This I think was about ten or eleven years ago. Said Stearns has continued to occupy the land to the present time. He has people living there and has cattle and horses and other stock. The number of cattle on the land at this time I think is about eleven thousand and the number of horses two thousand, the number of sheep about two thousand.

Filed in office, Nov. 11th, 1852

U.S. Land Commission Hearing Case 404, Abel Stearns claimant for the place named Los Alamitos

of the peace. Indians, of course, could not testify against white persons in court, so they were released on bond, bound over for a period of work not to exceed four months.[62] In August 1850, a Los Angeles city councilmember declared, "When the city has no work in which to employ the chain gang…a number of prisoners will be auctioned off to the highest bidder for private service."[63]

Horace Bell, a contemporary observer of the practice, likened it to the slave auctions in New Orleans, with a notable exception:

The slave at Los Angeles was sold fifty-two times a year as long as he lived, which generally did not exceed one, two or three years under the new dispensation. They would be sold for a week…at prices ranging from one to three dollars, one-third of which was to be paid to the peon at the end of the week, which debt due for well performed labor would invariably be paid in aguardiente.[64]

Ant. Gabrielino
Compana Indian Cowboy Taag—Indito
    [young Indian]
Luis Indito
Alejandro, cowboy
Fernando, cowboy
Martin, Labrador, Field worker
Cook
José San Janeño
Guadalupe Ruis
A Felipe Canedo
Ygnacio Vareles
José A. Ernande
Vitalano
Dolores Bermundez
José Yola
Pablo
Salvado Bermundez
Ramon Soto
José Angel

This list from Abel Stearns's payroll at Rancho Los Alamitos reveals that a few Native Americans, Tongva included, worked for Stearns (Stearns Papers, The Huntington Library, San Marino, California.)

Indian prisoners sometimes paid their fines and escaped the auction block—also acceptable from the city's perspective, since the revenue helped fill its coffers. The *Los Angeles Star* and some citizens routinely questioned the hideous spectacle of the auction, but through the 1860s, the white population of Los Angeles relied primarily on this procurement of Indian labor for their domestic and agricultural needs.[65]

Surviving payroll records, census data, and occasional bits of correspondence tell at least a partial story of the people who worked for Abel Stearns at Rancho Los Alamitos. According to the 1850 federal census, thirty-three of the thirty-eight people who lived at the Rancho were California Indians. Employees and their families lived in five separate structures, which suggests that there were five different families, four with children: Vicente Solters and María Antonia (no children); José Zoila and Lionicia (four children); Juan de Mapa and Materna (one child); Paulino and Malieriana (seven children); and Fernando and Carlota (two children).[66]

A decade later, the 1860 federal census showed thirty-three people living in two separate dwellings: twenty-six were rancho employees (laborers, vaqueros, or servants) and eighteen were California Indians. There was only one family at Alamitos at the time, at least officially: the male cook Paulino, two women (likely his wife and daughter-in-law), and three of his children. This extended family and their needs greatly irritated majordomo Brinley, who dashed off a letter of complaint to his boss on October 11, 1859:

> There are here a lot of women, children, and men (I believe, Paulino's crowd) that are eating here. Juan gave them a cart to go for their traps, and also, Guadalupe's house to live in. I do not know what to do with them, for if Juan takes it upon himself to lend them a cart, and a house to live in, without asking me about it, I suppose that he has a right to do so.[67]

On December 19:

> Paulino is here cooking and wants rations for his two daughters and rest of children, please write to Juan about sending them away.[68]

Neither census tells us if any of the Indians working at Alamitos were Tongva; by now the Tongva people were a minority among the region's native workforce. In 1852 Hugo Reid wrote that most of the Tongva had gone north to Monterey after secularization, though some still lived in San Fernando, San Gabriel, and "the Angeles."[69] Perhaps others had found ways to stay. Historian William McCawley suggests that Tongva people may have "renegotiate[d] their identity to a higher, non-Indian status where they would face less discrimination, have greater legal protection from crimes against their persons, and perhaps even get the chance to own land."[70] Some Tongva may have chosen to hide their native identity under Spanish surnames, perhaps even at Rancho Los Alamitos.

UNDER SIEGE

Hispanics fared better than the Native Americans under the new regime, but even the most prominent Californios were reduced in stature and under attack. The elimination, before the Treaty of Guadalupe Hidalgo was ratified, of Article 10, which specifically protected Spanish-Mexican land grants, ushered in new challenges to old legitimacy. To further complicate matters, state law permitted squatters to preempt uncultivated land grants until the owners could prove their title. If an owner were finally able to prove his grant satisfactorily, he was still required to pay for any squatter improvements.[71]

The Land Law of 1851 invested a three-man land commission with the power to authenticate grants given by the Spanish and Mexican governments and to ascertain which lands were "held, used and occupied by Indians."[72] Estimates vary, but somewhere between five hundred and seven hundred Mexican land grants were likely issued, though more than eight hundred claims were filed—the majority of them in the last five years of Mexican rule. Some land grants were signed by Mexican governors who had left office; some were multiple family claims; others were speculative or corrupt.[73] The burden of proof fell on the Californios, who were required to produce written records of ownership—this when the Spanish and Mexican notion of ownership came from occupying, working, and maintaining land loosely defined by natural features, not surveys and grids.[74]

To the Honorable United States Commissioners ascertaining and settling California Land Claims.

Your petitioner, Abel Stearns, resident of the County of Los Angeles, state of California, would respectfully represent that he claims to be the owner...of all that tract of land...called the Alamitos—said tract of land is part of the tract originally occupied by Manuel Nieto who possessed and occupied from about the year 1784 until the time of his death, which took place about the year 1807, all the lands now known by the name of the Ranchos Santa Gertrudes, Coyotes, Bolsas, Alamitos, Serritos [Cerritos] and Palo Alto in Los Angeles County.

Scott Granger for the Petitioner
Oct. 21, 1852

from the records of U.S. Land Commission Hearing Case 404,
Abel Stearns claimant for the place named Los Alamitos

(Even Yankee dons had difficulty proving title to their land grants. Los Coyotes had been split into five ranchos and individual title given to the heirs of Manuel Nieto. The decrees granting separate title were included in an espediente; however, Juan José Nieto's title to Rancho Los Alamitos was missing. The burden of proof fell on Abel Stearns.)

Unscrupulous lawyers represented Anglo squatters—particularly in the northern parts of the state—who believed that the large landholdings should be redistributed among the newcomers. Long, drawn-out proceedings in a language and a law that were unfamiliar forced Californios to drain away meager cash reserves, selling off land acre by acre to pay legal fees.[75] In 1852 the land commissioners reached Los Angeles and held hearings in the vicinity for the rest of the year, before going to San Francisco to continue their work through the end of 1856. In the end, the Californios lost 40 percent of the land they held prior to 1846.[76]

February 15, 1855

Opinion of the Land Commissioners to ascertain and settle the Private Land Claims in the State of California.

...The case before us is peculiar in its character. It was a division of property long held in possession by the family of the grantee....Under the decree of July 27 the Alamitos was decreed to be the property of Juan José Nieto....The difficulty...is however that there is no direct evidence of...a grant of the Alamitos to said Juan José Nieto...The title of the present claimant is deduced from said Juan José Nieto through a conveyance made by the latter to Governor Figueroa, which bears the date June 30, 1834. It cannot be believed that Figueroa should make this purchase with the knowledge he had of all the other facts unless the proper documentary evidence of the grantor's title had been duly delivered.

A decree of confirmation will be entered.

from the records of U.S. Land Commission Hearing Case 404,
Abel Stearns claimant for the place named Los Alamitos

(A decree of confirmation in favor of Abel Stearns's claim to title was entered in 1855; however, a counterclaim was filed in 1857 citing insufficient proof. Stearns successfully responded and on June 4, 1857, received formal title to Rancho Los Alamitos.)

Even Abel Stearns and his neighbor on the mustard coast, Jonathan Temple, whose Yankee smarts and business sense had survived the mellowing influence of a don's life, found themselves under legal siege. Temple had to prove his right to Rancho Los Cerritos in proceedings begun September 21, 1852. It wasn't until April 11, 1853, after presenting sufficient documents and calling six witnesses (including Stearns, who testified for him three times) that Temple's claim was confirmed.[77]

Don Abel Stearns was not nearly so lucky. Although his title to Rancho Los Alamitos had been confirmed by the U.S. Land Commission in 1855,

prying lawyers in San Francisco found that Governor Figueroa had not died intestate, as had been represented, but had three legitimate sons in Mexico who had been cheated of their patrimony. The legal jackals closed in on the richest man in Southern California and the Ranch of the Little Cottonwoods. In desperation, Stearns turned to his old friend Don Juan, using Temple's business contacts in Mexico. Acting as his old friend's confidential agent, Temple sailed to Mexico packing a payoff of $10,000 to quiet Figueroa's deprived heirs. Abel Stearns would not surrender easily the core ranch to what soon would be a cattle empire of awesome vastness.[78]

A LOSS OF LUSTER

Gold may be where you find it, but it doesn't stay there if you mine it. By 1856, even the ample ore of California was beginning to play out. Miners were heading elsewhere to new strikes in the Mountain West. That meant the demand for beef was falling even as the rancheros replenished their stock with purchases in Mexico and drovers of better Midwestern herds arrived to sell into the glut. Don Abel's fellow ranchers, several of them related to him by marriage, were devastated. Their own lack of foresight was partly to blame, as well as their joyous, extravagant lifestyle during the 1850s, when money from beef had been rolling in like a tidal wave down from the mines. They imported more longhorn cattle from Texas and northern Mexico than the scattered bunchgrass of their fragile lands could withstand; they borrowed heavily at misunderstood, outrageous rates of interest to hold onto their property and maintain the luxuries to which they had so quickly grown accustomed.[79] Surely good times would soon return.

They did not. Instead, the dons and their lifestyle started slipping away

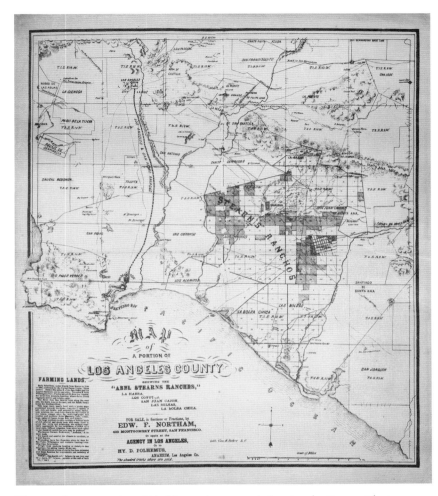

The map shows a portion of Abel Stearns's property in Los Angeles County. The tax assessment records of 1858 indicate that Stearns was the wealthiest man in Los Angeles County, but the environmental disasters of the coming decade would soon change his status. Courtesy of The Bancroft Library, University of California, Berkeley

as compound interest and notes came due. Abel Stearns, the provident and savvy Yankee, survived, even thrived—for a time. In 1857 he purchased the eleven-thousand-acre Rancho La Laguna for less than thirty cents an acre and gave it to Arcadia. That was only the start for the man who, the following year, opened his Arcadia Block at the corner of Arcadia and Los Angeles streets, a shopping complex of eight stores that was adjudged the fanciest business block south of San Francisco. According to tax assessment records of 1858, Abel Stearns was by far the wealthiest landowner in Los Angeles County; his friend and neighbor Jonathan Temple was a distant second.[80]

Over the next five years Stearns increased his standing as cattle king and land baron by acquiring, at auction or on defaulted loans, one ranch after another, until he owned more than two hundred thousand acres and perhaps thirty thousand head of tough, bony cattle. The holdings included properties in Santa Maria and San Diego and a vast acreage in San Bernardino County. But it was from his treasured home base, Rancho Los Alamitos, that he expanded north and east, until he had reunited all but two ranchos once owned by Juan Nieto.[81] Stearns had reached the zenith of his illustrious and multisided life. Nemesis was waiting in the wings.

IN THE NATURE OF THE PLACE

Perhaps Mother Earth had had enough of the mining and overgrazing. Perhaps the far western land was simply reacting sympathetically to the agony of the eastern half of the nation, where the Blue and the Gray turned the earth red with their blood. For whatever reason, the early 1860s and nature caught Abel Stearns overextended and surprisingly vulnerable.

Against a backdrop of economic recession made worse by low beef prices and high interest rates, a plague of grasshoppers arrived in the summer of 1861 to eat crops and the summer-fall pasturage. In November, things seemed to have turned for the better with the early arrival of rain. Unfortunately, it didn't stop. Through November and December, and another month after that, the rain fell unabated in the greatest recorded flood California has known. The deluge took human lives, ruined farms, and drowned cattle in uncountable numbers; losses were put at as much as one-quarter of the state's taxable wealth.[82]

Of course, the spring sward grew lusher and thicker than any vaquero could remember. But that good news evaporated in the fall of 1862 when the Santa Ana winds came and sucked the earth dry. Worse, no seasonal rains came to the rescue this time; instead, a smallpox epidemic ravaged those on the land, killing more than twenty a day in Los Angeles, leaving the poorer sections of town with "more corpses than gravediggers."[83]

The double misery of drought and pox lengthened through the winter of 1862-63, the havoc suitably summarized in these laconic messages to Abel Stearns from Los Alamitos majordomo C. R. Johnson and Cave J. Couts (Anglos who, like Stearns, had married daughters of Juan Bandini and gone into ranching):[84]

We have no rain yet. There is no grass and the cattle are very poor; your Rancho men report a great many dying.—Johnson, Feb. 6, 1863[85]

We have had very warm weather; and what little grass we had is all dry and burnt....In consequence of the shortness of grass and scarcity of vaqueros, no one has thought of Recogidas or Rodeos as yet.—Johnson, March 4, 1863[86]

What are the cattle raisers going to do? No rain, no grass, nearly as dry as in the month of August....Not only the want of pasture, but Small-pox allows no general recogidas this spring.—Couts, March 8, 1863[87]

There is absolutely no grass and it's the opinion of the ranch men, the cattle will begin dying within a month...the horses have no strength.—Johnson, March 14, 1863[88]

Gaunt cattle roaming the rancho holdings were being slaughtered for the few dollars their hides and horns would bring. The rest were left to rot in heaps where they fell. Die they did, in incalculable numbers as the drought stretched deep into 1864, with virtually no rainfall and prices plunging as low as thirty-seven and a half cents a cow.[89] Between 1860 and 1870, the federal censuses indicate, the number of cattle in Los Angeles County declined from seventy thousand to twenty thousand. Most of the drop occurred in the mid-1860s. One rancher declared later, "Before the year 1864 had passed away there was a perfect devastation—such a thing was never before known in California."[90] The assessed valuation of rangeland sagged to ten cents an acre.[91]

Stearns would lose as many as fifty thousand head of cattle at Rancho Los Alamitos alone.[92] In lieu of the green sea of grass that once rippled south from Los Angeles to the Pacific's blue, one observer saw only "a regular mass of dead cattle." In Los Angles County, as much as 70 percent of the stock lay rotting on the range, a number that approached three million head by the time the drought was done, late in 1864. The devastation was the closing act of an era as the Californio land grant ranches fell into American hands during the 1870s.

TWILIGHT OF A YANKEE DON

Though dry periods are a recurrent element of California's climate, Stearns and his fellow ranchers weren't prepared for the intensity and duration of this one. Hoping to salvage as much as possible before ruin was complete, owners would sell one property at a bargain price in the hope of holding onto another, while mortgage holders simply foreclosed on their hapless clients. In the fall of 1861, to complete the financing of his Arcadia Block, Stearns borrowed $20,000 against the jewel in his crown, Rancho Los Alamitos, from notorious San Francisco skinflint Michael Reese at 1.5 percent interest per month. His timing couldn't have been worse.[93]

Within a year of the ill-advised loan—and the onset of the drought—Stearns's exposed position became widely known. He borrowed heavily against his extensive lands as the list of his delinquent back taxes in three counties spread over two pages in the newspaper.[94] But he wasn't alone. Pío Pico, the last governor of Mexican California; José Sepúlveda, who in 1852 owned over one hundred thousand acres of land; and Manuel Domínguez, the owner of the Rancho San Pedro, were also among the newly burdened.[95] From all sides, creditors and their lawyers hounded Abel Stearns, who favored his vanished life too much.

On February 18, 1865, Michael Reese took the defaulting Abel Stearns to court—namely, the District Court of Los Angeles County, which issued a decree of sale against Rancho Los Alamitos. Despite a year's extension on the note, Stearns failed to raise the necessary funds. "The ranch of the 'Little Cottonwoods,'" like so many of its kind, passed into the hands of another money lender.[96]

Mercifully, in April 1865 the national agony of the Civil War ended

On the 20th day of February, A.D. 1866 in and by the District Court of the First Judicial District of the State of California, for the County of Los Angeles....in which Michael Reese was Plaintiff, and Abel Stearns was Defendant, a decree was made....Foreclosure of the mortgage deed... and sale of certain real property in said mortgage and decrees...in satisfaction...of the debts...doth grant...forever, the real estate sold...as described as follows: All that tract, piece or parcel of land situated, lying and being in the County of Los Angeles, State of California, known as the Rancho of "Alamitos."

—*Deed to Rancho Los Alamitos, Michael Reese, October 29, 1866*

with Lee's surrender at Appomattox. The Union, which Stearns had served well as a confidential agent, was preserved. But Stearns's agony continued; the courts weren't done with him. In both 1865 and 1866, Los Angeles County sued him for unpaid taxes, on his personal property as well as his ranches. Though the business climate had brightened, Stearns's personal situation did not. Reduced to a few hundred head of cattle, Stearns faced a court-ordered decree of foreclosure for $23,625 on the Arcadia Block in February 1867, and two months later the state brought suit for unpaid personal property and realty taxes in excess of $9,000.[97] Next his unpaid lawyers turned on the once wealthiest man in California, whose net income dropped to less than $300 in 1868.

Yet despite it all, through delay and the timely intercession of friends and speculators, Don Abel Stearns managed to hold onto his ranching empire by a frayed thread, save, of course, for that lost jewel, Los Alamitos.[98] A friend and former business associate going back to hide-trading days, Alfred Robinson, put together a group of San Francisco investors who advanced Stearns $50,000 to pay off his debts. In return, Stearns conveyed nearly 178,000 acres of his holdings into the Robinson Trust, which meant to subdivide the fertile acres into small farms, with Stearns having one-eighth interest in the syndicate and realizing $1.50 an acre as the land was sold.[99]

Stearns proved an obstinate and irascible partner, raising and racing horses and leasing the range to shepherds and their close-cropping stock, no matter the unsightly look of the land to prospective Eastern buyers. In spite of his obstructionism, the trust made sales and money. But Don Abel didn't share in it for long. On a rare trip to San Francisco he was stricken suddenly and died in the Grand Hotel on August 23, 1871.[100] His empire did not collapse completely, as had the bucolic domains of so many of his fellow dons. But cattle wasn't king anymore; that title was briefly usurped by a lesser, fleecy ungulate with sharp hooves that did great damage to the native grasses not already trampled to extinction.[101]

Stearns's neighbor, Don Juan Temple, had also somehow managed to survive the years of flood and drought and hang onto Los Cerritos, but he was badly battered and in failing health. When, in 1866, the Northern California firm of Flint, Bixby & Company offered Temple $20,000 for his twenty-seven thousand acres, he accepted with alacrity and moved to San Francisco. There he died suddenly at age seventy.[102]

On the other hand, Arcadia Bandini Stearns, Abel's wealthy and respected widow, survived quite well. With leagues of land and cattle still in tow, she married Colonel Robert S. Baker, a forty-niner. In this marriage she would continue her role as a gracious lady, called by some the most beautiful woman in California, and within the new generation of Southern California landowners her wealth would, as it had for Stearns, guarantee her new husband's status.[103]

FOUR

PIONEERS ON THE MOVE

H EEDING THE CALL OF MANIFEST DESTINY, restless Americans took to westering in the mid-nineteenth century. A considerable number of them were New Englanders, ambitious Yankees afflicted with wanderlust and moved by the entrepreneurial spirit. The Bixbys embodied this kind. The prolific family first settled in Massachusetts prior to the American Revolution. As the region grew crowded, the first Bixbys' ambitious descendants foreshadowed the westering urge by seeking fresh opportunities in Somerset County, Maine (while that state-to-be was still part of Massachusetts).

By the middle of the nineteenth century, Somerset County was full of Bixbys. One of them, Rufus Bixby, entertained 156 relatives at a single Thanksgiving dinner.[1] Rufus married Betsy Weston. His brother Amasa Bixby married Betsy's sister Fanny—a way of choosing wives that repeated itself later on. A third Weston sister, Electa, married William Reed Flint. It is with some of the many children of Amasa Bixby and of William Flint—those children were, of course, first cousins—that this section of our story will concern itself.

Most members of both families were farmers, not an enticing occupation where the soil is grudging and the growing season short. Moreover, there was not enough land within the Bixbys' reach to support their multitudes of offspring. Early in 1849, when twenty-two-year-old Benjamin Flint heard that vast quantities of gold had been discovered near the western edge of the continent, he took off like a shot. Maybe he knew that six thousand miners had already taken out $10 million from the California goldfields. But he couldn't have known that in the rush of forty-niners to come, more than forty thousand miners would increase that take by 200 to 300 percent.[2]

Despite the polyglot of people in California, the influx of Yankees during the Gold Rush gave Northern California a particular American flavor distinctly different than that of Southern California, where Spanish

Facing page: Benjamin Flint, ca. 1860s. In 1849, twenty-two-year-old Benjamin Flint of Maine headed to the California goldfields and Volcano. Courtesy of Rancho Los Cerritos Historic Site, Long Beach, California

A view of hopeful miners at the entrance to a Volcano gold mine, from a 1921 postcard. Courtesy of Rancho Los Cerritos Historic Site, Long Beach, California

Volcano, then a collection of tents and log huts crowded together almost without pattern, occupies a cup rimmed by evergreens and bisected by a tributary of the Cosumnes River. Its altitude is 2,100 feet. In spite of its name, the hollow is not the product of volcanic activity, though layers of lava do cap some of the hills to the northeast. Geology was of only peripheral interest to the stampeders, however. They wanted immediate gold, placer gold washed into the craterlike hollow by eons of foaming winter rains. And gold there was. By 1852, over one hundred thousand miners would extract about $80 million in gold from the region[4]—this in the days when a dollar amounted to something.

By the mid-1850s a reputed ten thousand people, having arrived via Sacramento or the emigrant trail that crossed the Sierra Nevada at Carson Pass (today's Highway 88), were scrambling away in the hollow, and one way or another most of them were making money—that is, as long as they weren't "foreign." In 1850 the California legislature passed a "foreign miners' tax." In theory the twenty-dollar fee was to regain a small portion of the profit made by

Dr. Thomas Flint, ca. 1857. The diary of Dr. Thomas Flint documents the 1851 journey he made with his cousins Lewellyn Bixby and Amasa Bixby Jr. from Maine to the gold mines in Volcano, California, and the remarkable sheep drive across the country in 1853. Courtesy of Rancho Los Cerritos Historic Site, Long Beach, California

style and traditions still prevailed.[3] However, Southern California was not immune to gold fever. Its contagious symptoms would foreshadow afflictions yet to come as new capital and populations affected Southern California with unexpected consequence.

Benjamin reached San Francisco, presumably by ship, at about the time rumors of a major strike at Crater City (soon to be renamed Volcano) were electrifying the easily electrified stampeders who were already rushing about like ants throughout the western foothills of the Sierra Nevada. Ben joined a group bound for the new Golconda, and the epic of the California Flints and Bixbys was underway.

Lewellyn Bixby, ca. 1859. Courtesy of Rancho Los Cerritos Historic Site, Long Beach, California

"foreigners," to offset the state debt (although the targeted miners were probably spending more on merchandise than they earned in profit).[5] It was also, in theory, to protect Californios and Chilean, Mexican, and Chinese miners from mob violence. The racially motivated law[6] was repealed after a year, but not before many of the intended targets, in particular the miners from Sonora, Mexico, and the Chinese, headed to Southern California with a newfound loathing of Yankees and their laws.[7]

We don't know what Ben Flint thought about the rough and ready mining country, but seeing the clamor for legitimate goods and services, he clearly knew a man did not need to dig to earn a living. With the bits of gold he was accumulating, he started buying a few of the bony cattle that the rancheros of Southern California were driving north for sale to the meat-hungry miners. He made arrangements to fatten them on a ranch near the southeastern edge of the Sacramento Valley and sell them as needed to the town butchers of Volcano. Ben Flint also realized that if his business was to flourish, he would need help. He wrote home, and as a result an older brother, Dr. Thomas Flint, and two cousins, Lewellyn Bixby and Amasa Bixby Jr., joined the swell of argonauts heading west by way of the Isthmus

of Panama. They began the long journey on May 21, 1851, the day Thomas Flint wrote in his diary, "Left my childhood home for California."[8]

The three young men made their way to Boston, on to New York City by train, and finally boarded the *Crescent City*, a crowded steamship carrying forty-five people from Maine and other assorted "growling, rowing" passengers. After sailing to the Bay of Chagres, on June 6 the passengers transferred to a small stern-wheel steamboat and started up Panama's Chagres River to Gorgona. Two days later, with pack mules in tow, they crossed the dividing ridge between the Atlantic and Pacific oceans, traveling on foot to Panama City, where they boarded a vermin-ridden steamship called the *Northerner*. They stopped at Acapulco and reached San Francisco on July 7, but the trade winds, as well as debris from a fire that had taken place in May, made for an uncomfortably brief visit. That afternoon three weary travelers boarded the steamer *Hartford* going to Sacramento. Three days later they caught a freight wagon headed to the Volcano Diggings, where they met up with Benjamin. On July 12 Thomas Flint concluded his travel diary thusly: "Arrived about noon in Volcano, the objective point when we started from Maine 53 days out."[9] Such was the understated pride and relief that thousands must have felt upon reaching gold country.

TO SEE THE ELEPHANT

A family legend claims that while the Bixby brothers and Tom Flint were sailing up the California coast to San Francisco in a decrepit, mismanaged steamer, the drunken captain came dangerously close to running aground in the vicinity of today's Long Beach. As the passengers crowded along the rail, watching in suspense, the brothers noticed several Mexican vaqueros

Jotham Bixby, ca. 1860. In 1852 two more Flints and two more Bixbys from Maine would head to California. Courtesy of Rancho Los Cerritos Historic Site, Long Beach, California

herding cattle on the low bluffs just back of a beach of the whitest sand. *Beautiful!* Lewellyn thought, or so the story goes. *Someday I'd like to have a ranch around here.*[10] The ship moved on and the dream faded...for a time.

Hopes may flourish in such idyllic dreams, but those who lived in Southern California suffered the waking reality of a regional discontent. Six cow counties in Southern California (population 6,000) were required to pay $42,000 in property taxes. But twelve mining counties in Northern California (population 120,000) paid only $21,000 in taxes. Worse, mining claims on U.S. land (the majority) were not taxed under California law.[11] In August 1851, the *Los Angeles Star* complained that the region "would be better off as a territory dependent upon the federal government than as six counties neglected by the state," since Southern California received nothing for its disproportionate taxes.[12]

Attempts to separate Northern and Southern California would become a regional sport in time, but in 1859 it was a serious matter. That year the legislature passed Assemblyman Andrés Pico's proposal to separate Southern California into a new Territory of Colorado. Regional voters approved, but Civil War fears of spreading slavery ended the matter in Congress. But the rift continued as other legislation benefited the mining counties in Northern California as well.[13]

After Thomas Flint, Lewellyn Bixby, and Amasa Bixby reached

Volcano in July 1851, they mined awhile—in that excitement it was impossible not to—and soon discovered they did not like the work any more than Ben did. Lewellyn took a job in a butcher shop, perhaps one to which Ben Flint had already sold cattle. Deciding the odorous place had a future, he persuaded Ben and Tom Flint to become partners with him and buy the establishment—partly on credit, one assumes, for the young men were already showing signs of the entrepreneurial bent that would characterize many of the family members in the future. Take Dr. Flint, for instance. He practiced no medicine in California but did, at a fee, put his accurate scales to work weighing gold dust, a principal medium of exchange between the town's miners and merchants. He may even have bought the metal at a discount from men in a hurry for cash. Anyway, he soon raised funds enough to build one of Volcano's first hotels, the National House.[14]

In 1852, two more Flints and two more Bixbys, Jotham and Marcellus, answered the blood's call to pioneer. (In time all of Lewellyn's seven brothers and two sisters would move to California.) The newcomers found employment in different places. Meanwhile, the loose partnership

Wedding portrait of Marcellus Bixby and his first wife, Mary Amanda Gould Bixby, August 3, 1857. Courtesy of Rancho Los Cerritos Historic Site, Long Beach, California

of Lewellyn Bixby and Ben and Thomas Flint stayed together, speculating more and more in cattle. Ben, accompanied at times by Jotham, made most of the buying trips, some as far as Los Angeles County. During the visits some knowledge of the area must have lodged in the back of their minds, ready to be drawn upon when the time came.[15]

THE GOOD SHEPHERDS

By the end of 1852 the Bixby-Flint enterprise was going so well that its partners were ready to engage in a new pursuit: raising quality sheep from breeding stock obtained in the Midwest. No record remains to explain why they decided on sheep ranching, but the general logic can be assumed. Southern California appeared to have an endless supply of cattle, and their price was plummeting at the mines as increasing numbers of herds took to the trail. The supply of sheep, by contrast, was limited. Aware of this, former mountain men living in New Mexico—Kit Carson, Uncle Dick Wootton, and Lucien Maxwell among them—were hurrying west with big flocks. The New Mexican sheep were scruffy animals, however, tough but small, with sparse, coarse wool.[16] The American Midwest abounded with higher-quality animals that should command good enough prices to offset the skid in value brought on by the herds from New Mexico. Sheep could be handled more easily and economically than cattle on the unfenced ranges in the rolling hills south of San Francisco Bay, a region close to several voracious markets. Moreover, sheep were more prolific than cattle, twin lambs being far more common than twin calves. Finally, sheep offered a twofold opportunity—wool and mutton. After the spring shearing, the male lambs could be butchered and the females kept to maintain the size of the flock.

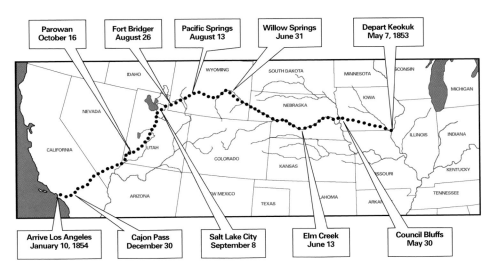

The route of the sheep drive made by Lewellyn Bixby, Benjamin Flint, and Thomas Flint in 1853. The map is based on the rough sketch accompanying Thomas Flint's diary. William S. Wells, 2009

Their decision was made on Christmas Day 1852, Thomas Flint recorded in his diary. The enterprising trio traveled east by way of Panama with thirty-six pounds of gold. Some was in the form of fifty-dollar slugs minted in California; the rest was freshly mined gold dust. (During the 1850s private mints in San Francisco had begun melting and extracting pure gold from the miners' ore, since gold dust was difficult to handle and gauge. Officially stamped with the private mint's name and seal of approval, California slugs circulated in the confusing array of coins from Mexico, France, England, and Germany, in addition to the U.S. currency required for all import duties. The U.S Mint in San Francisco would open in 1854.)[17]

A goodly portion of the Flint and Bixby metal had probably come from the sale of the butcher shop and the last of their cattle. When they turned in the mixture at the mint in Philadelphia, they realized between $10,000 and $11,000, no great treasure for three men, even in those days.[18] As Tom Flint said in his diary, however, they were undertaking the sheep drive as much for adventure as for profit.

On January 31, a little over a month from their start in California, the travelers arrived home in Maine. There Thomas Flint saw his old famil-iar homestead with a new perspective. He wrote on February 1 that at the first glance out of his window, he was "surprised in my recollection of the landscape before me. What was large and high to me when a child seemed dwarfed. The fields did not appear to be more than garden patches in Cali-fornia."[19] Moreover, the three adventurers had become "objects of interest" since they were among the first to return from the "far distant land of gold." They talked until their "vocal organs could stand the strain no longer and were glad to start west on March 8th."[20]

His diary recounts boarding the first of a series of uncomfortable trains that took them as far as Terre Haute, Indiana. There, after formally organizing the firm of Flint, Bixby & Co., they bought horses for the ride to central Illinois, where they put together, bit by bit, a herd of about eighteen hundred sheep to begin the epic journey. These they promptly sheared, and then they sold the wool for $1,570. On May 7 they paid an imperturbable ferryman sixty-two dollars to float the bleating herd, bunch by bunch, across the Mississippi to Keokuk, Iowa. They had one hired hand and three sheepdogs with them; they carried their supplies in two wagons pulled by oxen.[21]

After crossing the Missouri at Council Bluffs,[22] they added another wagon and several helpers, among them William and Mary Johnson, two work-your-way-west emigrants they picked up beside the trail.[23] The Johnsons lasted out the trip; most of the others quit as soon as opportunity offered. The party followed the busy Mormon route on the north side of the Platte River, which was about to get even busier: back in Missouri, they had seen 278 emigrant wagons ready to take thirty-four hundred European proselytes to Salt Lake.[24] The Bixby-Flint party passed by Indian villages and encountered Indians, some friendly, some not.[25] Along the way they met a huge herd of nine thousand sheep being driven west by William Welles Hollister of Ohio and some fifty drovers. (The town of Hollister in Northern California is named after him.) The two groups leapfrogged each other the rest of the distance to California, and their shared problems developed into firm friendships.[26]

It was a slower trip than they had anticipated, and they did not reach Salt Lake City until September,[27] too late to risk pushing straight ahead in the hope of crossing the Sierra before snow blocked the high passes. So they swung south through the then tiny hamlet of Las Vegas and on across the grim Mojave Desert. They lost sheep in the desert. They were often hungry, thirsty, and cold, and always tired. But surely easier times were com-ing. On January 1, 1854, exactly one year after leaving San Francisco, they pushed their herd across Cajon Pass and down into a region very different from what they had seen.[28] The sheepherders from Maine must have real-ized, as they moved their flock westward along the base of the San Gabriel Mountains, that here was a land of uncommon promise. The first rains had brought a vivid green to the undulating earth. Clusters of dark green live oaks stood like diadems on some of the knolls. Thickets of sycamores, alders, willows, and cottonwoods shaded the stream courses that drained the high mountains. On January 9 they halted their herd—now increased to twenty-four hundred through purchases—on the Rancho El Rincón de

> Tuesday [January] 10th. Went into Los Angeles to fit out supplies for a two-months stay in camp before taking the coast route north. From this time on we remained in the vicinity of Los Angeles...The last part of March we started along the coast for Northern California. Drove through Santa Barbara, San Luis Obispo—San Juan Bautista to Santa Teresa Rancho, one Spanish league S.E. of San Jose, where we remained 14 months. While on that ranch sheared our sheep and sold the clip...Purchased about 1,000 sheep...at $5.00 per head and brought them from near Petaluma. —*from the diary of Dr. Thomas Flint*

San Pascual, whose 13,595 acres they rented for the rest of the winter from the owner, Manuel Garfias, a former officer in the Mexican army.[29] Today the city of Pasadena sprawls across those acres.

What sightseeing trips Lewellyn, the Flint brothers, and William Hollister took while waiting for spring are mostly unrecorded. There must have been a few. After all, they were young, energetic, and professionally interested in farms and farmlands. And here they were in the heart of what would become and long remain the richest agricultural county in the United States, with its potential already being recognized and coveted by new arrivals.

The adventurers had already camped at Mission San Gabriel on their way to San Pascual, and the day after arriving they headed southwest into the county seat of Los Angeles to outfit their new camp for the long winter layover. The drab, dusty, violent town built mostly of adobe bricks boasted a mixed population of a little over sixteen hundred Mexicans, mestizos, blacks, Native Americans, and Anglo-Americans.[30]

If Ben Flint had come this far south on cattle-buying trips, as seems likely, surely they had references in Los Angeles. More than likely, these would have included two of the town's leading citizens, former traders and naturalized Mexicans—not to mention Yankees, like themselves—who had come before. Jonathan Temple had bought Rancho Los Cerritos in 1844,

land the Bixbys and Tom Flint may have looked at while coasting along the Long Beach shore in 1851;[31] Abel Stearns had bought its eastern neighbor, Rancho Los Alamitos, in 1842. Couldn't one suppose that Lewellyn might even have mentioned to them, perhaps over drinks one evening, his admiration for their properties?...Well, not even family legend goes that far, and for good reason: Abel Stearns was in the thick of ugly times.

UGLY TIMES

Southern California was an isolated, occupied, and sought-after frontier during the 1850s. There was no regular stagecoach to San Francisco or

Los Angeles, looking north from Temple Street, 1857. Lithograph by Charles Kuchel and Emil Dresel

Salt Lake; steamers arrived at Wilmington Harbor just a few times every month, and no telegraph line linked Los Angeles to San Francisco.[32] New news was old news by the time it arrived in Southern California. Yet despite the regional isolation, some people thrived. By most accounts, the rancheros—the Californios and Yankee dons—lived extraordinarily well off the expensive beef they sold up north and the inexpensive labor they used down south. Los Angeles, however, was more symptomatic of the decade, a town where murder was a daily occurrence and where punishment "graduated by the color of the skin, and not the color of the crime," as one journalist of the time said.[33]

In 1853 the *Los Angeles Star* reported that "there is no country where nature is more lavish of her exuberant fullness and yet with all our natural beauties and advantages, there is no country where human life is of so little account. Men hack one another in pieces with pistols and other cutlery."[34] The 1850 federal census (an incomplete record), identified 8,329 inhabitants in Los Angeles County, half Indians.[35] During the coming decade Native Americans would suffer their worst decline in population and Mexican numbers would decline as well: within a generation they would drop from 80 percent of the total population to perhaps 20 percent.[36]

As one historian has noted, "What had been the Mexican American War only a few years earlier became a war against Mexican Americans."[37] The Treaty of Guadalupe Hidalgo guaranteed that Mexicans who stayed in California would become full American citizens, but prejudice and the legal system denied their property rights and opportunities.[38] Upper-crust Californios were forced to fight for their land and the regional Mexican population at large became an underclass of dependent wage laborers. Those resisting met force.[39]

Although statehood did not beget the violence,[40] it drew the lines and the noose. Sonoratown, the Mexican barrio north of the pueblo (named for Sonoran miners ousted from the gold country) was Mexico proper in the eyes of many Anglos.[41] Self-appointed vigilante groups—the volunteer Rangers, the gang of Texans from El Monte, the "local capital of anti-Mexican word and deed,"[42] and Committees of Public Safety—led the charge to assert order through legal, and often illegal, force and violence.

The population split in fear and hatred. Juan Flores, leader of a band of outlaws, won the support and sympathy of the Mexican American population, but his capture and hanging in 1854 prompted over a hundred new lynchings. Californios who had tried to distance themselves from the general Mexican American population and defend their land by allying with Anglos now felt betrayed, and newcomers asserted their power.[43] The implications of the decade would play out for generations.

Yankee Don Abel Stearns, owner of Rancho Los Alamitos, lived squarely in the times. In February 1853 he and his wife, Arcadia Bandini, would host a party at El Palacio in Los Angeles for the "agreeable" elite Californios and Americanos. It ended disagreeably. As the *Los Angeles Star* reported, "certain parties took umbrage, because they were left out"—they were incensed that the invited Californios, not they, would be celebrating the birthday of George Washington at El Palacio, the social center of Los Angeles. On the night of the party a surly mob attacked the Palace to break up the festivities. A cannon was fired, a revolver discharged, but the outsiders continued their unruly protest. Around eleven p.m. bells rang out, firecrackers exploded, and the mob rushed again. Shots rang out. Then two people lay dead.[44] In the best of homes, the times were ugly. At least at

Rancho Los Alamitos, Abel Stearns's home away from troubled home, things were not quite as violent.

HEADED BACK NORTH

In any event, the drovers did not tarry long in the "promising" land below the Tehachapis. Spring was coming and the Bixby-Flint compass was pointing north to where other family members were waiting and where their far-traveled sheep, growing fat now, could be marketed to better advantage, in needy and well-heeled San Francisco.

So, late in March they pushed their herd slowly through hills velvety green from winter rains to rented pastures near San Jose. A year later, eager for a place of their own, they moved about fifty miles south to the vicinity

SAN JUSTO RANCHO, FLINT, BIXBY & CO. PROPRIETORS, SAN JUAN, SAN BENITO CO. CAL.

Rancho San Justo was the home of the extended Flint-Bixby family before the Bixbys moved to Southern California.

1855—July. Moved to Monterey Co. for sheep feed. In October bought the San Justo Rancho in name of Flint, Bixby & Co, though with the understanding that Col. Hollister would pay for half of it...The San Justo has been the home place up to this time of Thomas Flint and family. —*from the diary of Dr. Thomas Flint*

of the old mission of San Juan Bautista, founded in 1797. There they purchased, with William Hollister, the 34,620-acre Rancho San Justo.[45] Hollister owned one-half interest in the undivided property; Flint, Bixby & Co. (Tom Flint, Ben Flint, and Lewellyn Bixby) owned the other.

Other Bixbys and Flints soon clustered around. Jotham and Marcellus sold a ranch they had held only a short time, bought fifteen hundred sheep, and set up headquarters in the hamlet that had grown up around the San Juan Bautista mission. In 1857 the Flint brothers went back to Maine in search of wives, found them, and returned to California by way of the railroad that had been finished across the Isthmus of Panama two years earlier. Accompanying the bridal party were Ann Flint, a sister of Ben and Thomas; Nancy Bixby, one of Lewellyn's sisters; and two more Bixby males.

The married couples and the two unwed girls set up housekeeping in the ranch's four cabins. Lonesome? Evidently not. Nancy Bixby wrote that thanks to the remoteness of neighbors they were able "to make as much noise as we please...which I esteem a great privilege." They also had the privilege, during shearing season, of cooking three heavy meals a day for the thirty hands brought in to clip the sheep.[46]

Two years later Lewellyn Bixby's life took a domestic turn. While visiting his family in Maine, he attended a church meeting at the home of the

Wedding portrait of Lewellyn Bixby and Sarah Hathaway Bixby, 1859. Sarah, Lewellyn's first wife, died six years later. Courtesy of Rancho Los Cerritos Historic Site, Long Beach, California

Reverend George Hathaway, a liberal (for the times) minister who could trace his ancestry back to the *Mayflower*. Hathaway and his wife, Mary Susanna, were the parents of two boys and six girls. Lewellyn promptly wooed and won petite Sarah.[47] She was eighteen; he was just short of thirty-four.

Back on the California ranch, the three couples set up a housekeeping arrangement that is only a little short of mind-boggling. In 1861 San Justo was formally split in half because William Hollister wanted to sell part of his interest. The Bixby-Flint sextet then moved about five miles, to the buildings formerly occupied by the Hollisters. Gentle hills spotted with live oaks enfolded the site, which boasted a California rarity, a small lake. There the new proprietors built an elegant, many-gabled, Maine-style house decorated with early Victorian gingerbread and surrounded by a wide verandah. Several barns and outbuildings rose nearby.[48]

The house contained three apartments, one for each family. Both Flint families were producing children with down-Maine regularity, but Lewellyn and Sarah Bixby remained childless. All three families shared a common parlor, dining room, and kitchen, and a large office. Housekeeping rotated, each wife taking a turn every month. Guests were common, as were visiting relatives, mostly female, who stayed for months at a stretch.[49] The potentially explosive arrangement lasted for fifteen years, breaking apart only when Lewellyn Bixby moved a new wife and their children to Los Angeles in 1877.[50]

Sarah, Lewellyn's first wife, had died childless, six years after their wedding.[51] Five years later the forty-five-year-old widower married her younger sister Mary, then aged twenty-four. She died in Los Angeles seven years

Left: Mary Hathaway Bixby, the second wife of Lewellyn Bixby and the mother of Sarah Bixby Smith and her two siblings, ca. 1868. She died seven years after her marriage to Lewellyn.

Right: Sarah Bixby Smith, daughter of Mary and Lewellyn Bixby, and future author of *Adobe Days*, ca. 1885. Courtesy of Rancho Los Cerrito Historic Site, Long Beach, California

---

The San Justo house was newly built by the three partners-cousins, large enough to accommodate their families. It was reminiscent of Maine, with its white paint, green blinds and sharp gables edged with wood lace...perhaps meant to remind them of icicles.

—*Sarah Bixby Smith,* Adobe Days

Martha Hathaway, ca. 1860s. Martha declined to become the third Hathaway sister to marry widower Lewellyn Bixby, but she cared for his children.

Margaret Hathaway Bixby, wife of Jotham, ca. 1860s

I am a child of California, a grandchild of Maine, and a great-grandchild of Massachusetts. —*Sarah Bixby Smith,* Adobe Days

Bixby & Co. Like Lewellyn and the Flint brothers, he, too, visited Maine—in his case in 1862—and dropped by the Hathaway residence to meet his new in-laws, Sarah's sisters. Margaret caught his eye. She was nineteen then, two years younger than Sarah, who was still alive and learning her way around the new house at San Justo. Jotham was thirty-one; a ruff of whiskers circled his kindly face from ear to ear.[53]

It was a whirlwind courtship, and Jotham had to leave for California before Margaret could get ready for a wedding. She followed in November, traveling with friends by ship, the Panama railroad, and then ship again to San Francisco. They were married at San Juan Bautista on December 4, 1863, and settled into a house of their own.[54] Not for long, however. Because of a pair of catastrophes—drought in the West and Civil War in the East—new opportunities in livestock were opening up that made the fading goldfields of the Mother Lode country look pallid, at least in the eyes of the Flints and the Bixbys.[55]

NORTH AND SOUTH

You can't downplay luck. Not out west. It is an essential, if fickle ingredient of the myths that illumine California, and its smile certainly shone on Flint, Bixby & Co. the year they bought San Justo. The Civil War broke out. Union ships blockaded Southern ports to halt the shipment of cotton. Wool immediately became a necessary substitute—especially for

after the wedding, having borne three children. (Sarah, the oldest, grew up to be Sarah Bixby Smith, the renowned author of *Adobe Days,* published in 1925. Her classic account would recall the Bixby family story and life at San Justo, as well as life in a poetic, bygone Southern California at Rancho Los Cerritos and Rancho Los Alamitos.) Lewellyn next importuned sister Martha Hathaway to marry him. She resisted, but did come west to care for her young nieces and nephew.[52]

Younger brother Jotham soon strengthened ties to the Hathaways. It's probable that Marcellus and he had amicably ended their business associations, and Jotham had become a principal and valued employee of Flint,

March 1, 1860

Dear Brother,

...Yours of Dec 9th was received last week: it was at Jotham's a month before I received it, I was so busy I could not go over after my mail; we are working very hard taking care of young lambs, we have over one thousand lambs less than four weeks old, and if a man ever done hard work I have for the past months. You say that you wish that you was in California tending sheep....I forbid it: don't you ever come to this country.... It would be useless for you to go into the mines....If you were to come down here and tend sheep, you could not get but $30 per month, and be obliged to work very hard every day, rain or shine, hot or cold, Sundays not excepted....It is a dog's life to tend sheep....Times are getting harder every year in Cal. And I think that the majority who now come to this land will not make as much as they would if at home....I have not heard from home for some time. I received a host of papers the other day but there was nothing in any of them but John Brown John Brown....

From your Brother A. R. Bixby

(Letter from Augustus Rufus Bixby to Samuel Munson Bixby, March 1, 1860. Augustus Bixby came to California in the 1850s. His cousin John W. Bixby (a future partner in Alamitos) would arrive in 1871 with much better luck.)

the Union, which needed woolen uniforms and blankets for its armies. Prices soared.[56]

California had fewer than eighteen hundred sheep in 1850;[57] by the 1860s the number had increased to around a million, half in the southern parts of the state.[58] The profitable wool clip (the total amount shorn in one season) jumped from 5.5 million pounds in 1862 to 22 million in 1871[59] to meet the new demand. Sheepmen everywhere, not least in Northern California, began questing for additional land on which to graze enlarged flocks. Ahead of the vanguard was Flint, Bixby & Company. They had already purchased the fifteen-thousand-acre Huero-Huero Ranch near Paso Robles in 1858—a fine stepping-stone south—but with the onset

of the great drought of 1862 to 1864, even that swath of land proved inadequate. Where could more rangeland be had?

The answer was Southern California—if a man could wait out the recent weather, not to mention the grasshoppers, the scorching Santa Ana winds, and the heavy overgrazing that had helped turn a pastoral paradise to dry dust. For the American newcomers, the times were right for the taking. The Treaty of Guadalupe Hidalgo, the Land Act, and the belief that land, however gained, was an inherent right of California's conquest by a superior people and culture[60] churned through the 1860s and 1870s. The Californios and Yankee dons, who had for a time held sway after California became a state, succumbed to the new economy of Southern California—markets, production, and compound interest.[61] But other things would not change, including the pattern of large acreages owned by a few and the need for inexpensive labor.

Corporate banks were illegal in California, banned under the state constitution to avoid the problems arising from unregulated free middlemen and paper banknotes in the rest of the country. In spite of this, San Francisco and Sacramento banks existed long before the ban was lifted in the late 1870s.[62] Southern California was another story. In the isolated region, most people were not able to easily borrow working capital at reasonable rates (1.5 to 2 percent) until 1868, the year the first bank opened in Los Angeles; a second bank followed a few months later.[63] The cofounder of this bank, Isaias Wolf Hellman, had been sizing up land and buying properties since 1863.[64] Taking advantage of skyrocketing prices and sales (between 1868 and 1869, countywide real estate transactions increased 500 percent),[65] Hellman became a real estate mogul of the region, and he was, for a brief time, a part financier of and partner in

Rancho Los Alamitos.[66] The transfer and consolidation of land during the 1860s and 1870s equaled a national phenomenon: as Kevin Starr puts it, "Rarely in the history of the United States was so much acreage consolidated in so few hands."[67]

Whether Flint, Bixby & Co. carried word of this buyers' market to James Irvine, a wealthy San Francisco wholesale merchant and real estate dealer (who also did business with I. W. Hellman) or whether Irvine approached them because of their experience with livestock can't be said. In either event the new partners moved aggressively south and between 1864 and 1868 purchased ranchos San Joaquin and Lomas de Santiago and part of Santiago de Santa Ana—approximately 110,000 acres in all. As they had in their arrangement with Hollister, the three partners of Flint, Bixby & Co. held an undivided one-half interest in the property, while Irvine alone held the other half.[68]

Fortune smiled. Heavy rains fell during the winter of 1867-68, and the partners were able to graze upward of thirty thousand sheep on the combined holdings.[69] The herds produced forty thousand lambs, and the wool that was shipped from Newport Bay sold at roughly thirty cents a pound in New York. Since a single sheep could be maintained at a cost of about thirty-five cents a year and produced six and a half pounds of wool in the same period, the return on the investment well outstripped that from many a gold mine. Moreover, Irvine thought, his half of the landholdings could probably carry as many as a hundred thousand sheep a year, and the land was steadily rising in value, partly because of pressure from agriculturists who were immigrating into all parts of the Los Angeles Basin.[70] If only weather and prices held—but those items were not part of the foreseeable future.

During that time of rapid expansion, Flint, Bixby & Co. took a flyer on their own. In 1866 Jonathan Temple, the fading and ailing don, agreed to sell them his twenty-seven-thousand-acre Rancho Los Cerritos and surviving livestock for $20,000.[71] Unable to supervise the new holding because of their other activities, the owners proposed that Lewellyn's younger brother Jotham Bixby take charge of Los Cerritos in return for half of each year's profits and an option to buy half of the ranch for $10,000. Timing could hardly have been more opportune. Rains returned; wool prices climbed. By 1869 Jotham's Indian and Californio workers had sheared enough fleeces and he had shipped enough mutton to exercise his purchase option. A new firm, J. Bixby & Company, was set up to recognize the partnership comprising Jotham Bixby and Flint, Bixby & Co.[72]

That same year Jotham gave symbolic and perhaps unconscious notice that his family's pioneering days were drawing to a close.

Isaias Wolf Hellman, California's foremost banker and financier in the late nineteenth and early twentieth centuries. Hellman was a one-third investor in the Rancho Los Alamitos partnership, which also included John Bixby and J. Bixby & Co. (Jotham Bixby with Flint, Bixby & Company). Courtesy of the California Historical Society

Sheep shearers in front of the barn at Rancho Los Cerritos, spring 1872. Photograph by William Godfrey, courtesy of Rancho Los Cerritos Historic Site, Long Beach, California

way of knowing this, of course, but he did have reason to feel the years 1869-70 were going to be good for entrepreneurs and the new class of landowners who would use the capital that they had made elsewhere to buy land in California and make more. Such was the beginning of agribusiness.[75]

In May 1869, the joint Central Pacific–Union Pacific transcontinental railroad was completed, joining the Mississippi Valley to Sacramento, with connections to San Francisco Bay. The California Immigrant Union, seeing the railroad builders and developers intent on generating heavy traffic flows to all California, decided it was in the best interest of its membership to help promote new inbound travel and immigration—particularly to the still isolated cow counties of the south. One task

He became a major contributor to and a board member as well of a quasi-governmental booster organization named the California Immigrant Union.[73]

TRACKS TO THE PROMISED LAND

Statisticians used to believe (and perhaps still do) that spurts in real estate activity occur in California every twenty years or so.[74] Jotham Bixby had no

would be to prove that Los Angeles County really wasn't hard to reach. A traveler could catch one of the steamships that made regular runs between San Francisco and San Pedro Bay (a two-day trip), whose landing facilities had recently been improved by a bull-voiced transportation entrepreneur named Phineas Banning. For some years Banning had been running stagecoaches between San Pedro and Los Angeles and massive freight wagons to army posts and other destinations in the interior. As the probability grew that seaborne traffic between San Francisco and Los

Jotham Bixby in the gardens at Rancho Los Cerritos

Angeles would increase, he prepared himself by building a little twenty-two-mile railroad from his wharf at San Pedro to Los Angeles.[76]

Banning had no monopoly, with his sea-land route, on travel to Southern California. Some travelers would prefer journeying between the San Francisco Bay Area and southern points by stagecoach. The Overland Mail Company had operated a stage line between San Francisco and Los Angeles through the interior of California, but in 1861 the Civil War brought an end to the route.[77] Anticipating a renewed demand for stagecoach transportation, Flint, Bixby & Company bought the Coast Stage Line on January 17, 1868, for $70,000. The seller was William Lovett (state senator, gubernatorial candidate, assistant U.S. attorney general, Indian agent), who was married to one of Lewellyn Bixby's sisters—perhaps the company was foreclosing on Lovett as the only way to recover $70,000 in easygoing in-law loans they had made earlier. As for the stage line, it ran from San Diego through Los Angeles, Santa Barbara, and San Luis Obispo to San Jose, where rail connections could be made to either San Francisco or the Central Pacific's terminus at Sacramento.[78]

The next part of the California Immigrant Union's job was to make the still-arduous journey, whether by sea or Bixby stagecoaches, seem worthwhile. The Union's most powerful propaganda was provided by the Robinson Trust, the syndicate which had bailed out Abel Stearns in exchange for almost 178,000 acres of land meant for subdivision. Using

LOS ANGELES, CAL., 1873.

Los Angeles gives its name to the valley in which it is located, and where it occupies a charming location, nestling amidst orange groves and vineyards. The Coast Range with its accompanying valleys have forms a panoramic view of rare beauty.

A. L. BANCROFT & COMPANY, PUBLISHERS, 721 MARKET STREET, SAN FRANCISCO, CAL.

A bird's-eye view of Los Angeles by A. E. Matthews, 1873

the California Immigrant Union's outlets, the syndicate flooded the United States with hyperbole about climate, agricultural cornucopias, easily drilled artesian wells, and the ready availability of one-family farm plots close to the amenities and markets of the small towns that speckled the firm's maps if not the ground itself. As lots began to move, the implications became obvious to livestock operators. Sheep, cattle, and horses were fine until the land they ranged across became more valuable for other uses.[79] Created from the undoing of Yankee don Abel Stearns and a bygone time, the Robinson Trust was one of the first large-scale land developments in Southern California and a forecast of the future.

And yet, though the California Immigrant Union blew its promotional trumpet loud and far, it wasn't heard by all that many. To most Americans of the time, Southern California still seemed forbiddingly remote. Many land-owning Californians, among them Jotham Bixby, turned to new transportation facilities to bring in more people, especially farming people. Prominent banker I. W. Hellman and other movers and shakers agreed, knowing that the isolated Los Angeles region could never match or hope to challenge the economic power of Northern California and San Francisco without a connecting railway to the transcontinental line. Without this vital economic lifeline the city and region could not grow, only wither. In February 1871 the future of the region came to a vote—Congress authorized a new southern transcontinental route that was to include the city of Los Angeles.[80] In 1876 the Southern Pacific Railroad would finally arrive. Soon "the world rushed in."

FIVE

A PLACE TO SETTLE, A TIME TO BUILD

PERHAPS IT WAS BECAUSE JOTHAM BIXBY needed an extra hand on Rancho Los Cerritos that he sent the invitation to his cousin to come west. Perhaps a California Immigrant Union handbill caught the young New Englander's eye. Or perhaps he simply heard the siren call answered by so many Bixbys before him: California! Whatever the reason or reasons, John William Bixby, a first cousin of Jotham's and Lewellyn's, left Anso, Maine, for the promised land in 1870; there he would find a wife, found a dynasty, and die without realizing what he had accomplished.

In many ways John Bixby's timing would prove to be excellent over the coming years. In 1870 the population of Southern California was 32,032,[1] and during the decade it would increase over 100 percent.[2] California would join the ranks of the ten most populous states in the nation,[3] though the majority of its land would be owned by a few.[4] The Gold Rush had long since ended, but in 1872 the clarion call of *California for Health, Wealth, and Residence* by Charles Nordhoff attracted thousands more from the U.S. and Europe to its heralded good life and opportunity, which included easy ranching. "To one who likes a free outdoor life, I think nothing can be more delightful than the life of a farmer of sheep in Southern California,"[5] Nordhoff wrote after visiting Tejón Ranch (sixty miles north of Los Angeles),[6] where three hundred Indians eventually lived and worked as tenant farmers following the closure of the Sebastian Indian Reserve in 1862. Taking Nordhoff's unbridled praise to heart, 154,300 people would head to California between 1873 and 1875.[7]

By this time John Bixby had already made his stake. Dark-haired, slender, and more than six feet tall, he was twenty-two when he arrived in Los Angeles early in 1871 with thirty dollars in his pocket and ready to meet opportunity. Los Angeles remained a violent place in 1871. On October 24 the Chinese quarter in

Facing page: John William Bixby, ca. 1868. He was born in the same year that his cousins Benjamin and Thomas Flint and Lewellyn Bixby headed for the California Gold Rush.

The first entry on John Bixby's ledger page is to "Susie," who is Susan Hathaway Bixby.

01-30-1872	Commenced work for Jotham Bixby—one month's wages—$40
05-01-1872	20 days work at $2.00—$40.00
06-01-1872	Anaheim Landing and about range—$1.50
06-21-1872	One day hauling wood—$1.50
06-22-1872	One day doctoring sheep—$1.50
08-14-1872	Pants—$6.50, shirt—$2.00, Cigars—$2.25, necktie—.50, Watch chain & key—.75
08-17-1872	J. W. Bixby—3 days work on camp—$4.50
	Expenses of shearing fall 1878: Aug. 19th—40 lbs. sugar $5.06; 16 lbs. bacon—$2.24; 100 lbs. flour—$6.50; 10 lbs. coffee—$2.50; 100 lbs. potatoes—$1.00; 15 lbs. rice—$1.50; 2 boxes pepper—$4.50; 1 pkg. saleratus—.25; 2 pkg salt—.50; 1 box matches—$.25; 2 yeast powder—$.50
08-20-1872	She horse from Jotham which he gave me
09-07-1872	Hair cutting—.25
09-17-1872	Commenced work for J. B. & Co. and worked at shearing 14
days	

—from J. W. Bixby, Cerritos Ranch Ledger, Jan. 1872—Fall 1878

John Bixby knew little about ranching when he arrived at Rancho Los Cerritos, but his schoolteaching experience was a business asset. He managed accounts and documented ranching and personal expenses in ongoing ledgers.

| 06-04-1873 | Chinaman—washing 7 pieces—.75 |
| 08-01-1873 | Chinaman—1/2 doz clothes—.50 |

—from J. W. Bixby, Rancho Los Cerritos Ledger, July 24, 1872—Dec. 26, 1873

John W. Bixby, after helping his widowed mother pay off the mortgage on a State of Maine farm, started in his early twenties with $187 in his pocket and that good mother's blessing on his head, to join his Bixby kin in Southern California.

—Martha Hathaway, Long Beach Press Telegram, *n.d.*

Los Angeles's infamous Negro Alley would burn. At least nineteen people would be killed in what proved to be the worst incidence of anti-Chinese violence yet in California.[8]

Well educated, John Bixby had been teaching school when the impulse to move sent him West in 1870. He brought his infectious gaiety, a love of pranks, a violin he played with exuberance—and a capacity for persistent hard work. Already a skilled carpenter, he put his talent to work at Rancho Los Cerritos, where he earned up to forty dollars per month on a contract basis—twice the average worker's wages.

There, under cousin Jotham's supervision, he also learned how to run sheep; how to dip them in a homemade concoction of scalded tobacco soup, sulfur, and other ingredients to prevent disease; what supplies were needed to outfit the sheep camps; and how much to pay the men.[9] John Bixby knew little about ranching when he arrived at Rancho Los Cerritos in 1872, but no doubt his teaching background was a valued business asset. He began keeping business ledgers to document the Rancho's—and a few of his personal—expenses. The watch chain and key, pair of pants, shirt, tie, and haircut recorded might indicate that he was a well-groomed man with plans for the future.

When John arrived, wool prices were still rising. Because he was insightful by nature, he may have glimpsed the sadness underlying the glow

John W. Bixby...was a son of Simon Bixby and Deborah Flint... Several of his older brothers were in California...and his sister.... Like young men of today going into a new country he looked for a job...anything that was offered. He soon found a place with his cousin, Jotham, at the Cerritos, learning ranching, doing carpentering...making...cabinets and bookcases that are still in use.

—*Sarah Bixby Smith,* Adobe Days, *1925*

Dipping sheep at Rancho Los Cerritos, spring 1872. Jotham Bixby, who ran Rancho Los Cerritos on behalf of J. Bixby & Co., is standing in the center of the photo. Photograph by William Godfrey, courtesy of Rancho Los Cerritos Historic Site, Long Beach, California

of prosperity that buoyed the ranch during the two annual shearings that rewarded the labor of the preceding long months. Once Native Americans had handled the clippers, but as their numbers thinned, their places were taken by the displaced rancheros and vaqueros who had once proudly practiced the cowboy's trade as well.[10] Then again, many native people in Southern California had intermarried and were using Spanish surnames, so this is likely an oversimplification. For example, in the early twentieth century ethnologist John P. Harrington interviewed an Ajachemem (Juaneño) man by the name of José de la Gracia Cruz, or "Acú," who may have "sheared sheep at Los Alamitos ranch house" around this time.[11]

Bands of shearers followed a circuit from ranch to ranch, some still dressed in the finery of bygone days, riding hand-tooled saddles and reining their high-stepping mounts with silvered bridles. On reaching the site of a job, they made camp in an old barn, folded their finery into their bedrolls, donned brown overalls, and went to work. After seizing one of a group of penned animals, they threw it onto the shearing floor, denuded it, tossed the fleece onto a counter, collected a token worth five cents or so, and reached for another sheep. An experienced hand could shear more than forty animals a day, but all too likely he lost his earnings by lantern light after supper to poorer clippers but better gamblers.[12] On the larger ranches

Twice a year, spring and fall, the sheep came up to be sheared, dipped and counted....The shearers would come in, a gay band of Mexicans on their prancing horses, decked with wonderful, silver-trimmed bridles made of rawhide or braided horsehair, and saddles with high horns, sweeping stirrups, and wide expanse of beautiful tooled leather....They would...live and work at the ranch for more than a month.

—*Sarah Bixby Smith,* Adobe Days, *1925*

03-08-1872	J. Bixby & Co—To cash paid Shearer Dominguez—$1.25
02-01-1881	Shearing & Dipping 5239 Sheep—$550.09; Dipping 2200 Lambs—$440.09

—from Expense Ledger, Jan. 1881–June 1882

the shearing season might last longer than a month. But after a few such jobs, destitution returned until the next season.

ALL IN THE FAMILIES

In addition to learning how to supervise the handling of the herds, John Bixby worked at the constant chores of hauling, repairing, and building that are endemic on any ranch, and in the process he refined his native talent for carpentry. He also took a fancy to Susan Hathaway, sister of Jotham's wife, Margaret. Susan had come to Los Cerritos for a protracted visit. Her being three years older than John proved no impediment to the romance, and they were married on October 4, 1873. She was the fourth Hathaway to wed a Bixby.

The couple set up housekeeping in Wilmington near Phineas

Banning's wharf and railroad station and almost next door to his big New England–style house. It was a convenient location, and John Bixby would have future business with Banning. In 1875 a son, Frederick Hathaway Bixby, was born. It was also in Wilmington, according to family legend, that Susan stirred John's ambitions, though it wasn't the best of economic times to be ambitious.[13] Wool prices had broken at last and entrepreneurs were looking for other ways to use the land and beat the depression that had gripped the nation in 1875 and arrived full steam in California the next year.[14] Over on the Irvine Ranch, Lewellyn and the Flint brothers were feeling the pinch of another drought, a mysterious epidemic among their lambs, and an unwise mining investment. To rescue themselves they sold their interest to Irvine for $150,000 in 1876. A little later they disposed of the Coast Stage Line.[15]

Rancho Los Cerritos courtyard with Bixby family members, spring 1872. Jotham Bixby is standing in the courtyard. His wife, Margaret, is thought to be the woman in the doorway, and her sister Susan Hathaway (the future wife of John Bixby) may be the woman standing on the roof. Photograph by William Godfrey, information courtesy of Rancho Los Cerritos Historic Site, Long Beach, California

The three families were doubly related, Hathaway mother and Bixby fathers, Mary and Llewellyn, Margaret and Jotham, Susan and John.—*Sarah Bixby Smith, Adobe Days, 1925*

05-25-1872   Ring for Susie—$4.50

—*from J. W. Bixby, Rancho Los Cerritos Ledger,*
July 24, 1872—Dec. 26, 1873

09-29-1888   P. Linarez—Engagement ring—$2.50

—*from Alamitos Day Book #3, July 2, 1888—July 25, 1889*

On rare occasions John Bixby's ledgers reveal the personal lives of both the owners and workers at the ranchos, in this case the engagements of both John Bixby and Pilar Linarez, an Alamitos ranch hand.

Left: Susan Bixby, ca. 1873. Courtesy of Rancho Los Cerritos Historic Site, Long Beach, California

Right: Susan Hathaway Bixby and her sisters, ca. 1865. Standing, left to right: Susan Hathaway Bixby (married John Bixby); Martha Hathaway (cared for the children of widower Llewellyn Bixby); Margaret Hathaway Bixby (married Jotham Bixby). Seated: Mary Hathaway Bixby (second wife of Llewellyn Bixby and mother of Sarah Bixby Smith).

Yet in spite of portents and reversals, some Bixbys remained expansionist. Jotham had struck out on his own by buying into the Palos Verdes Ranch. Then, urged on by Susan, on June 24, 1875, John purchased 2,155 acres of La Cañon de Santa Ana, south and east of the river of the same name.[16] (The land grant is in present-day Orange County and had originally been awarded to Bernardo Yorba by Governor José Figueroa in 1843. Well known, Bernardo Yorba was the son of José Antonio Yorba, who, like Manuel Nieto, had been a leatherjacket soldier on the Portolá expedition of 1769.) Gradually John added another 4,000 or so acres to the holding. Since he spent little

From Bernardo Yorba in 1875 my uncle, John W. Bixby, bought a ranch extending from the beautiful cañon of the Santa Ana up over rounded grassy hills.—*Sarah Bixby Smith,* Adobe Days, *1925*

03-31-1881   Balestor Mex on Santa Ana—hauling 15 tons barley—$25.

—*from Expense Ledger, Jan. 1881—June 1882*

time at Cañon de Santa Ana, one presumes the purchases were an investment and that he leased the land to others until it could be profitably subdivided, as was already happening at the towns of Tustin, Orange, and Santa Ana, no great distance away at the edges of the Irvine Ranch.[17]

In 1871 John Bixby became a lessee himself: in his case, of a piece of Rancho Los Alamitos. Beyond doubt he had ridden over those lovely plains and hills several times since first arriving at Los Cerritos. Out of his musings—and out of yet another harsh drought, in 1876 and 1877, which

In 1866 Gabriel Allen was living in the old adobe on the Alamitos, and had several thousand head of cattle and horses. In 1873, Mr. Mellus' brother-in-law…leased the ranch from Michael Reese for ten years…. About 1878 these men sub-leased one or two thousand acres to John W. Bixby. He and his wife, Susan Hathaway, and their small son Fred moved in at once.

—*Sarah Bixby Smith,* Adobe Days, *1925*

John Bixby, ca. 1873

was souring him on sheep—came a plan to create something new for Los Alamitos. The ranch was being operated at the time by sheep ranchers who were renting the land from Michael Reese, the San Francisco financier who had finally wrested title from Abel Stearns in 1866. The drought had hurt Reese's tenants badly, and they were willing to sublease to John Bixby as much of Los Alamitos as he desired.[18]

A good opening, John thought, perhaps sensing that agriculture was the economic power behind California (it would be through the first two decades of the twentieth century as well).[19] He was also well aware that the Southern Pacific Railroad had reached Los Angeles in 1876 on its way to New Orleans, and he believed the new link to the East and Midwest would bring more immigrants to Southern California than the Immigrant Union and Robinson Trust ever had. So why not put part of the ranch to more intensive use? Introduce new crops. Add dairy cows. Make cheese: it kept well and could be sold to advantage in growing Los Angeles.[20] As a sideline he could try his hand at raising a few of the sleek-coated Hambletonians and trotting carriage horses that had become a passion with him. And maybe use the old Stearns adobe as headquarters for both pursuits?[21]

| 5-25-1872 | Photographs—$4.00 |
| 07-05-1872 | Fare to Wilmington with Susie—$1.00 |

—from J. W. Bixby, Rancho Los Cerritos Ledger, July 24, 1872—Dec. 26, 1873

| 10-01-1874 | Sugar Susie used 16 lbs—.50 |

—from J. W. Bixby, Wilmington, Cal. Day Book & Journal, May 25, 1874—Dec. 1875

| 02-01-1876 | Wilmington—Susie—To Cash—$30 |

—from J. W. Bixby, Alamitos, Cerritos & Wilmington Ledger, 1876—1879

After their marriage, John and Susan Bixby moved from Rancho Los Cerritos to nearby Wilmington. John's ledgers record a few of their household expenses before he, Susan, and their son, Fred, moved to Rancho Los Alamitos.

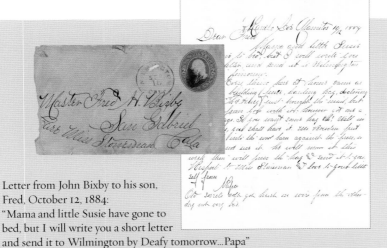

J. W. Bixby state and county taxes, 1889

12-31-1878   County & State Taxes—$1,396.60

—from Expense Ledger, Jan. 1881—June 1882

Letter from John Bixby to his son, Fred, October 12, 1884:
"Mama and little Susie have gone to bed, but I will write you a short letter and send it to Wilmington by Deafy tomorrow...Papa"

Susie was Susanna Bixby (Bryant), the young daughter of John and Susan Bixby, and Deafy was an Alamitos ranch worker whose name appears in the ledgers.

06-16-1887 W. Spencer [Deafy] to pay Chinamen—$325

—from Alamitos Day Book, Sept. 1887

Jotham Bixby, ca. 1866

The firm [Flint, Bixby & Co.] first entered Los Angeles County in 1866, with the purchase from John Temple of Rancho Los Cerritos. Later, with Jotham Bixby, they bought seventeen thousand acres of the Rancho Palos Verdes....We had cattle on both the Alamitos and the Cerritos but the greater range was on the Palos Verdes.

—Sarah Bixby Smith, Adobe Days, 1925

Winter of 1884-85   Jotham Bixby—pasturage on Palo Verdes—2,000 sheep—$400

—from J. W. Bixby & Co., Los Alamitos Ranch Day Book, Sept. 1887—June 30, 1888

The firm of Flint, Bixby and Co. (and Jotham Bixby) sold their Rancho Palos Verdes acreage in 1915.

Most people...have seen the old house...on the brow of a hill out on Anaheim Road....When my uncle and aunt first went there to live it was almost a ruin having fallen...from the high estate it was when it was the summer home of the lovely Arcadia de Bandini de Stearns.

—*Sarah Bixby Smith*, Adobe Days, *1925*

So, with Jotham and Susan agreeing, John Bixby sought out the current tenants. They had signed a ten-year lease with Reese in 1871, which meant that any sublease they entered into with John Bixby would expire with theirs in 1881; but the dream was so strong and Susan so supportive that John was willing to take a chance that his lease would be renewed. In 1878 he signed papers renting something over a thousand acres. The transaction had scarcely been completed when John learned Reese had just died. That meant the entire ranch would probably go on the market during the settlement of the estate. All of Los Alamitos—if he could raise the money!

Buoyed by the thought, something really big to aim for, Susan and John moved with their three-year-old son, Fred, into the crumbling old adobe on the knoll above the Povuu'ngna spring—the adobe that dated back to the days of Governor Figueroa, or even to Juan José Nieto, the heir of the original grantee.[22]

Out of the ramshackle remains, John and Susan Bixby created a new kind of permanent home, the likes of which no one in the region—certainly not the various natives and newcomers who had inhabited the hill from the time of Povuu'ngna—had ever seen. Making the old adobe livable again took hard work and imagination. Part of the roof had fallen in since the days Don Abel and Arcadia had spent here; the front room had been used as a pen for livestock; rats abounded.[23] Over the course of 1878 and 1879 John and Susan hired at least three workers (referred to as "Scotchman No

1," "Mexican," and "Frenchman" in John's ledger) to help divide one room into a dining room and a bedroom. They enlarged the tiny windows that had been set into deep recesses in walls two feet thick, and in 1882 they purchased windows for eighteen dollars at Perry & Woodworth (a planing mill in Los Angeles) as well as elaborate moulding at Guy Smith & Company. They covered the rough adobe walls with newspapers and pasted floral wallpaper on top of that. To find more space for their two children—Fred's sister, Susanna, was born at Los Alamitos in April 1880—they paralleled Stearns's wing with one that extended out from the southwest corner of the main building.

Q. Do you know how much the house where you live in is worth up there on the hill?
A. My home?...I don't know what my home is valued at.
Q. How long has it been built?
A. Nearly one hundred years. But I have repaired it. I have put it in modern condition.
Q. It is a two-story house?
A. Part of it one story.
Q. It is a frame house, is it?
A. One story adobe.
Q. The main part of it is?
A. I have four rooms in the adobe.
Q. The original house was an adobe house?
A. It was.
Q. Four rooms in that. Then you have added some frame buildings to it?
A. Yes, I have some frame....My husband added them.
Q. The frame part has been there how long?
A. Perhaps fifteen years; more than fourteen.

—*from Susan Bixby's testimony, April 18, 1901, in Susan P. H. Bixby et al. vs. Los Alamitos Sugar Company*

At the end of the new wing, John built a tall, round cooling tank. It contained a pair of compartments, one above the other. The top one was kept filled with water pumped from the Povuu'ngna spring by a hydraulic ram that was adjusted so that overflow continually oozed down the tank's rounded sides, keeping the rooms inside cool through evaporation. The bottom one kept cool the stored dairy products, meat, fresh fruits, and vegetables.[24]

| 02-11-1878 | Mexican at house—11 ds. work—$20 |
| Dec. 21, 1883 | house fixing—$3.00 cr. |

—from Expense & Income Ledger, Aug. 1, 1881–June 23, 1886

| 02-10-1879 | Scotchman No 1 15 ds work at house—$12.45 |

—from J. W. Bixby, Alamitos, Cerritos & Wilmington Ledger, 1876–1879

Ledger entries note the workers who transformed the rundown adobe into Susan and John Bixby's ranch home.

Certain doors were cut...windows enlarged....A bathroom shortly followed...a little later the house sprouted a wing, containing two bedrooms, and the moving of dining room and kitchen three times marked the expansion of the home....One of the first [changes] was the building of a high tank with its cooling house underneath....To supply this tank with water a busy ram down by the spring steadily chug-chugged its days and nights away.

—Sarah Bixby Smith, Adobe Days, *1925*

The Ranch House and nearby water tank on top of the hill, ca. 1909

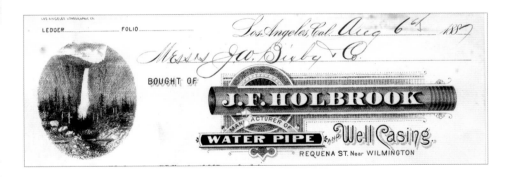

| 05-02-1882 | Robt Bothwick $316—for 1 well & pulling pipe |

—from Rancho Los Alamitos Ledger, July 1, 1881–Dec. 31, 1883

The Ranch House, ca. late 1880s. The hidden core of John and Susan's renovated ranch house was the old adobe, which was built sometime between 1806 and 1833. Note the enlarged windows and door and the new non-native plantings.

02-28-1882	Guy Smith & Co—Moulding—$3.60	
03-29-1882	Perry & Woodworth windows—$18.	

—from Rancho Los Alamitos Ledger, July 1, 1881–Dec. 31, 1883

Some of the expenses for renovating the adobe.

09-22-1888	Window curtains—$2.40	

—from J. W. Bixby & Co, Los Alamitos Ranch Cash Book, Sept. 1, 1887–1890

Enlarging the adobe windows soon required new curtains.

Susan Bixby, the "notable housewife,"[25] as Sarah Bixby Smith would describe her aunt later, had help transforming the crumbling hilltop adobe into a permanent home for her family. Between 1872 and 1888 only a few women are listed by name in the ledgers, but it appears that they worked in the house, also helping with the corn harvest or the cheese factory. A Miss Owens, for example, earned twenty dollars a month, according to the Cheese Accounts. A letter written by John Bixby to his son on January 11, 1885, may give a clue to the identity of another of these household workers:

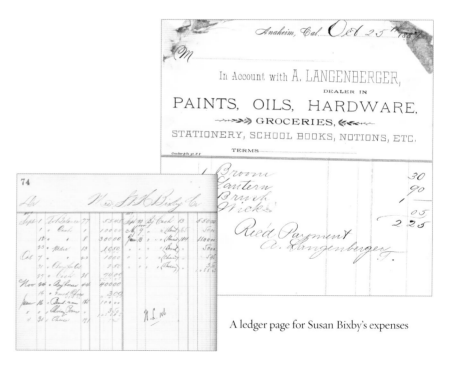

A ledger page for Susan Bixby's expenses

It was a "notable housewife" that undertook the rehabilitation of that wreck of a house.—*Sarah Bixby Smith*, Adobe Days, *1925*

"Am going to Los Angeles tomorrow...Mary goes to L.A. Tuesday, another woman comes home with me tomorrow to take her place. Susie says she is glad for knows the other woman will let her have more presents and everything. She acts like-the-dickens some times..."[26] "Mary" may refer to Mary Phillips, a name that recurs over time in the ledgers in conjunction with buying supplies and helping with the harvest. In any event, like many "notable housewives," Susan had help.

Household help at Rancho Los Alamitos, winter 1912

From a January 11, 1885, letter from John Bixby to his son, Fred: "Mary goes to L.A. Tuesday, another woman comes home with me to take her place.
Your affct. Papa
J. W. Bixby"

07-23-1881	Mary Phillips—"having" corn—$25.00
	—from Rancho Los Alamitos Ledger, July 1, 1881—Dec. 31, 1883
01-26-1878	Josie Synder—cash—$10.85
	—from J. W. Bixby. Feb. 28, 1871—Jan. 1, 1881
05-1882	Miss Owens commenced May 16th, 1882 at $20 per month
	—from Cheese Accounts, 1881—Dec. 31, 1883
08-09-1886	House girl—$20
	—from Alamitos Day Book, July 1, 1886—May 6, 1887
01-19-1888	Mrs. J. W. Bixby—board of seamstress—$10.00
	—from Alamitos Day Book #3, July 2, 1888—July 25, 1889

ADOBE DAYS

BEING THE TRUTHFUL NARRATIVE OF THE EVENTS IN THE
LIFE OF A CALIFORNIA GIRL ON A SHEEP RANCH AND IN
EL PUEBLO DE NUESTRA SEÑORA DE LOS ANGELES
WHILE IT WAS YET A SMALL AND HUMBLE TOWN;
TOGETHER WITH AN ACCOUNT OF HOW THREE
YOUNG MEN FROM MAINE IN EIGHTEEN HUNDRED
AND FIFTY-THREE DROVE SHEEP AND CATTLE
ACROSS THE PLAINS, MOUNTAINS AND DESERTS
FROM ILLINOIS TO THE PACIFIC COAST; AND
THE STRANGE PROPHECY OF ADMIRAL
THATCHER ABOUT SAN PEDRO HARBOR

BY
SARAH BIXBY-SMITH

REVISED EDITION

THE TORCH PRESS
CEDAR RAPIDS, IOWA
1926

Left: *Adobe Days* title page

Left: Sarah Bixby Smith, ca. 1885. The picture was probably taken near the time of her description of Rancho Los Alamitos in *Adobe Days*. Courtesy of Rancho Los Cerritos Historic Site, Long Beach, California

Right: Sarah Bixby Smith, ca. 1890. Courtesy of Rancho Los Cerritos Historic Site, Long Beach, California

She also had an astute young girl watching her. Sarah Bixby Smith, the motherless daughter of Llewellyn Bixby and Mary Hathaway (Susan's sister had died of typhus), relished the precious time she spent with her extended Bixby/Hathaway family at Rancho Los Alamitos and Rancho Los Cerritos. Ever engaged and curious, Sarah stored away her young impressions until the year 1920, when she published an article based on her memories which led to *Adobe Days,* her classic autobiographic account of Southern California ranchos. Her affectionate portrayals of her large intertwined family and her lyrical descriptions of the family ranchos of her childhood reveal much about the labor practices and biases of the times, as well as the role of women and changing attitudes toward children.[27] "Aunt Susan...was most hospitable especially to children and Uncle John, with his jokes and merry pranks, a delight to them all," Sarah recalled fondly. "I shall always hear the sound of his voice as he came in the back door of the hall, danced a sort of clog and called some greeting to his little wife."[28]

A PLACE OF THEIR OWN

In 1881 the entire 26,395-acre Alamitos rancho was offered for sale at $125,000. The extended Bixby family was prepared; a three-way partnership was formed. John Bixby took one third; a friend and business associate of Jotham's, the Los Angeles banker Isaias W. Hellman, became the second partner; and J. Bixby & Co. (Jotham together with Flint, Bixby & Co., which included his brother Lewellyn Bixby and cousin Thomas Flint), completed the group. The new company obtained an initial $80,000 mortgage and began business under the confusing name of J. W. Bixby & Co.[29]

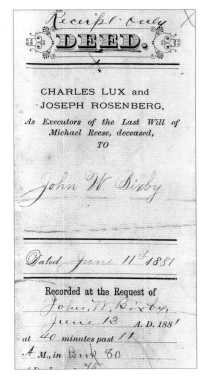

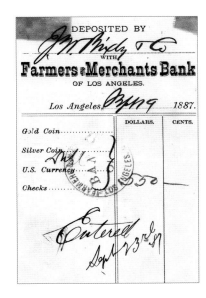

The whole property came on the market at a tempting price. The young people to whom this had already been home for five years saw an opportunity...but it was too much to be undertaken alone. The wife had been in California for a number of years and had seen the process by which Jotham with help had been able to change from a small rancher to the prosperous manager and half-owner of the Cerritos and encouraged her husband.

—*Sarah Bixby Smith,* Adobe Days, *1925*

Left: The partners' deed to Rancho Los Alamitos, June 11, 1881

07-01-1881	Profits for Alamitos Ranch—$1,600.24
	—from Expense Ledger, Jan. 1881—June 1882
12-31-1881	Farmers & Merchants Bank—$5,209.77
12-31-1882	J. W. Bixby—6 mo salary—$600
	—from Rancho Los Alamitos Ledger, July 1, 1881—Dec. 31, 1883

John, as opportunistic as the rest of the family, had glimpsed the future shrewdly. The nation's economy was strong enough and the Los Alamitos rangeland was in good enough shape that Jotham and he promptly introduced several thousand sheep and would introduce choice merino rams for maintaining the excellence of their herds. To the sheep they added several hundred beef cattle. By 1880 the worldwide drop in sheep prices also prompted John, like others, to look for new ways to use his range.[30]

When my husband was running the ranch, a businessman, he got a good income out of the property.

—*from Susan Bixby's testimony, April 18, 1901, in Susan P.H. Bixby, et al vs. Los Alamitos Sugar Company*

Lithograph of Rancho Los Alamitos by William Elliot, 1887. In accordance with European tradition, this work both documents and exaggerates the family "homestead." Susanna Bixby is driving the pony buggy and her brother, Fred, is herding the sheep. However, John and Susan Bixby planted California pepper trees, not firs as illustrated, to divide the open landscape.

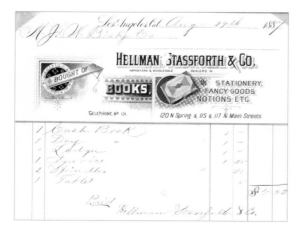

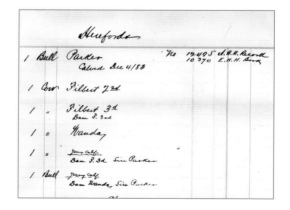

Left: A receipt from the stationery store owned by a cousin of Isaias Hellman, who was a one-third partner in Rancho Los Alamitos.

The Rancho Los Alamitos brand used by John Bixby and his son, Fred

09-05-1881	Property sold to J. W. Bixby & Co. by J. W. Bixby Cattle—$18,657
12-23-1881	36 head of cattle at $20 ea—$700
05-27-1882	Tom Elliot Texas herder—stockings—.25
09-23-1883	Joe Lazy Cowboy—to cash by acct—$8.35
10-15-1883	5 head steers—$2450

—from Rancho Los Alamitos Ledger, July 1, 1881—December 31, 1883

| 06-17-1882 | Paid Mexican for branding—$10.00 |

—from Income & Expense Ledger, August 1, 1881—June 23, 1886

| 06-06-1885 | Smith & Powell for cattle $2,887 |

—from J. W. Bixby & Co., Rancho Los Alamitos checkbook, June 2, 1885—January 27, 1886

John Bixby raised both cattle and sheep at Alamitos.

DISEASES OF DOMESTIC ANIMALS SCIENTIFICALLY TREATED.

Los Angeles, Cal. 6 1889

M. Alamitos Ranch

To **DR. COWPER**, Dr.

Graduate Ontario Veterinary College, Toronto, Canada

VETERINARY SURGEON

RESIDENCE, 255 HILL STREET, Corner Fourth.

Office at CALIFORNIA STABLE, No. 279 N. Main Street.

| 06-30-1881 | Wages of herders—$40 |

—from Expense Ledger, Jan. 1881—June 1882

| 08-09-1881 | Coyote Frenchman—coyote scalps—$2.00 |

—from Rancho Los Alamitos Expense & Income Ledger, 1881—84

09-05-1881	To W. J. Montgomery for sheep pasturage to Jan. 1882—$40
06-09-1883	B. P. Flint to wool & pelts—$15,336.76
10-30-1883	Augustine Old Basque—tobacco—.80
	Q. Story: doctoring 5858 sheep—$51.40

—from Rancho Los Alamitos Ledger, July 1, 1881—December 31, 1883

| 07-20-1887 | F&M Bank—deposit wool money—$11,380.07; F&M Bank—deposit for wool—$17,641.36 |

—from Alamitos Day Book, May—Sept. 1887

Sheep was the main interest of the ranches...on the Cerritos alone there were often as many as thirty thousand head, and upward of two hundred thousand pounds of wool were marketed annually in San Francisco. The sheep prospered under favorable climatic conditions. Coyotes were the chief hazard and the effort to outwit them must have offered the only spice in the life to the sheep herder and his dogs...These men lived lonely lives...Many of the men were Basques.

—Sarah Bixby Smith, Adobe Days, 1925

Sheep-shearing sheds southwest of the Alamitos Ranch House, summer 1887

Every week a man from the ranch made the rounds of the sheep camps, carrying mail, tobacco, and food,—brown sugar, coffee, flour, bacon, beans, potatoes, dried apples...

—*Sarah Bixby Smith,* Adobe Days, *1925*

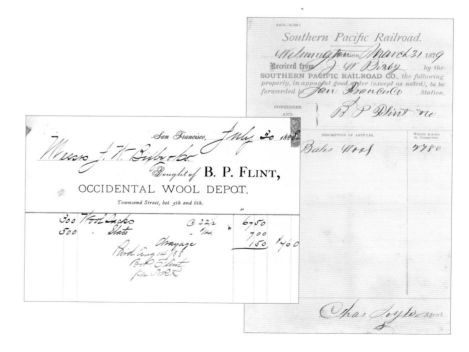

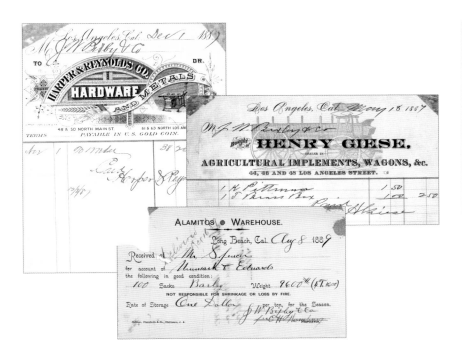

Threshing at Rancho Los Cerritos

During the 1860s and 1870s, harvests from the vast wheat fields up and down California (as well as other states) had been shipped to Liverpool, England, to take advantage of the extravagant prices there resulting from crop failures in Europe.[31] The drought-resistant crop did not need much care, and new technology and equipment—headers that cut grain from the stem and threshers that separated the grain kernel from the head—ushered in corporate agriculture.[32] Like other big outfits, John Bixby's used a portion of his great acreage to grow wheat during the 1870s and 1880s, earning almost $1,500 from one wheat harvest alone in November 1884. Of course, high returns meant up-front costs: in July 1886, to give an example, he paid $3,500 for a thresher. To help offset these costs, Bixby also hired out his threshing crew to others. This was big farming and big business.

Threshers with sacks by the scale

07-01-1881	Property sold to J. W. Bixby & Co. by J. W. Bixby— harnesses—$95
01-02-1882	J. W. Bixby 1 plow—$40
01-06-1882	Keifharber blacksmith—$26.20
12-10-1883	Plow chains—$3; double trees—$8.00

—from Rancho Los Alamitos Ledger, July 1, 1881– Dec. 31, 1883

| 11-17-1884 | Rec'd for wheat—$1,458.15 |

—from Expense & Income Ledger, Aug. 1, 1881–June 23, 1886

| 07-15-1886 | Thresher to 1st cost—$3,500 |
| 10-21-1886 | Chas Thornburg—threshing wheat & barley $233.90; heading wheat—$125; heading barley—$75; sacks—$48.50; hauling grain—$24.60 |

—from Alamitos Day Book, July 1, 1886–May 6, 1887

John Bixby's ledgers show profits made from wheat, corn, hay, and barley.

04-1873 To J. W. Bixby—cash paid Old Jose—$4.00

—from J. W. Bixby, Rancho Los Cerritos Ledger, July 24, 1872– Dec. 26, 1873

Several of the characters mentioned in Adobe Days also spring to life from the pages of the ledgers.

There were many other interesting men working at the ranches. There was always a Jose.

—*Sarah Bixby Smith*, Adobe Days, 1925

Land was at a premium, especially in Southern California, where the population would explode during the decade. Throughout the state in the 1880s, wheat yielded to crops that produced more volume and more profit per acre—lush orchards and vineyards especially, but also plentiful vegetables and cereals.[33] At Alamitos, closer to the house than Susan perhaps liked, John's farmworkers broke ground for barley, hay, and alfalfa to feed his livestock and sell on the open market.

Like Abel Stearns, Governor Figueroa, and the Nietos before him, John had a vision for his land that required a ready, inexpensive supply of labor to produce real profit. During the 1840s and early 1850s Abel Stearns had used unpaid Indian labor bought at the Los Angeles auctions that were legal at the time. But he also paid Mexican and Indian vaqueros, as well as his household help. Almost forty years later, John Bixby's workers would come from around the world—China and Japan, Northern and Southern Europe, elsewhere in the U.S., Puerto Rico, and perhaps from Mexico, but more likely from California, Were any descendants of Povuu'ngna or other native people still working at Alamitos? Maybe. But like the sheepherder Acú, their Spanish surnames may have hidden their identities from outsiders.

John Bixby's workers—men, women, and children included—cultivated and harvested the fields, herded sheep and cattle, guarded against coyotes, milked cows, made cheese, dug ditches and wells, built barns, renovated the Ranch House, and in the process made a profit for Alamitos. Ledgers reveal that among the changing cast of characters during the 1870s and 1880s were Augustine Old Basque, Old Charlie Swede, Old Sandy Kansas, Old Black Frenchman, John Italian, Old Irishman, Manuel Portuguese, Old Glory Mexican, Andrew Mexican Boy, Foolish Boy, George Big Dutchman, Tom Elliot Texas herder, Joe Lazy Cowboy, and Old Deafy, as well as

| 09-28-1881 | Paid Japanese—$14.10 |
| | *—from Expense & Income Ledger, Aug. 1, 1881—June 23, 1886* |

09-14-1881	To Old Swede—work at $25 a mo.
10-20-1881	Leimo Romero for 1 pair girls shoes
01-15-1882	Manuel Portugese—corn work at $25 mo
01-15-1882	Joe Sherman—rubber boots—$4.50
07-21-1882	Italian John by corn work July 20th at $25
08-01-1882	Casure Mexican—to cash paid wife—$30
09-01-1882	Old Irishman—corn work
02-22-1883	Black Frenchman at Raphaels—corn work at $20
	—from Rancho Los Alamitos Ledger, July 1, 1881—Dec. 31, 1883

A sampling of John Bixby's ledger entries reveals the international work force at Rancho Los Alamitos.

workers with less descriptive names, like Capt. Raphael, Charles Pattish, John Alexander, George Reinbeck, and A. Lundenberger.

These names and familiar nicknames reveal the ethnically diverse backgrounds of workers, not to mention the common biases of the era. Most of these laborers earned less than a dollar a day, less the cost of board in some instances, and many spent as much on tobacco or personal supplies at the ranch, which functioned almost like a company store, it seems.

Several of John Bixby's workers—Ah Fan, Ah Han, Ah Yoon, Ah Keen, and Jim Chinaman—came from China. Some worked in the kitchen or, like "Vegetable Chinaman," sold produce to the ranch kitchen, but most worked in the fields, and this was in accord with the larger pattern throughout the state. By 1880 immigrant Chinese field-workers, the latest source of inexpensive farm labor, constituted one-third of the state's agricultural workforce.[34] Their experiences farming in China helped shape the landscape of the state, especially in Northern California.[35]

| 12-23-1881 | G. W. Parlin—cash paid for watch—$3.50 |
| | *—from Rancho Los Alamitos Ledger, July 1, 1881—Dec. 31, 1883* |

Then there were all sorts of other nationalities represented in one way or another: Parlin, a Maine man, always predicting disaster.
—Sarah Bixby Smith, Adobe Days, *1925*

09-23-1874	French boy—.50
	—from J. W. Bixby, Wilmington, Cal. Day Book & Journal, May 25, 1874—Dec. 1875
02-28-1878	Mexican boy—work commenced in morn—$10
	—from J. W. Bixby, Alamitos, Cerritos & Wilmington Ledger, 1876—1879
07-04-1883	Jim Jackson foolish boy—2 days work—$1.50
	—from Rancho Los Alamitos Ledger, July 01, 1881—Dec. 31, 1883

Paid labor at Alamitos included children.

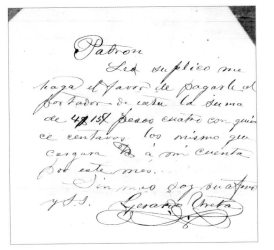

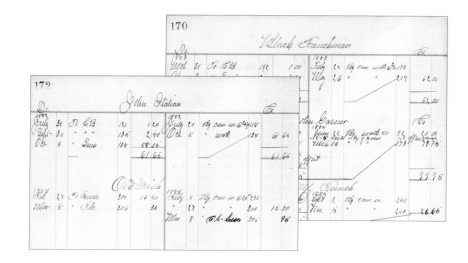

04-07-1878   Jim Chinaman—2 mos. and 1 ds. work at $20

—from J. W. Bixby, Alamitos, Cerritos & Wilmington Ledger, 1876—1879

04-14-1882   Ditch Chinamen—work 691 days, 7 hours at $1.25—$864.62
08-31-1882   Ah Fan Chinaman—corn work Aug. 2nd—$35
05-25-1883   Han Chinaman—corn work—$15

—from Rancho Los Alamitos Ledger, July 1, 1881—Dec. 31, 1883

08-02-1886   Keen Chinaman—$40

—from Alamitos Day Book, July 1, 1886—May 6, 1887

Goon Chinaman—4 mos. work at $40—$80

—from Expense & Income Ledger, Jan. 1, 1884—May 31, 1886

Skilled Chinese farm labor was highly valued and common until the Chinese Exclusion Act of 1882 barred Chinese immigration to the United States.

When anti-Chinese sentiment and mob violence erupted in the 1870s, legal discrimination soon followed, and provisions in the new state constitution of 1879 declared Chinese immigrants "dangerous to the well-being of the state." Three years later, the federal government bowed to pressure from California by passing the Chinese Exclusion Act, which prohibited further immigration from China to the U.S. This law was extended for another ten years in 1892 and made "permanent" in 1902. Chinese farm labor in California quickly declined, a fact John Bixby's son, Fred, would sorely lament during his time as Alamitos owner in the early twentieth century.

Plowing, planting, and tending crops on the large Alamitos acreage meant the early introduction of tenant farming, in 1878. These farmers toiled in the fields for a share of the produce; each sharecropper could pay one-fourth of his crop to the ranch as rent and sell the rest. Again, this reflected the larger state of affairs: by 1890, almost 18 percent of California farmers would be tenant farmers.[36]

04-21-1882	Chinaman for veg.—$3.00
	—from Expense & Income Ledger, Aug. 1, 1881–June 23, 1886
05-25-1887	Men's Chinese Cook—$5.00
09-01-1887	Vegetable Chinamen—10 sacks potatoes—$10
	—from J. W. Bixby & Co., Los Alamitos Ranch Cash Book, Sept. 1, 1887–1890

The vegetables...were bought once a week from the loaded express wagon of a Chinese peddler, whose second function was to bring news and company to the faithful ranch cook and his helper. There was always a plentiful supply of vegetables and the quality was the best. I remember hearing Aunt Susan tell that her man had brought strawberries to the door every week in the year and she had purchased them except on two January occasions when the berries were not quite ripe.... Ying reigned supreme [at Cerritos] and Fan was his prime minister. Later Fan, having passed his apprenticeship, moved on to be head cook at the Alamitos.

—*Sarah Bixby Smith*, Adobe Days, 1925

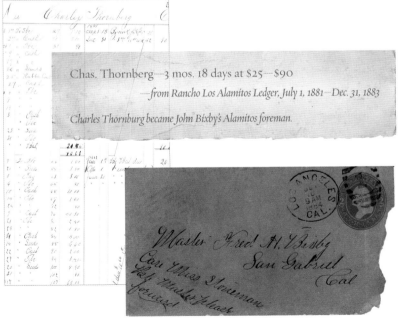

Chas. Thornberg—3 mos. 18 days at $25—$90

—from Rancho Los Alamitos Ledger, July 1, 1881–Dec. 31, 1883

Charles Thornburg became John Bixby's Alamitos foreman.

01-01-1878	Rent from farms—$277.50; Rent from N. Myer—$600
	Total in rents for 1878—$6,508.98
	—from J. W. Bixby Ledger, Feb. 18, 1871–Jan. 1, 1881

John Bixby rented his land for pastures and farming as well as his Alamitos water landing.

Left: John Bixby's January 11, 1885, letter to his son read, "...We have had another nice rain haven't we? Charley and I and Tom are plowing out on the mesa. Charley has his grays, old sorrel, Minnie, one of the gray mares, and Tom his six mules, and are plowing, sowing, and harrowing, about 15 acres per day..."

The Alamitos cheese factory, ca. 1880s

John Bixby was nothing if not resilient, seemingly open to the use of his land in any way he could imagine. He cultivated the soil, rented out pastures, charged for the coastal water landings, and sometime during the early 1880s, he built the dairy barn and cheese-making complex he had been thinking about toward the northeastern foot of the knoll on which the house stood. He imported some of the first registered Holsteins in California to improve the grade, and in time the ranch would be running about two hundred milk cows and employing eight to ten milkers. John Bixby's dairymen came from Switzerland, the home of expert cheese makers. It wasn't long before Alamitos cheese was a sought-after item in Los Angeles markets: as one newspaper reporter noted, it was a "gilt-edged article, that sells readily at a gilt-edged price."[37]

An invoice from John Bixby's prosperous cheese factory

I was fifteen and had been for several days at the Alamitos, among other things making diagrams of spots of some Holstein calves on the blanks of application for registration, that being a privilege reserved for me, the wielder of the pencil among us.

—*Sarah Bixby Smith*, Adobe Days, 1925

05-01-1881	Property sold to J. W. Bixby & Co. by J. W. Bixby—cheese factory (vat press, hoop, buckets, shelves)—$220
07-23-1881	To E. Germain for 1 month cheese proceeds —$106.08

—from Rancho Los Alamitos Ledger, July 1, 1881— Dec. 31, 1883

01-30-1881	Net from cheese sales—$698.84

—from Expense Ledger, Jan. 1881— June 1882

09-03-1881	Farmers & Merchants Bank for advertising bill— $15.00 cr.
01-11-1887	Expenses— 2 trips cheese to L.A.—$5.50

—from Rancho Los Alamitos Ledger, July 1, 1881— Dec. 31, 1883

Q. Did you have a cheese factory adjacent to your residence there?
A. No sir.
Q. Never did?
A. Certainly, we had. My husband had, and it was kept up afterwards for some time.
Q. It isn't there now?
A. It is not.

—Susan P. H. Bixby, et al. vs. Los Alamitos Sugar Company, April 18, 1901

In 1901 Susan Bixby filed a lawsuit which claimed environmental damage to the Rancho by the Los Alamitos Sugar Company. Her testimony offers details about the physical ranch and the times, including the fact that the lucrative Alamitos Cheese Factory was gone by 1901.

The Drum Barracks in Wilmington was moved to Alamitos and converted into the Big Red Barn.

John Bixby's Big Red Barn at Alamitos, with the Ranch House in the distance, ca 1887. Note the newly planted row of California pepper trees. Some are still growing.

A SYMBOL ON THE LAND

John craved a barn in which to store hay for his horses and cows. "Building it" was to give him great satisfaction. During the Civil War the U.S. Army had erected, at the port of San Pedro, an installation known as Drum Barracks, a forwarding point for supplies destined for Union forts in Arizona. Following the war, transportation magnate Phineas Banning bought a major warehouse at auction. In 1882 John bought the empty warehouse shell from Banning and with his workers cut it into sections, marking the positions of the beams, planks, and braces. After hauling the material from San Pedro over to Los Alamitos, John paid his carpenters a little over fifty dollars (a cost offset by the tobacco and cheese they bought from John) to put the barn back together on the hill, about thirty yards west of the Ranch House. They added three ventilators capped by cupolas and painted the barn red trimmed with white, creating a famous landmark for the future, visible for miles.[38]

The central part of the barn's interior, almost as high as a three-story house, was capable of holding an almost inestimable amount of loose and baled hay. John put in stalls for cows and his prized stallions and horses along the sides, and walkways above them so workers could pitch hay into the mangers.[39]

A favorite resort was the great barn, a still familiar sight to passers-by on the Anaheim Road. It was made from an old government warehouse taken down, hauled over from Wilmington and rebuilt at the ranch, forty-odd years ago.

—*Sarah Bixby Smith,* Adobe Days, *1925*

Q. No barns or outbuildings collected around the house?

A. I have a large barn.

Q. Any stock corrals there?

A. None very near the house...they are west. There is one southwest. There is one west...the barn proper where the horses are kept, my carriageway from my carriage houses, are perhaps forty feet.

Q. Never noticed any odors from those corrals?

A. No. Never.

—from Susan Bixby's testimony, April 18, 1901, in Susan P. H. Bixby, et al. vs. Los Alamitos Sugar Company

The Big Red Barn with a team hauling lumber, 1887. Barns are practical structures that usually reflect cultural traditions and regional environments. During the Spanish-Mexican era small adobes on the hilltop may have housed livestock and equipment, but John Bixby's big multipurpose barn housed livestock, wagons, buggies, harnesses, and farm equipment and was also used to store feed and harvests. The next generation of barns at Alamitos were each built for a specific use.

04-07-1882 Barn carpenters—$50

—from Expense and Income Ledger, Aug. 1, 1881—June 23, 1886

01-30-1880	Lumber for corral—$25.50; 40 lbs nails—$3.20; moving lumber and corrals halls—$2.50

—from Alamitos Ledger, Jan. 1, 1880—Jan. 1, 1881

02-01-1881	Putting up corral & well—$3.00

—from Expense Ledger, Jan. 1881—June 1882

| 04-10 | By a/c flea powder—$5.00 |
| 06-04-1888 | Fruit & fly paper—$1.50 |

—from J. W. Bixby & Co., Los Alamitos Ranch Cash Book, Sept. 1, 1887—1890

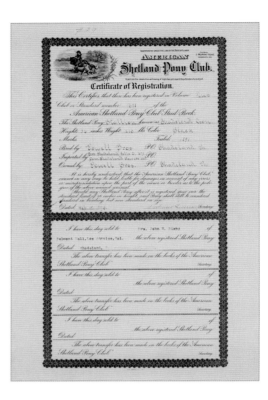

Fred and Susanna Bixby driving a team of Susan Bixby's Shetland ponies, ca. 1887

12-31-1882	J. W. Bixby—8 heat mare horses—$1,200
08-19-1885	J. W. Calkins for carriage—$260

—from J. W. Bixby & Co. Alamitos Check Book, June 2, 1885— Jan. 27, 1886

03-19-1887 Photographs of horses—$25

—from Alamitos Ledger, July 1, 1886— April 23, 1887

Mrs. S. P. H. Bixby: 2 bay horses—Dill and Dan—$400

—from J. W. Bixby & Co., Los Alamitos Ranch Day Book, Sept. 1887— June 30, 1888

Another addition unfamiliar to the region was several Shetland ponies. The children quickly learned to ride them, and Susan took to driving behind matched pairs in a small cart. Soon all the ranch's equines, big and little, were known and admired at the horse auctions John frequented. Perhaps to promote sales or to make a personal keepsake, in 1887 John spent thirty dollars to have his horses photographed.

Standing tall on the hilltop, John Bixby's Big Red Barn was the working symbol of the ranch, an icon on the surrounding landscape, representing entrepreneurial vision, wealth, connections, and the hard work of many who would never know its future returns. John Bixby's success was astounding. In 1886, J. W. Bixby & Co. finished paying back the $80,000 the three original partners (John Bixby, I. W. Hellman, and J. Bixby & Co.) had borrowed to buy the Rancho six years earlier, plus another $58,000 loaned by Hellman's Farmers and Merchants Bank for stocking the ranch.[40]

GREENING THE LANDSCAPE

Not everything could be practical. In keeping with her New England background and her desire for a sheltered, more intimate landscape, John's wife, Susan, had her husband plant rows of pepper trees to shield the hilltop house from the enormous plain of fields and pastures that sometimes looked ready to engulf it.

On the opposite side to John's great barn and industry, she managed to nurse a small green lawn into being and protect it from the ranch animals with a white picket fence. There she grew a few incongruous-looking palms and, eventually, two Moreton Bay fig trees that would grow over the years to gigantic size, becoming her living legacy. In true Victorian fashion she also

The Ranch House and its picket fence, 1887. Picket fences surrounding adobes reflected the new cultural overlay of the era, and in time Susan and John Bixby also planted their Victorian sensibilities on the landscape. They may have planted the Australian eucalyptus shown in the photo. The species dominated the regional landscape by 1863, but Susan would replace the trees with the two great Moreton Bay figs that grace the front lawn today.

| 03-29-1884 | trees—$31. |
| 04-06-1884 | Paid J.W.B. for trees—$10.45 |

—from Expense & Income Ledger, Aug. 1, 1881–June 23, 1886

Susan Bixby's Moreton Bay fig trees, 2009. Cristina Klenz Photography

Grandchildren of John and Susan Bixby, 1911, some forty years after the pepper trees were planted to divide the open landscape which seemed to engulf the Bixbys' hilltop home.

planted a few banana trees in the North (Old) Garden outside the house, it being the style to display exotic specimens outside and inside. She lived in a coastal Mediterranean climate (one of five in the world), the spring of Povuu'ngna still flowed, and six other artesian wells at Alamitos gushed with water. She could plant, water, and watch her exotics grow to her heart's content.

During the nineteenth century, this urge to green the semi-arid landscape of Southern California met with few objections. Drought-resistant California peppers were readily available, but by the early 1860s the more thirsty Australian eucalyptus covered the region. In the coming decade other landowners would promote the exotic, semitropical look, and brilliant florals and waving palms would come to symbolize the redesigned regional landscape and Rancho Los Alamitos in the early twentieth century.[41] Most required water.

However, a few farsighted individuals were thinking about the implications of using the scarce supply of water. For example, Frederick Law Olmsted, the preeminent landscape architect of the nineteenth century, would seek alternatives to the Victorian preference for green gardens.[42] In the early twentieth century, Susan's future daughter-in-law would work with the Olmsted Brothers, the sons of Frederick Law Olmsted, to extend the gardens at Rancho Los Alamitos, but Susan in her own time preferred her comfortable Victorian setting. These first plantings, including the original line of California peppers that she and John planted across the hilltop, would become the foundation of Los Alamitos' famous gardens.

HEART AND HOME

As the interior space of the Ranch House expanded, Susan brought from Maine some of the heavy mahogany furniture she had inherited. John carefully crafted cupboards and glass-fronted cabinets in which she could show off her china and glassware, perhaps purchases made from City of Paris, the noted dry goods store in San Francisco where she sometimes shopped. In her parlor and possibly throughout her home, Susan also displayed her collection of Indian baskets, already gaining value, and somewhat later, a striking Ojibwe beaded bandolier bag from the Great Lakes region. Her floral wallpaper hid the old adobe underneath, but Susan's eclectic decor exemplified both the Victorian taste for "exotic" specimens and the romanticized version of Southern California's past brought on by the publication of Helen Hunt Jackson's *Ramona* in 1884.

A romantic tale about the treatment of mission Indians under the "old Spanish aristocracy" of Southern California and its Yankee usurpers, the book's influence extended far beyond the realm of interior decorating. Jackson wrote *Ramona* to provoke serious discussion and reform, but most readers were instead distracted and seduced by her nostalgic and romantic envisioning of Old California. The best-seller launched a new regional identity—Mission Revival. Popular through the early twentieth century, the style reflected the Mediterranean influence found in Spanish mission architecture, with features such as thick plastered walls, arches and arcaded corridors, and clay tile roofs. Organizations like the Association for the Preservation of the Missions and the subsequent Landmarks Club of Southern California (the latter started in 1895 by Charles Fletcher Lummis, editor of *Land of Sunshine*) were founded to preserve—if not the reality,

The Ranch House parlor. Hidden beneath the Victorian decor of Susan and John Bixby's parlor is the old adobe.

then the romantic idea of—an idyllic mission past.[43] Even if Susan Bixby herself didn't read *Ramona* (and it's very likely that she did), she would have felt its effects. It was Jackson who made basket collecting fashionable and worthy of Victorian parlors like Susan's: she introduced the art form in *Ramona* as evidence of the fine moral character of its practitioners.[44]

Were any of Susan's baskets made by Tongva women? Probably not, since many Tongva left the region after the missions were secularized. Those who stayed in the urban environment or surrounding ranchos kept a low profile by necessity, and still more followed work elsewhere. Some native people used baskets to barter with shopkeepers during the 1880s. The influx of baskets that were made by native peoples from outside the region into private collections would reveal the diversity of the native population in the area and perhaps the limited number of available Tongva goods.[45]

01-20-1882 Meyer Crockery Store—$23.55

—*from Rancho Los Alamitos Ledger, July 1, 1881—Dec. 31, 1883*

10-23-1885 City of Paris—$90

—*from J. W. Bixby & Co., Alamitos Checkbook, June 2, 1885—Jan. 27, 1886*

The City of Paris, a noted dry goods store in San Francisco, opened in 1849 aboard La Ville de Paris. The store relocated to 152 Kearney Street in 1851 and to Geary and Stockton streets in 1896. Today, with its Beaux-Arts rotunda and glass dome, it is a state and national landmark.

01-1889   Clock for kitchen—$4.50

—*from Alamitos Day Book #3, July 2, 1888—July 25, 1889*

Expense for 1 man to unload Mrs. Bixby's furniture—L.A.

—*from J. W. Bixby & Co., Los Alamitos Ranch Cash Book, Sept 1, 1887*

Susan's home was well furnished and funded. This entry may refer to the mahogany pieces that she had shipped from her old home in Maine for the new music room she had added to her Ranch House in October 1885.

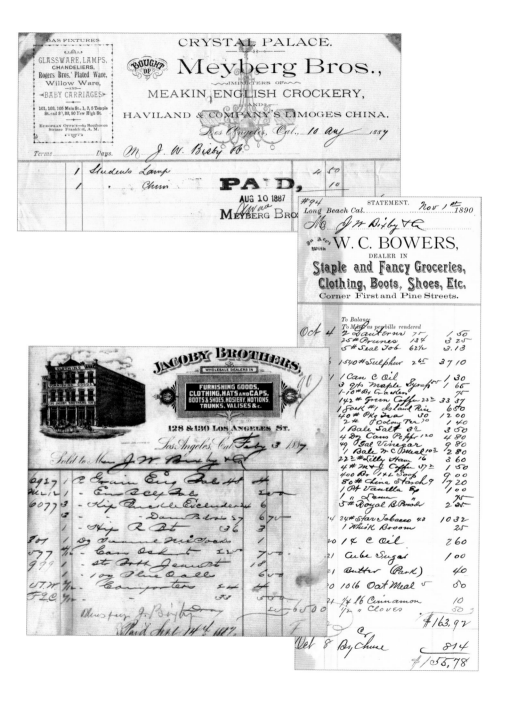

The Ranch House parlor, ca. 1888. The photo suggests the cross-cultural style common to the Victorian era. The framed portrait pays homage to John Bixby, who had died in 1887. The banana leaves in the fireplace probably came from Susan's garden, typifying the use of exotic plants at the time. The Indian basket at the lower right of the fireplace was one of many in Susan's collection.

As Indian baskets increased in popularity, the native population continued to decline. Did Susan Bixby know this? Is it possible that her Indian collection reflected a deeper value than Victorian decor? Susan's father, the Reverend George Hathaway, was a respected New England Congregational minister who put his beliefs and his family to the test in the days leading to Civil War by opening his home to the Underground Railroad, providing an illegal temporary refuge for slaves escaping to freedom.[46] Such a moral lesson is not easily forgotten, and perhaps Susan Bixby knew of the ongoing plight of Native Americans—including the Tongva from Povuu'ngna.

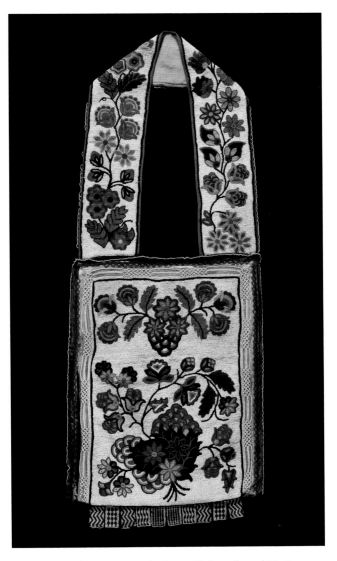

In keeping with Victorian style, Susan Bixby collected Native American baskets and other objects, including this bandolier bag (decorative shoulder bag) from the Ojibwe tribe of the Great Lakes region. Cristina Klenz Photography, 2009

The Ranch House parlor, ca. 1888. The parlor was probably the scene of Sunday night get-togethers with John Bixby's family and the Alamitos workers.

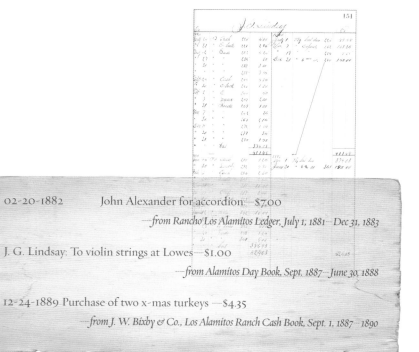

02-20-1882	John Alexander for accordion—$7.00
	—from Rancho Los Alamitos Ledger, July 1, 1881—Dec 31, 1883
J. G. Lindsay: To violin strings at Lowes—$1.00	
	—from Alamitos Day Book, Sept. 1887—June 30, 1888
12-24-1889 Purchase of two x-mas turkeys —$4.35	
	—from J. W. Bixby & Co., Los Alamitos Ranch Cash Book, Sept. 1, 1887—1890

I recall Sunday evenings at the Alamitos when Uncle John got out his fiddle, and men who had other instruments came into the parlor and we had a concert that included Arkansas Traveler, Money Musk and Turkey in the Straw.—*Sarah Bixby Smith,* Adobe Days, *1925*

"Dear Fred," John Bixby wrote to his son in this 1884 letter, "...Thanksgiving is the 27th, one week from tomorrow. You can come into Los Angeles Wednesday on morning train, where I will meet you....Mama and little Susie send love to you. Suppose we shall get a letter from you Sunday."

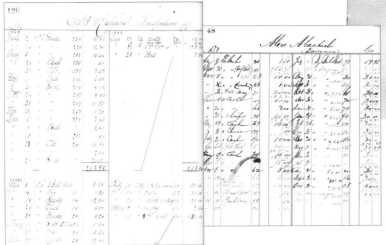

02-02-1882   Capt. Raphael—cash sent to San Juan—$20
—*from Rancho Los Alamitos Ledger, July 1, 1881–Dec, 31, 1883*

09-07-1887   Alois Abacherli—To money sent home to Switzerland—$75
—*from Alamitos Day Book, July 31, 1889–April 23, 1890*

Perhaps these men also dreamed of bringing their families to California to make a new home. In the meantime Alois Abacherli was probably one of John Bixby's Swiss cheese makers, while Captain Raphael worked in the Alamitos fields and about the ranch.

In any case, in their stylish parlor and renovated home, John and Susan enjoyed the evidence of their success. They settled into the reassuring rhythms of family life that sometimes included their extended family, when workers like John Alexander and John Lindsay brought their accordion and fiddle to the Ranch House on Sunday night and played along with John. John and Susan transplanted the traditions they had known in the East. They celebrated the holidays with relatives from Los Angeles and began to hold an annual Christmas party sometime in the 1880s.[47] Doubtless with the children in mind, the young couple took to setting up a big evergreen tree in the parlor. The lighted candles on the branches wavered, presents were passed out to the children, and Fred's and little Susanna's eyes grew big and round. John struck up a tune on his violin; banjos and guitars followed, and as the shyness of their guests wore off, there were singing and dancing, refreshments and fun.

BIRTH OF A TOWN

For John and Susan, the world was coming their way; a nascent community had begun to form around the sustaining land called Los Alamitos. The gregarious couple, with their many friends and a strong feeling of responsibility, entered the wider community. With cousin Jotham, they listened to a proposal that would spread scores of homes across the Los Cerritos hills to the ocean. The idea had originated with a plump, pink-faced, balding man named William E. Willmore, an agent for the California Immigrant Union. With Jotham's blessing, he obtained from J. Bixby & Co. an option to several thousand acres that could be divided into many small home sites, the nucleus of a new city. As fast as he sold the lots, he would pay the company for the land. The name of his dream: Willmore City.

For nearly four years he worked desperately, sinking a few wells, plowing the brush out of the way of a few streets, auctioning off a few lots, and overseeing the building of a small hotel. It wasn't enough. In May 1884, he sadly relinquished his option to a better-financed real estate firm that changed the name of Willmore City to Long Beach. Building on his foundations, they attracted enough families with children that a school was necessary. To John and especially to Susan Bixby, parents of a nine-year-old boy and four-year-old girl, this was proof that civilization was reaching them; after all, their Los Alamitos home was only five miles from Long Beach.

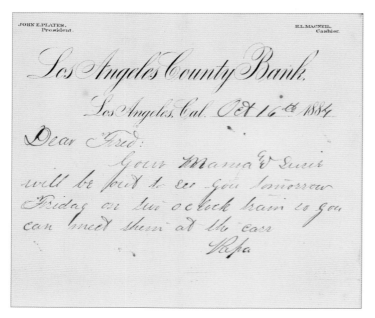

From a letter from John Bixby to Fred, October 16, 1884: "Your Mama and Susie will be out to see you tomorrow Friday on two o'clock train so you can meet them at the cars."

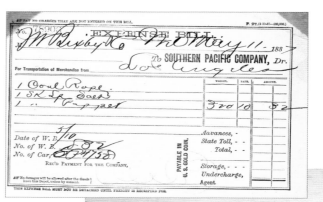

07-20-1881   Railroad ties—$22; telegraph pole—$68; railroad building—$250

—*from RLA Ledger, July 1, 1881—Dec. 31, 1883*

01-19-1888   Mrs. J. W. Bixby—r.r. ticket (30 trips)—$10

—*from Alamitos Day Book #3, July 2, 1888—July 25, 1889*

In the booming times, the growing infrastructure included transportation and communication.

People were coming into Southern California more and more, especially after rail connection with San Francisco came in 1877.... We became resigned to the town that had first called itself Willmore City and then Long Beach, though we did think it might have kept its own old name, Cerritos Beach.—*Sarah Bixby Smith*, Adobe Days, *1925*

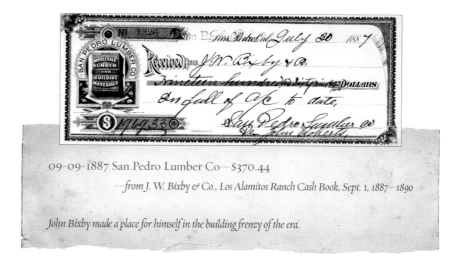

09-09-1887 San Pedro Lumber Co—$370.44

—*from J. W. Bixby & Co., Los Alamitos Ranch Cash Book, Sept. 1, 1887—1890*

John Bixby made a place for himself in the building frenzy of the era.

12-23-1881	Paid for Alamitos school—$55.49
	—*from Expense & Income Ledger, Aug. 1, 1881—June 23, 1886*
04-19-1889	Mrs. J. W. Bixby—teacher's bd.—2 wks
	—*from Alamitos Day Book #3, July 2, 1888—July 25, 1889*

John and Susan Bixby's priorities included a school for the growing community.

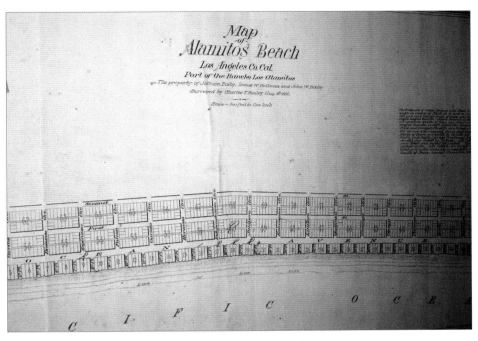

Plat of Alamitos Beach, Los Angeles Co., Cal., August 6, 1886. The development created along the coast by John Bixby and his partners was, as the map notes, "Part of the Rancho Los Alamitos."

Together Susan and Mrs. W. W. Lowe, whose husband owned the only store in town, prevailed on the county superintendent of schools to authorize a school district. The town, however, would have to provide, as a starter, a building and a teacher. A collection raised seventy-five dollars. With this the organizers hired a sixteen-year-old high school graduate, Grace Bush, to serve as teacher for three months. Classes began in a shack at the corner of Pine and Second Street but were transferred to a tent when the building was sold over the students' heads. Meanwhile a school board was elected. Thirty-five votes were cast. John Bixby was one of the three members unanimously chosen.

The tempo of Southern California quickened in the 1880s, then became a near-frenzy when the Southern Pacific Railroad, which had millions of acres to sell, and the Santa Fe Railroad, eager for a share of the traffic, joined forces with hundreds of promoters of fragmented old Spanish and Mexican grants to create the region's first great stampede for land. The completion of the Atchison, Topeka and Santa Fe Railroad connected Southern California to the East in 1885[48] and ushered in a rousing rate war, which dropped fares to as low as one dollar from the Missouri Valley to Southern California.[49] The offer was too good to refuse. The population of Southern California would increase 212 percent during the decade and reach 201,352 by 1890.[50]

John and Susan and Jotham sensed that the dynamics of land use were changing the face of America. And they were for it. Get people to cluster. Build trading centers beside seaports and crossroads. Let commercial buildings rise out of feedlots and citrus groves; let residential tracts spread across grain fields and pastures. Bringing it closer to home, shouldn't Los Alamitos share in the profits? Others were. Over the short span of two years, 1886 to 1888, there would be 1,770 maps and plans for tracts and subdivisions and revised plats filed in Los Angeles County.[51]

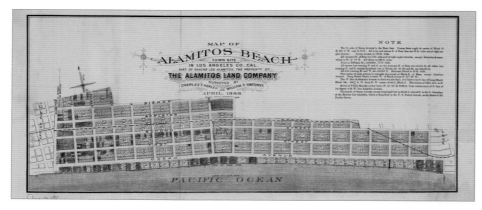

The Alamitos Beach Townsite villa and farm lots, Los Angeles Co., 1888, a development of the Alamitos Land Company.

"Alamitos Beach" is an extension of Long Beach on the East. Together, they are destined to form the UNRIVALED SEASIDE RESORT of the world....Alamitos Beach is the only beach in Los Angeles County where Lots are laid out on the Bluff and extend to the Pacific Ocean....Artesian water, pure and abundant, will be piped along the streets by next winter or spring. The finest location on the beach is reserved for a cosmopolitan hotel.—*John W. Bixby & Co., 1886 advertisement*

After many discussions with Susan and his partners, John took the initiative in developing 5,000 of the ranch's 26,393 acres. The townsite he called Alamitos Beach bordered blossoming Long Beach on the east and ran along the coast. Near the site's middle he set aside a plot for a park and planted saplings. Small farm lots popular in the subdivisions of the time would be laid out east and north of John's projected town. On the map these suburban lots rose north in a lopsided pyramid splicing into a ridge called Signal Hill, more than three hundred feet above sea level. As

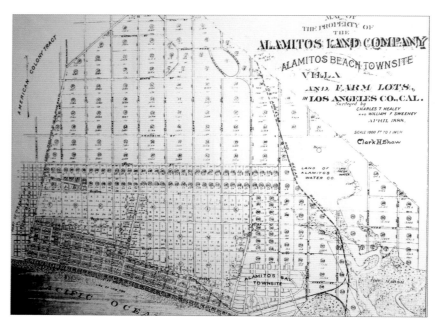

Map of Alamitos Beach, the Alamitos Land Company, 1888. A year after John Bixby's death, the remaining partners organized the Alamitos Land Company.

12-19-1885	E. T. Wright for survey—$200
	—from J. W. Bixby & Co., Rancho Los Alamitos checkbook, June 2, 1885–Jan. 27, 1886
09-25-1886	Paymt. on tideland—$86.25
	—from Alamitos Ledger, July 1, 1886—April 23, 1887
01-14-1888	Alamitos Townsite Co.—Fan Fong—1/3 payt on 2 lots—$266; Ch. Thornburg—3 lots deed & 1/3 payment 1 lot—$500; Ramon Bisques—1/3 payment 1 lot—$100; Jes Ramero—1/3 Payment—$100
05-19-1888	Bixby—cash paid for swampland for recording deed—$40.38
	—from J. W. Bixby & Co., Los Alamitos Ranch Day Book, Sept. 1887—June 30, 1888

distance from the proposed town increased, so did the size of the farm lots, up to a maximum of 160 acres.[52]

The three partners hoped to capitalize on the thousands of new residents and tourists coming to the region in search of sunshine, health, and romance. Residential and farm lots were sold with the promise that water would be delivered. No problem: John had seven artesian wells on the ranch. In early 1887 he planted eucalyptus trees (the site is now Long Beach's Recreation Park) to provide fuel for the boilers needed to pump the water to the fields; he also provided the machinery needed to pump the water. In keeping with the age of tourism, John Bixby's plans for the Alamitos Beach townsite included a luxury hotel.[53] (As it turned out, the posh Virginia Hotel beach resort and tropical gardens would have to wait for the next century.)

It was all going so fast and so well! In an interview by a representative of the H. H. Bancroft Company early in 1887, John provided an inventory of Rancho Los Alamitos: 24,000 sheep, 1,500 cattle, 100 horses, and several hundred head of smaller animals; it also had 2,700 acres planted to grains and 250 in alfalfa.[54] And that didn't include the Alamitos Beach development.

Then, in the spring of his life and the year, he was suddenly stricken with severe intestinal cramps—probably acute appendicitis. In a matter of days, on May 6, 1887, John William Bixby was dead at age thirty-nine. Susan's world all but died with him.

John Bixby's sudden death necessitated the division of Rancho Los Alamitos among its owners, and the creation of the Alamitos Land Company and Alamitos Water Company to finish the pipes, reservoirs, and pumps needed to move the water to the development and plan future developments.

In keeping with the era of tourism, a resort hotel was to be part of John Bixby's project, but the posh Virginia Hotel in Long Beach would not be built until the early twentieth century. The extended Bixby family would be investors in the later project.

John Bixby ordered the machinery for the pumping station needed to deliver water to the Alamitos Beach development, but he died the night it was delivered.

All the eastern portion of Long Beach, including Bixby Park... came from the Alamitos, and it was John Bixby himself who bought and planted the trees...

—*Sarah Bixby Smith*, Adobe Days, *1925*

In early 1887 John Bixby planted eucalyptus trees to provide fuel for the boilers that would be needed to pump water to his development lots as promised. Today the site is Recreation Park in Long Beach.

05-31-1888   Miss Alinda Feathers—water 1 month—$1.50

—*from J. W. Bixby & Co., Los Alamitos Ranch Day Book, Sept. 1887—June 30, 1888*

Flowering Trees in Bixby Park. In 1903 the land bounded east and west by Cherry and Junipero streets and north and south by Broadway and Ocean Boulevard would be deeded to Long Beach and named Bixby Park in honor of John Bixby. It became the scene of an annual picnic for Iowans which grew into a statewide phenomenon.

Cherry Avenue and Entrance to Bixby Park, Long Beach, Cal.

S. W. Entrance to Bixby Park, Long Beach, Calif.

John W. Bixby, ca. 1887

Death of John W. Bixby—Sudden Loss of a Respected Citizen

At his home, near Long Beach, Cal., John W. Bixby departed this life Friday May 6. His death was quite unexpected. Mr. Bixby was born at Anson, in the State of Maine, May 25, 1848, and was in his thirty-ninth year. At the age of 23 he came overland to California, coming directly to this county, where he has ever since resided. He went into the stock and land business immediately upon his arrival, and had acquired a considerable amount of property....About fourteen years ago he married Susan, the daughter of Rev. G. W. Hathaway, of this city, who survives him. He also leaves a son and daughter. Mr. Bixby was the second youngest of a family of ten children....He was in his usual health up to within about ten days ago, and had only been confined to his bed about a week...when he seemed to grow suddenly worse and passed away....Mr. Bixby was a very active, energetic and successful business man. Strictly honorable and upright in all his dealings, he won the esteem of all with whom he became acquainted, and leaves a large circle of friends as well as relatives to mourn his early death. The funeral takes place at the residence of Jotham Bixby, at Long Beach, at 12 o'clock today, and interment to be at Evergreen Cemetery upon the arrival of the 4:00 train at the Commercial Street Depot. —Los Angeles Times, *May 1887*

His death is a calamity...—Los Angeles Herald, *May 1887*

Jotham Bixby, owner of the Cerritos ranch, received a telegram at 1:15 this afternoon, stating that...John Bixby was dying at his residence on the Alamitos ranch. He at once left in a carriage for the dying man's bedside. John Bixby was...one of the owners of the Alamitos ranch, a tract of 28,000 acres of land near Long Beach.—*Long Beach newspaper, May 16, 1887*

I was fifteen and had been for several days at the Alamitos....In order to be back in school Monday morning, I had to be taken over to Long Beach to meet the first Los Angeles train....This foggy morning Uncle John was driving and as it was April there was a pearly light over everything. Every hair of his beard and eyebrows was strung with tiny drops of water; we had a most happy hour....The next day came word of sudden sickness. In ten days my merry young uncle was dead. It did not seem possible.—*Sarah Bixby Smith,* Adobe Days, *1925*

After the five thousand acres destined for real estate development had been set aside under the newly formed Alamitos Land Company, the rest was appraised and surveyed. Each participant ended up with seventy-two hundred acres. I. W. Hellman received the land along the coast, and J. Bixby & Co. took the inland section. But John's heirs (Susan and his children, Fred and Susanna) received the central part; it embraced the house and barns and was given, permanently, the name Rancho Los Alamitos.[55]

No one knows if John and Susan would have chosen to stay at Rancho Los Alamitos had John lived. His cousin Jotham and his wife had already moved from their home at Rancho Los Cerritos in 1881, and not long before John's death, Susan Bixby had overheard the land speculators who were visiting her husband in the sitting room talk about buying the Rancho. John's unexpected death changed matters all around. And by the late 1880s the Southern California boom had gone bust.

Q. Do you remember of an offer being made for that ranch and refused before it was subdivided?

A. I do...I think it was a million dollars....I heard men discussing it in my sitting room. My husband's office was my sitting room.

Q. Who was discussing it when you heard it?

A. Two men with my husband....They were the men who wished to handle it at that figure. They expected to make a commission off of it.

Q. That must have been in '86 or '87, was it not?

A. It was in '87.

Q. That was the year of the boom also.

A. The Witness—No, the boom was abating. I don't consider the boom was at its height then.

Q. Mrs. Bixby, do you know the value that the ranch was in the year 1890?

A. I know what my husband valued it at in his lifetime.

Q. Do you claim that land was worth as much in 1890 as it was in 1898?

A. I think as our country settles up our land is more valuable.

—*from Susan Bixby's testimony, April 18, 1901, in Susan P. H. Bixby et al. vs. Los Alamitos Sugar Company*

John Bixby and his two partners planned to develop five thousand acres of Alamitos, but other speculators were also interested in buying land at Alamitos during the 1880s boom. In her testimony Susan revealed her knowledge of the regional economy and the changing value of land relative to growth.

William F. Sweeney has just finished a big job of surveying the Rancho Los Alamitos, preparatory to a division amongst its respective owners. The rancho will be divided in three equal parts, each of the owners taking one-third.

—Los Angeles Times, *July 23, 1890*

SIX

HOME ON THE RANGE

J OHN BIXBY'S DEATH LEFT SUSAN WELL OFF FINANCIALLY. She inherited half of Rancho Cañon de Santa Ana and half of her husband's share in Rancho Los Alamitos. John's interest in the Alamitos Beach township development was translated into shares in the Alamitos Land Company when it was organized in January 1888. Each of Susan's children received an undivided one-quarter interest in the same three properties, with their mother as guardian. Susan, however, took little interest in the radical changes that were accompanying the divisions.

Her grief was intense. But strong-willed and deeply devout, strengthened by her Maine ministerial heritage, she would not let her emotions show—except symbolically. And that she did. She dressed herself and her daughter in black for John's funeral, and to the day of her own death, nineteen years distant, she never again appeared in public except in black, whether driving through Long Beach behind her Shetland ponies or taking the train to Los Angeles to visit relatives—or consult her lawyers. She also kept little Susanna in black for more than two years. Only her gardens outside the house on the hilltop seemed to bring her peace.[1]

Susan held no seat on the board of directors of the emerging Alamitos Land Company, but depended on Jotham and her nephew George Bixby to keep her informed about what was going on. Moreover, after John's estate had been settled in 1891 and she and the children were the unrestricted owners of the central seventy-two hundred acres of Rancho Los Alamitos, Susan was content to rent the holding to Jotham for a cattle-raising enterprise.

With the children she was more decisive. As a youngster Fred was exceptionally tall and thin. He spoke with a slight stutter and was painfully shy. What he needed, she decided, was new surroundings. Both Susanna and he, moreover, would benefit from wider cultural contacts. Accordingly she removed them from the Long

Facing page: Susan Bixby, ca. 1890

113

Fred on his horse El Calandrio, ca. 1895

His education at home and, for a brief time, at the Long Beach school had not been adequate for the college degree she was determined he have.[4] As a result he repeated several courses at Belmont and did not graduate until he was nineteen.

Next he was enrolled in the University of California, where he majored in history and jurisprudence, which suggests that he, too, was uncertain about his future. He got on well, though. He was merry by nature, like his father, and lost enough of his shyness as he matured to be initiated into a fraternity. At the end of his sophomore year he made a small declaration of self-sufficiency. He strapped on a trusty six-shooter and rode on horseback alone from Berkeley to Los Alamitos, taking time to record events and the passing landscape in his penciled diary. "O but the scenery," he rhapsodized about Monterey County, "beautiful oaks, sycamores, pine, a brook full of trout. And quail—millions of them."[5]

Fred Bixby's early years on the ranch naturally drew him to the open countryside, and his genuine appreciation of land and wildlife was in step with

Beach school she had been active in promoting and in the fall of 1889 traveled to the San Francisco Bay Area. There she entered the fourteen-year-old Fred in a military school at Belmont, on the Peninsula, south of San Francisco. Susanna, aged nine, was placed in Anna Head's prestigious girls' school in Oakland. The pupils wore uniforms, and so the child at last escaped the black she had grown to hate, especially the black stockings. Susan took a house nearby and stayed there whenever school was in session, returning to the ranch only for summer vacations—in black. It was as if the color cried grief not only for her husband but also for the more urbane life that might have been theirs if fate had dealt a different hand.[2]

Apparently she hoped Fred could be weaned from the ranch she blamed for his father's death.[3] As a youngster he did not seem suited for the work.

Thursday, May 28 Warm—not hot—warm. Started out for Jolon at about 7:30. El Calandrio was pretty tired....Well by inquiring every mile or two I succeeded in getting about 20 miles on my way....Oh Ye Gods! No more short cuts for me. Got lost and had to spend the night up on the top of the mountains. Nearly did up El Ca. too—poor horse. In the course of my wanderings had to knock down a fence. Oh but the scenery—beautiful, oaks, sycamores, pine, a brook full of trout. And quail—millions of them.

—Fred H. Bixby diary, 1896

In 1896 Fred Bixby rode from Berkeley to Rancho Los Alamitos on horseback. He stopped in the town of Jolon, located in the Salinas Valley and once the commercial and social center of southern Monterey County. In 1916 Fred and his three daughters would retrace Fred's adventures on horseback and stay at the "family hotel" in Jolon.

the new turn-of-the-century perspective being fostered at the University of California. There, in 1892, faculty members along with famed naturalist John Muir established the Sierra Club with 182 charter members. Students and professors traveled to the High Sierra over the coming decade to explore and chart the terrain, name its peaks, and protect the treasured landscape.[6] In the coming century, President Theodore Roosevelt, Chief Forester Gifford Pinchot, and John Muir would sound the cry for environmental conservation, preservation, and protection.[7] Was young Fred Bixby influenced by these new viewpoints during his years at Berkeley? Certainly his journal of the horse-back ride from Berkeley to Alamitos, along with his later correspondence and efforts to protect the heart of Alamitos, suggest an enthusiastic view of land and open space. And possibly the value of a lasting education.

Susan and her children saw the ranch only during vacations, and it is not likely they concentrated very intently on management procedures during their visits. It should be noted, perhaps, that Susan was afraid of horses and never learned to ride.

Inevitably Fred fell in love. She was Florence Elizabeth Green, often called Polly, daughter of Adam Treadwell Green, a merchant who had made his way to San Francisco via Nicaragua in 1852. Green had lost his first wife in a shipwreck and had waited twelve years before remarrying, so that Florence was a daughter of his middle age. She was a small, quiet, beautiful city girl with a passion for reading, especially poetry. She majored in English and Latin and was active in the German Club, having begun German practically in kindergarten. And she was in the same graduating class as Fred Bixby. Family tradition says that the marked difference in their backgrounds worried her, and he had to propose three times before she accepted. They were engaged immediately after graduation and were married in Berkeley on August 31, 1898.

Frederick Hathaway Bixby, ca. 1890

Susanna Bixby, ca. 1890

Top to bottom: Leslie Green (Huntington), Florence Green (Bixby), and Susanna Bixby (Bryant) at Miss Head's School in Berkeley, 1896

Florence Bixby, ca. 1898

Mr. and Mrs. Adam Treadwell Green
invite you to be present
at the marriage of their daughter
Florence Elizabeth,
to
Mr. Fred Hathaway Bixby,
Wednesday afternoon, August the thirty first,
eighteen hundred and ninety eight,
at four o'clock.
Dwight Way,
Berkeley, California.

Berkeley, June 8—The engagement of Miss Florence Green and Frederick H. Bixby has just been announced. Miss Green was educated at a private seminary at the State University. She is a brunette, pretty and petite. Young Bixby was one of the most popular men at the University in the College of Social Sciences. Since his graduation he has undertaken the management of the large property interest of his mother and sister at Long Beach. After their marriage the young couple will make their home in the southern part of the State.

The engagement announcement most likely appeared in the Berkeley Daily Advocate *or the* Berkeley Evening World.

Fred Bixby, ca. 1898

Florence and Katharine, 1899

Western Union Telegram

June 18th, 1899

Mr. D. Davenport, 2323 College Ave.

Berkeley, Cal.

You are uncle to ten pound girl who arrived yesterday.—*Fred H. Bixby*

Dixwell Davenport was a Berkeley classmate and friend of Fred Bixby.

Florence Bixby and her daughter Katharine, 1899

ENDS AND NEW BEGINNINGS

Following their honeymoon, the newlyweds headed to Rancho Los Alamitos, which Fred was to manage under a lease from his mother. The weather and other more domestic factors did not make for an easy transition, according to Fred, who later recalled his bumpy start: "I entered the farming and cattle business in 1898, but I was so busy trying to fight a dry year that I paid no attention to it until about 1906."[8] 1906 was the year his mother, Susan, would die, but at the time she maintained her residence at Rancho Los Alamitos, and she traveled extensively. Fred was in charge, but not quite. Practical considerations may also have determined the couple's choice to live at the ranch. Florence was pregnant. Nine months and sixteen days after the wedding, the child, a daughter named Katharine, was born in the adobe that John and Susan had so lovingly enlarged and refurbished.

I entered the farming and cattle business in 1898, but I was so busy trying to fight a dry year that I paid no attention to it until about 1906.
—*Fred H. Bixby, 1947*

1907   Fred H. Bixby—Manager's Salary—$3,000
—*Los Dos Ranchos, 1907–1911*

Sister playing on the South Drive. The Bluff House, in the distance, was moved from its ocean-view perch to the Rancho to house the Fred Bixby family so Fred would not have to commute. The house is no longer on-site.

Susan was not there to witness the birth of her first granddaughter, but was traveling—with her daughter this time. When she accompanied Fred and Florence south, she had transferred Susanna from the Anna Head School to Miss Hersey's finishing school in Boston, where cultural advantages were strong and the family home in Maine was near enough for frequent visits. The Boston schooling was topped off with a mother-daughter tour of Europe.

More than a year later, in 1901, when a passionate courtship ended in a tempestuous breakup, Susanna was urged by her mother to console herself with a Grand Tour, properly chaperoned, around the world. Returning, Susanna refused to live at the ranch but instead used part of her inheritance from her father to take an apartment on Russian Hill in San Francisco and hobnob with artists and writers.[9]

Susan did return to Los Alamitos, though, to the house she and her husband had shared. And Fred and his baby and his again-pregnant wife moved out—to an ocean-view house in Long Beach that Susan leased, or gave, to the young parents. They had their own private beach until, on July 4, 1902, the new Pacific Electric Railway—the Red Car line—came to Long Beach, carrying people from throughout the region to the popular Long Beach public beaches, pier, saltwater plunge, and Pike entertainment area (the "Coney Island of the West").[10] "All roads lead to Long Beach," reported the *San Francisco Pacific Underwriter and Banker* in 1923,[11] adding that it had become "the mecca of all tourists."

For several years Fred commuted from his Bluff House, sometimes on horseback, sometimes in a buggy pulled by high-stepping trotters, the six miles to the ranch.[12] He was making some difficult adjustments. Since age fourteen he had spent only a few months each summer at the ranch, and he had treated the stays as vacations, which they were. His lengthy schooling in

The Los Alamitos Sugar Factory, 1901

The Alamitos ranch house is situated on the point of the high ground. Eastward is the Alamitos sugar factory, Anaheim, Fullerton and other towns bordering this great ranch. To the south is the Pacific Ocean, while to the north and west is the picturesque Signal Hill Country.

—*unidentified Long Beach newspaper, February 10, 1905 (In 1905 Long Beach had three newspapers: the* Press, *the* Tribune, *and the* Daily Telegram.)

the San Francisco Bay Area had made him a "city boy." His mother naturally deferred to Jotham and to Los Alamitos' foreman, Charles H. Thornburg, concerning problems of management even after Fred settled in with his bride, ready to step into what he considered his proper place. Perhaps his greatest problem arose from a long conflict with a sugar beet company that built a factory just outside Los Alamitos' eastern boundary. The company proposed to harvest its beets from land acquired in part from Los Cerritos and to a much smaller extent from Los Alamitos, turn the pulp into sugar at the factory, and thus introduce industry into the pastoral countryside.

To Fred, who was in college when the operation began in 1897, the idea sounded fine. He felt that the factory and the town of Los Alamitos that grew up beside it enhanced the value of the ranch. And he foresaw the possibility of putting tenants on some of the 160-acre plots that William F. Sweeney had surveyed and letting them raise mountains of beets, on a sharecrop basis, for sale to the sugar people. Young Fred willingly signed an easement, as did his mother, that permitted the factory to discharge the waste from the refining process into Coyote Creek. From there it would drain through ranch property into the nearby San Gabriel River and on to the ocean.[13]

Interior of the Los Alamitos Sugar Factory, 1901

Q. Don't you know sugar beets are cultivated all along that creek north of you in large numbers; large number of acres, by people living there?

A. They don't live there from choice.

Q. Well, they do, don't they?

A. They live there for they have to...Because they are obliged to support their families, as my husband was his family.

—from Susan Bixby's testimony, April 18, 1901, in Susan P. H. Bixby, et al. vs. Los Alamitos Sugar Company

---

Q. Since that factory has been in operation, have you at any time noticed any odors about your house and about this river?

A. Yes. An exceedingly vile and filthy odor of decayed vegetation, and like decaying cattle on the plains, that had died in dry seasons or died from disease.

Q. Prior to the construction of this factory what use, if any, did you make of the waters of the Coyote Creek and of the New River?

A. My husband watered stock there, sheep and cattle and horses, when there was water. I have often given my boy a drink in the rim of his hat from the [sloughs], from the tule swamps; the water was perfectly clear. Now it is blue-black like indelible ink. I have lived there thirty-five years and on Cerritos. There never was any disagreeable odor from the tules, swamps that I perceived. I have observed it yellow like the water at Long Beach, the artesian wells, the old wells. That water was not perfectly clear.

—from Susan Bixby's testimony, April 18, 1901, in Susan P. H. Bixby, et al. vs. Los Alamitos Sugar Company

---

We had a quarter-share lease, which we still do when we're farming now. It's very good, particularly if you're dealing with honest people, everyone gains.—*George Watte, Belgian tenant farmer's son*

And so Belgian tenant farmers were introduced at Rancho Los Alamitos, with names such as Vlasschaert, Cosyns, Otte, Watte, des Pauls, and Lerno. "I can't be sure of the year," recalled Walter Vlasschaert, the son of one Alamitos tenant farmer, "but it was either 1898 or '99 that [my grandfather Petrus Vlasschaert] came and started farming for Mr. Bixby."[14] Like other immigrants before, the Belgian tenant farmers, in typical chain migration, followed each other out of their native land: "The group of Belgians that were in this Los Alamitos area came from an area in Belgium, with few exceptions, within ten miles of one another," remembered George Watte.[15] Albert Cosyns recalled that "the Bixbys were good businesspeople. Rental agreements were drawn up and most all crops were 25 percent rent to the landowners, 75 percent for the farmer, and what financing [the farmer] couldn't get from Mr. Bixby [for growing sugar beets], the sugar factory would finance."[16] The trend of tenant farming wasn't unique to Alamitos: by 1900, 23.1% of California farmers were tenants; by 1935, 35.6%.[17]

Belgian tenant farmer, ca. 1930

Belgian tenant farmers at Rancho Los Alamitos, ca. 1920

| 11-14-1908 | Land rental crop (¼ beets Oct.)—$4,678.72 cash |
| 12-15-1909 | Land rental crop (beets for Nov.)—$4,558.59 |

—Fred Bixby and Susanna Bixby Bryant Partnership,
Los Dos Ranchos, April 1907—1911

10-15-1918	Alam Sugar Co.—$6,703.56
Oct. 15, 1920	J. Cosyns—$2,206.08
	H. W. Orrick—$3,113.70
	J. De Pauw—$1,759.08

—Fred H. Bixby Cash Book, Jan. 1, 1918—Dec. 31, 1920

| 12-30-1930 | Land rental crop—$23,161.46 |

—Fred H. Bixby Ledger 14, 1931-32

Sugar beets were one of the main crops because the factory was here in Los Alamitos. When it came time for harvest, a horse-drawn plow would loosen the beet in the ground. At the time we got Mexican labor in Los Alamitos. They would hook that sugar beet, hold it in one hand, cut the top off, throw it over, and hand-pitch the beets on the horse-drawn wagon.

—Albert Cosyns, Belgian tenant farmer's son, 1997

We always had sugar beets on the Alamitos. The tenants would harvest their beets, cut off the tops and leave them on the ground for the cattle. When they cleaned up one pasture, they'd be moved to the next, having fertilized the field for the next planting. Beet-tops are fattening and good for cattle.

—Sister (Florence Elizabeth) Bixby, 1975

Belgian tenant farmer, ca. 1908

The Fred Bixby family on the South Drive, 1911. Left to right: Fred, Florence, Katharine, Sister, Deborah, John and Frederick. The California pepper trees lining the drive were planted by Susan and John Bixby in the late 1870s and 1880s.

In spite of the good feeling between owner and tenants, the operation didn't go smoothly. There was enough ambiguity in the easement document to open the way to a protracted and bitter dispute between factory and ranch.

The problem was the almost negligible fall in the creek beds. The once "perfectly clear" water from the tule swamps was now "blue-black like indelible ink."[18] Factory waste, sludge-like, clogged the channels, stagnated, and stank to high heaven, leaving "an exceedingly vile and filthy odor of decayed vegetation...like decaying cattle on the plains,"[19] Susan would later testify in court. She ordered the discharge stopped, which in effect would shut down the factory. The managers declined, and a lawsuit ensued. The

factory produced a horde of witnesses who swore they found the odor no worse than that emanating from the large-scale cattle operations that had centered on the barns and feedlots behind the main home. On Fred's settling down at the ranch following his wedding, his mother insisted on taking the matter to court.

Susan and Fred's environmental impact lawsuit was before its time and did not receive much public sympathy; company lawyers predictably scorned the Bixbys as being more interested in their personal comforts than in the economic welfare of a large part of Orange County's population. (Orange County had been carved out of Los Angeles County in 1889, embracing a sizable part of the ranch in the process.) Fred was roughly handled on the witness stand; the whole affair shook his self-confidence to the extent that he contemplated selling the ranch. One suspects his mother would not have been displeased.

In the end, in 1901, the jury found for neither side. Rather than embark on a second suit, both parties backed off and the factory kept operating until 1926, with no more formal complaints about the smell, perhaps because of improvements made in the drainage[20] but more likely because of the tenant farmer profits.

A second, happier event had helped the Bixbys through the legal dispute. Susan had fully expected Fred and Florence's first child to be a boy, who would be named John after his departed grandfather. Instead it was Katharine. The next child, due toward the end of 1900, would of course be a boy. No one even bothered thinking up names for a girl. It was a girl, however, born in November in the shingled Craftsman-style house on the ocean bluff across from Bixby Park that Susan had given her son and his bride. For lack of anything else, they called the infant girl Sister. In time she was christened Florence Elizabeth—but too late. For the rest of her life she would be Sister, to the polite amusement of visitors who heard her many nieces and nephews calling out for their "Aunt Sister!"

Well, surely next time. Not to be. In 1904 Fred and Florence had little Deborah—another girl! Fred, though, doted on them. Girls they might be, but they would grow up learning to help around the ranch just as though they were boys.[21] As Sister would later say, "We three girls were brought up to get in there and work—saddling our own horses as soon as we were tall enough...We did the same work as the men because Father treated us like sons. He trusted us."[22]

In that same year Susan's prodigal daughter, Susanna, came home to be married. A plump, prosperous young doctor, Ernest Bryant, unexpectedly won her on the seacoast of Bohemia and brought her back to more conventional ways. She agreed to be married at the ranch on July 12, 1904, but rejected somberness. She filled the house with flowers, and after a honeymoon in Alaska settled in Los Angeles, the most promoted city in the country, poised for greatness and growth as Midwestern tourists and new residents flocked to the sunny winter wonderland in the "great circus without a tent."[23] In the coming decade the population of Los Angeles would jump from 102,479 to 319,198[24] and its area expand to 89 square miles. (The original 1781 pueblo grant was 28.1 square miles.)[25] The city's infrastructure grew in kind. Construction boomed and freshwater flowed through the new Owens Valley aqueduct, enough to serve two million people. The Red Car connected Los Angeles to the beach towns, where part-owner Henry E. Huntington envisioned the destiny of the city within the greatness of the region: "It can extend in any direction as far as you like," he predicted. "Its front door opens on the Pacific, the ocean of the future...

There is nothing that cannot be made and few things that will not grow in Southern California."[26]

Susanna's nearby Los Angeles residence must have pleased her mother back at Rancho Los Alamitos, but Susan's other hope, for a new grandson to name for her departed husband, met with disappointment again. On May 29, 1905, John's fourth grandchild was born. She was named Susanna Bryant—the sixth Susanna in the family line.[27]

Florence Bixby and her children, ca. 1916. Back, left to right: Katharine, Sister, and Deborah. Front: John, Florence, and Frederick

The Bixby children, ca. 1919. Left to right: John, Sister, Katharine, Deborah, and Frederick

John and Frederick Bixby standing near the back of the Ranch House, ca. 1920

Katharine, Sister, and Deborah Bixby on the front lawn, May 1913

1914—Rancho El Cojo—Sunday Sept. Something—lost track of time

Dear Katharine,

Your Mother, Deborah, John & Frederick have just gone. Chapo & Indiano are turned out up in the hills here and have given absolute instructions for no one to ride them till you kids get out of school. How are you both getting along—hope you are doing well in your different studies, as one of all things that is an abomination is a girl that doesn't know anything—get every bit of knowledge you can while you have a chance—I hate a silly dress-talking party-talking dance-talking silly girl—If you don't learn anything, want you to keep clean and think about your appearance because that is very necessary; but don't exclude every other tho't.

Well be good—love to Sister

Letter of advice from Fred Bixby to Katharine and Sister at school, September 1914

Though a John would eventually be born to Fred and Florence, his grandmother did not live to see him. On February 3, 1906, Susan Bixby, who had been spending more and more time at the ranch as she aged, fell ill there and died at age sixty-one. She was buried two days later in Los Angeles. Shortly thereafter, Fred, his pregnant wife, and their three daughters moved into the main house to make it their own. It was not a long trip. Sometime between 1901 and 1906 Fred had grown tired of spending the time it took to commute to the ranch six days a week—time that he could have spent with his family. So he cut the Bluff House in half and moved the pieces to the knoll a short distance from the Alamitos adobe, much as his father had moved the Red Barn years before.

September 30, 1919

Masters John and Frederick Bixby

Dearest Boys,

I am anxious to know how you are behaving. Please tell me—Do you get up on time? Do you go to bed on time? Do you go to school on time?

Love, Mother

Letter from Florence Bixby to her sons, John and Frederick, admonishing all good behavior, September 30, 1919. The Bixby boys attended Thatcher School in Ojai; the girls attended Miss Ransom's School for Girls in Piedmont, California, near their mother's former home in Berkeley.

The move into the old ranch house probably signaled a major decision. During his early days at Los Alamitos, while the ranch was teetering on the edge of financial trouble, Fred had wanted to sell.[28] His mother and his very independent sister would have agreed. Florence, too, would probably have complied if such had been Fred's decision. But it wasn't. By steps we cannot trace, Fred changed his mind. His uncle Jotham and the ranch's able foreman, Charles Thornburg, may have exerted some influence. Memories of Fred's father probably had an effect. Maybe the land did as well. We can only guess.

THE RANCHER HIMSELF

Fred and Florence's fourth child and first son—the grandson Susan had always yearned for—was born April 15, 1906, and named John Treadwell Bixby. Another son, Frederick Hathaway Bixby, followed in 1910.

Upon Susan's death, Fred Bixby and Susanna Bixby Bryant, brother and sister, jointly inherited the Alamitos and Santa Ana ranches from their

One of the Alamitos ranch hands, ca. 1920

Alamitos ranch hand, ca. 1920s

Alamitos ranch hand, ca. 1930s

02-1906 To cow barn & corrals, horse barn & corrals, calf barn, bunk house

—*Fred H. Bixby ledger, 1906*

On the big ranch he keeps from eight to fifteen hands during the season consistently employed. Altogether he is demonstrating the possibilities of fine farming in California and is so far eminently successful.

—*unidentified Long Beach newspaper, February 10, 1905*

mother. For the first five years Fred managed the partnership enterprise, communicating regularly, if curtly, with his sister as the ranches struggled to survive financially. Susanna spent little time on ranch affairs until around 1911, when she decided to take an active interest in the management of the Santa Ana ranch. She planted citrus there and succeeded well, eventually becoming the first female director of a Sunkist cooperative. But disagreements over farming methods grew, and in 1911 Fred and Susanna decided to go separate ways. That year the Alamitos was partitioned. In 1925 Susanna bought out Fred's interest in the Santa Ana ranch.[29]

Having committed himself to being a rancher, Fred was forced to deal with profound population pressures from the outset. In 1900 the city of Los Angeles boasted 102,000 inhabitants occupying forty-three square miles.[30] By 1920 that population would surge to almost 577,000, and much of it was moving Fred's way. Over that previous decade Long Beach had emerged as a city in its own right, resisting attempts by the rapidly spreading City of Angels to absorb it. What gave the city of mostly transplanted Midwesterners the strength to hold off the northern Goliath was its early

Dear Sir,

I desire to notify you that your bay horse put in my pasture on February 6 died today. Enclosed herewith please find pasture bill.

Yours very truly, Fred H. Bixby

Letter from Fred Bixby to M. E. Lambert, March 15, 1906.

civic attention to building a seaport. Around the dredged mouth of the San Gabriel River a shipbuilding industry took root, canneries moved in to process the fishermen's abundant catches, and city fathers looked longingly to the completion of the Panama Canal, which promised to put the burgeoning harbor on the world's map.

Ironically, it was World War I that made the greater difference, with Long Beach becoming a funnel for food and clothing heading toward needy Europe, and a maker of submarines for Uncle Sam. During that same decade Long Beach played less-than-hospitable host to a nascent motion picture industry, while at the same time aviators found Long Beach's "stable" marine air to be more receptive than that of Los Angeles.

Though Fred Bixby could not have foreseen the dramatic growth, right along he felt its impact. As more and more people clamored for land, real estate values soared. Taxes and operational costs followed suit. The ranch simply could not survive unless it increased its per-acre financial yield.

Fortunately for him, nature had made Los Alamitos eminently suited for the production of a wide variety of feed crops. Barley and alfalfa were two common types, and by 1919 California would produce more of these two crops than any other state. But unlike John Bixby's hefty corn yields in the nineteenth century, California's corn harvest would no longer compete with that of the Midwest.[31] More exotic were lima beans, whose straw after threshing was highly nutritious animal fodder. Sugar beets were valuable, too. Before the white roots were sent to the factory just outside the ranch boundary, the green tops were cut off, with a little bit of the sweet beet clinging to the stems. Cattle, horses, or hogs turned in to feed on beet tops, barley stubble, and the other leftovers, which not only put weight on but also fertilized the fields for the next year's crops.

An Alamitos ranch hand posing "Golgotha," ca. 1915. There are very few photos of the Alamitos ranch workers and most are unidentified, since photos usually documented the prized livestock and not the workers. Many of the surviving snapshots were taken by Katharine Bixby (Hotchkis), an avid teenage photographer.

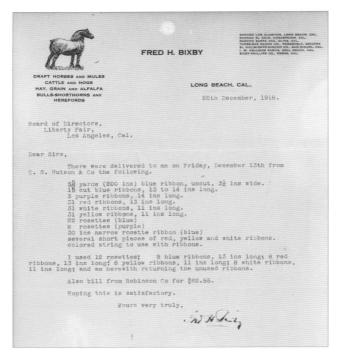

Fred Bixby's stationery featured "Omer."

Rancho Los Alamitos was all flat, four big pastures covering six or seven miles. You could just see what you had to round up and ride over and get it. The Alamitos mostly had steers feeding on beet-tops to get fat and shipped to market nearby at Los Angeles, but the Cojo, the Santa Ana, the Nacimiento, those ranches were cow-calf operations. The new calves would have to be branded in the spring and then weaned off in the summer.

—*Sister (Florence Elizabeth) Bixby Janeway, 1975*

On the home place there are approximately thirty-seven hundred acres. In his stock-raising he breeds Shorthorn and Hereford cattle and draught horses, Omer, at the head of his stud, having been imported from Belgium.—*James Miller Guinn,* A History of California

The view south from the Rancho Los Alamitos barnyard, 1915. Cattle were brought to Rancho Los Alamitos from Fred Bixby's outlying ranches for fattening before market.

Satisfactory rotations were maintained by dividing the farmlands into pastures with temporary fences. When the animals had cleaned out one patch, the fences and movable water troughs were shifted to another spot. The farming was done by a number of tenants who turned over one-quarter of their harvest, or proceeds from its sale, to the owners as rent and sold the rest either to the ranch, the sugar factory, or the cannery that contracted for the lima beans.[32]

For all that, Los Alamitos was destined to be a place meant for "finishing" animals for the explosive market in Los Angeles. In a sense the decision to break away from old patterns was facilitated by the reduction of Rancho Los Alamitos' size from 26,395 acres in 1881 to 3,600 acres in 1912—for it did away with the temptation to graze large unimproved pasture. Back in 1909 Fred and Susanna had established Dos Ranchos Company to run the properties, which meant raising cows and calves on Rancho Santa Ana and then bringing the young steers to Los Alamitos for their last suppers. In effect the "new" ranch was being transformed into an oversized feedlot in which cattle imported from outside ranches got fattened close to market.

Shortly after Fred split with Susanna to go it alone, he began acquiring a changing sequence of ranches in Arizona (the Clear Creek Cattle Co., Three Links, Moqui, El Desierto) and in the other parts of California—the Cojo, Jalama, and Rowland. In addition he managed ranches for others, notably two Hellman properties, one adjacent to his Los Alamitos holding and the other the magnificent Nacimiento, 36,000 acres on the eastern slope of the rugged Santa Lucia Mountains northwest of Paso Robles.

Sister (Florence Elizabeth) Bixby (Janeway) a lifelong cowgirl and rancher, roping a steer, 1921

One time I was helping Juan Dominguez work on a cow, but when we wanted to get back on our horses, we had to run and hide behind a piece of tumbleweed. We got back on just in the nick of time. At lunch that day Mother was busy with her brood as usual. At the table I never said more than three words in succession, but that morning I'd almost been killed, so I said, "A cow was mad today and tried to hook us." Poor Mother, she tried so hard to listen to everybody and understand. She said, "And did the cow's anger abate?"

—*Sister (Florence Elizabeth) Bixby Janeway, 1975*

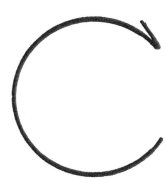

The Fred Bixby Cojo Brand

Cattle at the Cojo Ranch owned by Fred Bixby, 1920

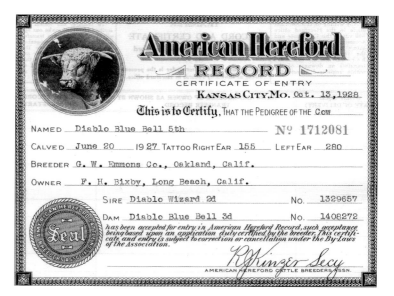

American Hereford Record, Certificate of Entry, 1928

Dear Wheelers:

I wish to report that finally after twenty years I have been able to annex the Rancho Jalama which, as you may remember, joins the Cojo on the north. I tried to buy this, as you know, twenty years ago...I got possession on August 1st and am now in the throes of rehabilitating, renovating and stocking the whole place. Showing what? I think perhaps the principal thing this purchase of the Jalama shows is that once a damn fool, always a damn fool! I have always wanted this particular piece of property, which is on the north side of the hills adjoining the Cojo, and at an age when I should be resting at a spa or in Havana or Miami Beach or some other health resort, I have acquired it and the retirement, which should have come about now, is herewith being postponed for several years.

Letter from Fred Bixby to the Wheelers, August 14, 1940.

The crown jewel of Fred's own satellite ranches was the Cojo, 8,750 acres located about forty miles from Santa Barbara. The coast there doglegs abruptly from east-west to due north at the great headland of Point Conception. Cojo itself lies just east of the point, falling steeply from timbered ridges and wild canyons to broad, grassy terraces facing the ocean. Enough ground for some farming was tucked into the folded terrain, but mostly the Cojo was used for another cow and calf operation and as grazing land for stock.

12-1930 Inventory balance—cattle (steers, cows, bulls)—$40,477.53
—*Fred H. Bixby Ledger 13, 1931-32*

Branding cattle at Nacimiento Ranch, 1920. Fred Bixby managed the ranch for I. W. (Warren) Hellman, a nephew of Isaias Hellman, an original Alamitos partner with John and Jotham Bixby.

On Rancho Los Alamitos [Fred Bixby] raised beef cattle, draft horses, mules, hogs, grain, sugar beets and alfalfa. On the Cojo Ranch, Concepcion, Calif., acquired in 1913, and the Jalama Ranch, Lompoc, Calif., acquired in 1940, he raised cattle, horses, beans, hay and walnuts; on the Shorb Ranch, Olive, Calif., acquired in 1905, he raised oranges and at the Rancho El Desierto, Mesa, Ariz., acquired in 1926, he raised grapefruit and operated a feed yard for cattle.—*Preston Hotchkis Sr., 1957*

Dearest Children,

We are just about to leave for Mustang Springs, for the rodeo. Now don't all shriek with anguish for your time is coming in May. They branded 75 calves yesterday & 100 the day before. I do not approve of "round-up" methods, & unfortunately, I have been saying so. Steve agrees with me on many points. Father on none!!

Woe is me!

Letter from Florence Bixby to her children about the roundup at Nacimiento Ranch. November 1914.

Sister working the cattle at Cojo Ranch, ca. 1916

05-04-1932   F. E. Bixby [Sister]—Apallucia stallion—$90
                                    —*Fred H. Bixby Journal 13, Jan. 1, 1932–Dec. 31, 1937*

Dear Icky:

We have been gathering cattle today on the Fuller Ranch. It was lots of fun, and we have three more days of it. From "the Queen of the Cowboys." Wow!!

Letter from Sister to her youngest brother, August 3, 1921. Frederick was nicknamed "Icky" by his siblings.

COWGIRLS

Those ranches—Los Alamitos, Cañon de Santa Ana, the Cojo, and Nacimiento—were the working grounds of the cowgirls, Katharine, Sister, and Deborah. Surely one of the most unusual labor forces ever put together by a fond but demanding father, the girls learned to ride when they were so small they had to lead their horses to an old pepper tree circled by a bench and stand on that to get a foot in the stirrup. "Deborah went on her first roundup at seven, riding behind me and hanging onto my waist. When she was eight she graduated to her own horse," later remembered Katharine, the eldest daughter.[33]

These were not Old West roundups sweeping across unfenced miles with men from a dozen outfits attended by chuck wagons and remudas of bucking broncos. Rather, they involved gathering cattle that ranged inside fenced areas, albeit large areas, in order to brand, castrate, dehorn, vaccinate, and so on. Still, some headlong riding and roping were involved at times to separate a mother cow from a calf destined for weaning, to keep steers being driven down a brushy hillside from doubling back into an almost inaccessible gulch, or to catch a calf by both hind legs and drag it to the branding fires. Fred himself was a hell-bent roper, going full tilt, lasso loop swinging over his fedora hat as he took aim at his target, and he expected no less from his daughters, once they had reached their teens. "Up at 5:15. Got a lot of cattle in the river bottom. The brush was so thick we had to walk and lead our horse, my chaps were so heavy I fell down about 6 times. It was hard work. Home by about 6:00,"[34] Katharine recorded in her diary that evening—an amazing feat of energy in itself.

Front to back: Katharine, Sister, and Deborah Bixby, on horseback near the Ranch House, 1907. The water tank was taken down in 1927.

Left to right: Sister, Katharine, and Deborah Bixby riding in the roundup, 1912. "Deborah went on her first roundup at seven, riding behind me and hanging onto my waist. When she was eight she graduated to her own horse."—Katharine Bixby Hotchkis, 1975

They slept not on the ground as in olden times but in beds in the different ranch houses. But they were up at 5:30 to help prepare breakfast, wash the dishes, and make their own and their father's beds before running out to saddle their horses. Fred had a notion, acquired perhaps from Florence, that they should not ride during their menses, and he always asked beforehand if each was "all right." They knew what he meant and, wanting to join the ride, they often lied if the timing was wrong. Since they made their own napkins, moments occasionally occurred when they were sure they would be caught, but Fred either did not notice or pretended he didn't.

Friday, May 12, 1922—In town all day. Horse Show in the evening. Sister & Deb both rode in the Stock-Horse class. Sis got 1st prize and Deb 4th. Deb staid to dance.

Tuesday, April 3, 1923—Practiced riding in the ring for the Horse Show tonight. To my perfect amazement I won second prize. —Katharine Bixby (Hotchkis) diary

04-02-1906   Pasadena Horse Show—$35
                                        —Fred H. Bixby Ledger, 1906

Fred Bixby, 1938.

His hat was always the same—a conservative city hat tipped at an unconservative angle.

—*Katharine Bixby Hotchkis, 1975*

For cattle work on the home ranch Father always wore his French cuffs starched and gold cufflinks, impeccably dressed in his monogrammed shirt and necktie, but he was much more in with his men, working with them, than a lot of bosses are. He was a crackerjack roper, always at a dead gallop, always dramatic.

—*Sister (Florence Elizabeth) Bixby Janeway, 1975*

Fred Bixby on his horse "Oriole," 1925

It was unusual for girls to ride in the roundups. We three girls were brought up to get in there and work—saddling our own horses as soon as we were tall enough. You rode by yourself and looked for the cattle. We got awfully tired day after day. We did the same work as the men because Father treated us like sons.

He trusted us.

—*Sister (Florence Elizabeth) Bixby Janeway, 1975*

This horseback trip from San Francisco to Los Angeles riding 500 miles was entirely different. Down the quiet back streets of Oakland we went and then to San Francisco, straight out Market Street. The horses were jittery because of the automobiles and clanging street cars. They jumped and skittered about on the slippery cobblestone pavement. At last—dirt roads! Father could set our pace, about six miles an hour. All we had to keep in mind was that we wanted to go south.

—*Katharine Bixby Hotchkis,* Trip with Father

Trip with Father *by Katharine Bixby Hotchkis, first published by the California Historical Society in 1971, recounts the adventure the three Bixby girls had with their father, Fred, as they rode from Oakland to Rancho Los Alamitos on horseback.*

Katharine Bixby on the "Trip with Father," 1916

Another problem was relieving their bladders—finding a bit of shelter (except that on Los Alamitos there was none), dismounting, dropping chaps, riding skirt, bloomers, and underpants while holding tight to the bridle reins of the horse as it tried to pull away and join the others. The only way to avoid the problem was to drink no water in the morning, which meant desperate thirst later in the day. One exception came when the crew was driving a plodding herd to or from some shipping point. It was a hot, dusty business, and the drovers now and then passed a communal canteen back and forth, though by the time it reached the girls it was likely to contain more secondhand tobacco juice than water.[35] They loved it all, especially when their mother told them privately, "Your father is really proud of you."

The zenith of those carefree cowpoke days came in 1916 with what became known as the famous "Trip with Father." Until then, the children had been taught at the ranch by a tutor who commuted from Long Beach. But as the girls reached college preparatory age, Florence chose to put them in a private school in Oakland, next door to Berkeley, where both parents had attended the University of California. How many times did they hear the story of their father's solo ride from there to Los Alamitos? Enough, certainly, so that they clamored to repeat it. Mother would not go, of course. She didn't like horses. John and Fred Jr. were too young and preferred riding tractors. But the three girls would, if Father acted as guide, and they would invite their cousin Susanna, daughter of Fred's sister, to come along.

Whether Fred was indulging himself more, or the girls, is hard to say. At the end of the school term, he shipped the necessary equipment and each rider's favorite mount to Oakland. "This horseback trip from San Francisco to Los Angeles riding 500 miles was entirely different...Father could set our pace, about six miles an hour. All we had to keep in mind was that we wanted to go south,"[36] Katharine wrote later. They crossed the bay on a ferry and clattered nervously across the cobblestone streets of San Francisco. They did not feel they were really on the way until they reached dirt roads, where there was less danger of their horses falling. They rode fourteen days. Their shortest ride was 12 miles; the longest, 52; the total, 522, for a daily average of a little more than 37. They spent as many nights as possible at some ranch or another, including Nacimiento, which their father managed, and the Cojo, which he owned. The Bixby girls were already familiar with both of those, as was cousin Susanna, who joined them at Nacimiento for the balance of the trip.

They spent one night in a flea-trap room back of a saloon and one at a luxury hotel in Santa Barbara, where on other occasions they often dressed in red-and-white costumes and rode silver-laden saddles in the fiesta parades. They got lost among thick trees and giant boulders in the dark, though Fred never admitted it; they pitched up and down mountainsides, shivered in fog, hunched against high winds screeching across the ridges, and trotted along one stretch of beach with surf lapping at their horses' feet. Along the way they learned of the respect with which their father was regarded by his fellow cattlemen. In nearly every farm town they jogged through and at the ranches they passed, men called out greetings and invited him to pause for an exchange of talk. The young women and all those who saw them would never forget the "Trip with Father."[37]

L-622   OIL FIELDS AT SIGNAL HILL, LONG BEACH, CALIFORNIA

HUDDLESTON PHOTO   94935

THE OILMAN

During the first two decades of Fred's management, the Alamitos ranch came closer to financial collapse than anyone, except Fred and Florence, realized. It had not been in good shape when he took over its supervision in fall 1898. Transforming patterns of operation and reaching out to buy other ranches had increased his burden of debt. The agricultural depression that began about 1920 deepened the mire.

But the sustaining land, plus a good measure of California luck, served Fred as well as it had his Bixby progenitors. Dwight Thornburg, a son of Alamitos foreman Charles Thornburg, studied geology in college.[38] What he learned convinced him there was oil under Signal Hill, which rose along the border between Los Cerritos and Los Alamitos. Other companies had punched down dry holes in the vicinity, however, and Thornburg had trouble getting a hearing from his employers at Shell. A sensational strike at nearby Huntington Beach changed some minds, and Shell leased from the Alamitos Land Company 240 acres that had been put into that holding firm as unsuited for either farming or residential plots. Drilling began March 23, 1921. Exactly three months later, when the well had reached a depth of 3,114 feet, a geyser blew up 114 feet over the crow block of the derrick. Alamitos No. 1 began pumping its liquid black gold two days later.[39]

A wild time followed. Except for the Alamitos lease, the hill was checkerboarded with small lots held by many owners, and soon a well was going down on every one of them lest a neighbor reach the pool first and drain away an unfair share of the booty. The mecca for Midwestern retirees turned into a speculator's paradise. In 1927, Upton Sinclair—writer, muckraker, and politician—described the frenzied scene in his novel *Oil*: The road into Long Beach was "lined with placards big and little, oil lands for sale or lease, and shacks and tents in which the selling and leasing was done...somebody would buy a lot and build a house and move in, and the following week they would sell the house, and the purchaser would move it away, and start an oil derrick."[40]

Even Shell got caught in that race. By the end of 1922, there were 850 derricks on the hill; some of their legs actually interlocked. Endless trains of wagons and trucks hauled in lumber, pipe, sheet metal, machinery, and whatnot. Tank farms, office shacks, machine shops, warehouses, and telephone poles proliferated. On the single day of October 24, 1923, the field turned out 259,000 barrels. By 1924, oil, not agriculture, would be the primary state industry and nourishment.[41] Yet the Alamitos Land Company found only frustration in these figures. It owned only a small part of Signal Hill and received only a small portion of the royalties, even though the discovery well had been drilled on its

Signal Hill Oil Fields   Long Beach, California

There is scarcely a place where one cannot see against the sky the fretted tower that means oil. —*Sarah Bixby Smith,* Adobe Days, *1925*

Thursday, August 17, 1922—Bob took me to one of the oil wells & staid there with him till about 11:30. Signal Hill is fascinating at night—about 225 busy oil wells.

—*Katharine Bixby (Hotchkis) diary*

Although Katharine Bixby Hotchkis mentions "Bob" several times in her diary, in this case his identity remains a mystery, although he may be the future husband of her sister Deborah.

01-19-1921 Land rental cash, Shell Co.—$743.85

01-27-1921 Land rental, Standard Oil Co.—$1,211.57

—Fred H. Bixby Cash Book 10, Jan. 1921—Dec. 1923

Profit & Loss Act: land rental cash—$8,024.50; land rental crop—$23,161.46; cattle—$2,961.42; crop—$6,398.11; oil—$647,132.63

—Fred H. Bixby Ledger 14, 1931-32

property. Meanwhile the noise, grime, traffic, and unsightly structures spreading in every direction—to say nothing of occasional oil well fires that threatened to torch the neighborhood—were crippling the sale of nearby lots.

Bixby luck, a believer in four-leaf clovers might say, decided to remedy matters. In 1926, even as the new rich flaunted their fortunes in an eclectic and opulent row of architectural wonders along Ocean Boulevard, new strikes were made at Seal Beach, in the southeast corner of Rancho Los Alamitos, where Bixbys and Bryants held rights to over two hundred acres. Seal Beach was not as rich a find as Signal Hill, but for Fred Bixby and his family it sufficed. Fred became a wealthy man, and the ranch no longer had to depend on itself for survival. Fred held no illusions about this truth. When asked, as he occasionally was, to what he attributed his success as a livestock operator, he would reply with a grin, "Oil. There's nothing puts fat on the ribs of a steer better than rubbing up against the legs of an oil derrick."[42]

12-1907 Omer (1/4 interest)—$1500—*Fred H. Bixby 3, Apr.—Dec. 1907*

12-1911 Stud barn—$2104.76—*Fred H. Bixby Cash Book 5, Jan. 1, 1911—Dec. 31, 1911*

THE HORSEMAN

Fred had one overindulgence—horses. Way back in 1903, three years before the death of his mother, Fred Bixby had bought a huge stud draft horse named Omer, of a breed known as Belgian. It had recently been judged best of its class at the Chicago International Livestock Show. Later he designed a ranch letterhead that showed a picture of Omer standing on the words "Draft Horses and Mules, Cattle and Hogs, Hay, Grain, and Alfalfa." This was just a starter. In time, for reasons not known, his preference in draft horses would shift from Belgians to even more statuesque Shires. Generally brown or bay, Shires originated in the central counties of England and are believed to be descendants of medieval warhorses bred to carry heavily armored knights into battle. Their greatest popularity in the United States followed the Civil War, when there was a constant demand, especially in the Midwest, for stronger animals for transportation and farm work. Not the least of the Shires' desirable attributes were the powerful mules that could be crossbred from them.[43]

Fred loved his Shires. He raised them by the hundreds. And after a circular driveway had been built around the enlarged front lawn, when guests were sitting on the front porch he would lead out some of his prizewinners to show them off, their fluffy fetlock hairs bouncing above their high-stepping hooves. He worked them around the ranch and used them, too, to produce the tall, tough mules for which Los Alamitos became famous. He sold both species in Los Angeles and other cities as motive power for big freight wagons—until gasoline engines eroded the market in the 1920s. Fred balked at the trend. When farmers and draymen learned how unreliable motors were, he argued, they would turn back to the animals that had been perfected by centuries of selective breeding for pulling and carrying heavy loads.

Showing a Shire, 1930

Fred Bixby's prized Shire "Gallant Prince"

I am sending a picture of my English Shire Gallant Prince. This horse is six years old, weighs 2280# and the opinion of all the judges that have looked him over is that he is probably the best shire on the Pacific Coast.—*Letter from Fred Bixby to the American Horse Association describing his Shire Gallant Prince, March 2, 1934.*

05-11-1932   Stallions—Gallant Prince $300
                   —*Fred H. Bixby Journal 13, Jan. 1, 1932—Dec. 31, 1937*

A ranch hand with one of Fred Bixby's prized mules

Fred Bixby, sporting his customary white shirt and hat, helping brand the cattle at Nacimiento Ranch, 1917

On the home place he breeds draught horses, Governor, at the head of his stud, having been imported from England. Among his other fine horses are Charlemagne and Louis, a Tennessee Jack. Mr. Bixby occupies a high place among the western breeders of fine stock.—*James Miller Guinn*, A History of California

12-1907	Charlemagne—$4500	
12-1907	Louis Jack—$2500	
		—*Fred H. Bixby Ledger 5, 1909*
03-25-1911	Governor (1st Prize Pasadena)—$50	
	—*Fred H. Bixby Cash Book Receipts, Sept. 1, 1909—Dec. 31, 1910*	

Governor

1911

An inescapable irony is that Fred's first major purchase of Shires came after the Signal Hill oil discoveries in 1921. Already Shire breeding farms in the Midwest were disappearing, though a number of owners were still hanging on in the West. Notable among them was Jack London's Black-hawk Ranch in Burlingame, California. In the mid-1920s, almost surely using oil royalty money, Fred bought practically all the Blackhawk stock. Methodically, Fred Bixby set about producing unrivaled Shire stallions for breeding purposes. That he succeeded is evidenced by the crowds that gathered around the Red Barn each time he held a horse auction. In 1938 his stallions were bred to over five hundred mares; his own herd of pure-bred animals rose to eighty-five.

Alamitos bookkeeper Bert Bell posts a flyer for one of Fred Bixby's livestock auctions at Alamitos, ca. 1928.

Talk about barbecues and auction sales! My brother and his wife, they sent them all over the country with signs, as far as Palm Springs—tacked them on telephone poles—"Going to have a big auction!" They killed two steers that were big and fat. They dug a great big hole up by the bunkhouse and buried them, and barbecued them underground. Most people didn't come to buy horses, they came for the barbecue. Oh, the barbecued beans, the beef! Oh man!! They were out of this world.

—Lino Sisneros (ranch worker), 1998

04-24-1915   Beef for barbecue—$25

—Fred H. Bixby Cash Book 8, Jan. 1, 1915–Dec. 1917

The ride of the Rancheros Visitadores, 1930. The annual ride of ranch owners to neighboring ranchos commemorated a tradition which, according to lore, dated from the Spanish-Mexican era.

04-1-1936 Rancheros Visitadores—$20

—*Fred H. Bixby Cash Ledger 15, Jan 1932–Dec 31, 1937*

The crowd at a Fred Bixby auction at Rancho Los Alamitos, ca. 1938

Riding front and second to the left in the photo, Fred Bixby is taking part in the annual Rancheros Visitadores occasion in Santa Barbara, ca. 1930.

Bixby Rancho Scene of Gala Barbecue Fete

Real old-fashioned out-of-door barbecue suppers are coming back into vogue. And revival of this early California method of entertaining will be heartily welcomed by society. At the Rancho Los Alamitos near Long Beach on the night of June 10 Mr. and Mrs. Robert Green (Deborah Bixby) entertained a host of friends at such an affair. Mr. and Mrs. Fred Hathaway Bixby assisted his son-in-law and daughter receive guests. Over red-hot coals in a large grate erected in front of the picturesque ranch house Mr. Bixby, aided by his son, Fred Jr., barbecued the beef and lamb for the seventy or more guests. Afterward a huge bon-fire was lighted and while guests reclined on new-mown hay that was scattered around it, music was played by a Mexican string orchestra. If you will read your history you will see that just this sort of social event was the popular method of entertaining in pioneer California days. And who isn't hopeful that such parties will be given often?

—*"Princess Marie de Bourbon,"* Long Beach Press-Telegram, *ca. 1930s*

Fred's barbecues, a part of his ongoing public auctions and, far more so, his private parties, were in keeping with the thirties, a time when "the privileged classes...revived the barbecue of the rancho era...a rite of celebration of their identity as heirs to the dons of Old California....For a smashingly successful pit barbecue, it helped to have a ranch."[44] The local papers agreed: "Seldom have jaded souls been entertained in such a free, gracious, novel and old-time Spanish hacienda manner as last Saturday at the Fred Bixby Los Alamitos ranch," gushed a Long Beach society columnist. Fred Bixby took his role seriously. He rode with Rancheros Visitadores in the annual social occasion of Anglo landowners, galloping from ranch to ranch to commemorate the romantic rancho tradition of Old California.

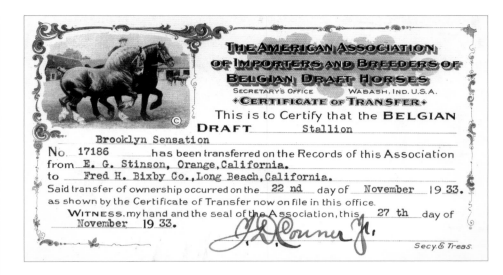

I am sending about a carload of my Shires to the San Francisco Treasure Island Fair and then to Stockton (San Joaquin County Fair), Sacramento (California State Fair) and then here to Pomona, which is the Los Angeles County Fair. This probably will be my grand finale or swan song, as far as sending my stock to all these fairs. The bottom has dropped out of the draft horse business here in the west to a marked degree.

Letter from Fred Bixby to Mr. Truman of the American Shire Horse Association, May 17, 1933, expressing concern about the declining market for draft horses.

Believe me, it is a hard proposition to sell a stallion of any kind in this part of the country. I have held four auction sales this year and have sold two or three stallions at each. The day of the draft horse for farm power is about over. The small tractors that are being sold to the farmers on the installment plan and at a price about the same as the farmers would have to pay for a good team (cash), is putting a crimp in the business. I am, of course, keeping my pure-bred Shires producing.

Letter from Fred Bixby to Mr. Fox of the American Shire Horse Association, May 8, 1940, regarding the impact of technology and credit on the sale of draft horses.

Nostalgia aside, and times being as they were, Fred could not afford to live in the past. The rush of farmers during World War II into what Fred considered mechanized madness would shake him, and he, too, saw the economic future: "Believe me, it is a hard proposition to sell a stallion of any kind...The day of the draft horse for farm power is about over," Fred woefully acknowledged in a letter to the American Shire Horse Association in 1940.[45] "The small tractors that are being sold to the farmers on the installment plan and at a price about the same as the farmers would have to pay for a good team (cash), is putting a crimp in the business. I am, of course, keeping my pure-bred Shires producing."[46] Like Rancho Los Alamitos, and indeed the entire state of California, Fred's Shires were nourished by oil. By 1950 he was one of the few breeders of Shires left in the United States.

A MAN OF LABOR

Diverse ranching and stock raising, and time devoted to the Alamitos Land Company, had turned Fred into a constantly active businessman, urban rancher, and oilman. His daily success, and his personal well-being, depended on a steady supply of trustworthy ranch labor.

The men who worked for Fred Bixby's father had come from across the country, Europe, Asia, and Mexico, and many had probably been in the area much longer than John Bixby. Labor patterns and hiring at Rancho Los Alamitos for the most part followed regional trends. Beginning in the 1880s, workers from Mexico were recruited through El Paso, Texas, to lay and maintain track for the Southern Pacific and Santa Fe railroads across the Southwest.[47] Fred Bixby followed suit in

I was born in Durango, Mexico. We came to the United States in 1929, the whole family. [My uncle] wrote letters to my father telling him that he could get work here, that a man had a ranch and was hiring people. Because of that letter he came here. I was only four or five.

—*Antonia Machuca Castillo (ranch worker's daughter), 1998*

the early twentieth century, recruiting workers from the rural area of Michoacán. These men usually had relatives working at the ranch or knew of the Fred Bixby Ranch via the grapevine. "A lot of people in Mexico were directed to come over here to Mr. Bixby," remembered Mike Hernandez, son of an Alamitos ranch worker in the era. "I guess my father starting working in '89. A lot of people came from the place Janamuato [in Michoacán]."[48] Fred Bixby usually paid for their hotel rooms in El Paso and loaned his new workers money for the remaining trip to Alamitos.[49] By 1911, a small and tidy cluster of houses had sprouted down the hill from the Ranch House, built for the families of the Mexican ranch workers living at Rancho Los Alamitos. Recruitment at Alamitos followed this pattern throughout the early twentieth century, as word spread during lean years. Antonia Machuca Castillo recalls how her father found work at Rancho Los Alamitos: "I was born in Durango, Mexico," she says. "We came to the United States in 1929, the whole family. [My uncle] wrote letters to my father telling him that he could get work here, that a man had a ranch and was hiring people. Because of that letter he came here."[50]

Manuel Machuca-Ramirez, an Alamitos ranch hand

Lina Salazar de Machuca, wife of Manuel Machuca-Ramirez

Fred Bixby really looked after the workers. On many occasions he acted as banker so you could save money to send back to Mexico. I have been told that if you worked for Mr. Bixby and returned to Mexico, as many people did at that time, if you got to El Paso on the return trip, you could stay at a hotel. Mr. Bixby would send money to pay your hotel and get you to the ranch.—*Ray Rodriguez (lease farmer's son), 2000*

I'm sure in our day and age it would be called paternalism and people would look down their nose and talk about unions or something. It may have been paternalistic but it was not demeaning. They really took care of the people.

—*Elizabeth Schugren (ranch foreman's daughter), 1991*

Daughters of Manuel Machuca-Ramirez and Lina Salazar de Machuca, from left to right: Antonia, Ignacia, and Pedra.

> *This is to certify that*
> MANUEL MACHUCA-RAMIREZ
> was admitted to the United States on **11-17-27**
> at **El Paso, Texas**
> as a **n-quota** immigrant for **perm.res.**
> under Sec. **4(c)** of the Act of **1924**
> and has been registered under the Alien Registration Act, 1940.
> *Visa Application No.* X **6351**
>
> | DATE OF BIRTH | SEX | HAIR | EYES | HEIGHT |
> | --- | --- | --- | --- | --- |
> | 6-7-02 | Male | Grey | Brn. | 5-2 |
>
> *Commissioner of Immigration and Naturalization.*
> GPO   16—48499-3

145

Monday, February 27, 1922—The Day of the Bachelors' Ball. Chan was the world's surprise Spanish cavalier—rouge, blackeyes etc. Wat, Frank Browne & Pres were Spanish likewise. —*Katharine Bixby (Hotchkis) diary*

Angie Sisneros with her parents and family, ca. 1920

Left: The Sisneros children standing behind the ranch workers' family housing, ca. 1943

The children of Alamitos ranch workers, ca. 1944. The photo was taken at the lower end of worker housing, below the hill, where the ranch workers' children were taught arts and crafts.

I came here when I was married. I was sixteen years old. We lived here until about 1962. He used to run all the errands—they used to call him Joe Bixby. He was born November 6, 1915, here on the ranch. His parents had been living here for years.

—*Angie Sisneros Mariscal (ranch worker's wife), 1988*

A lot of people in Mexico were directed to come over here to Mr. Bixby. I guess my father started working in '89. A lot of people came from the place Janamuato.

—Mike Hernandez (ranch worker's son), 1979

05-1911   A. Hernandez—2 days—$3
05-1911   José Hornellos—27 days—$40.50

—Fred H. Bixby Cash Book 5, Jan. 1, 1911—Dec. 31, 1911

One-third of all California farm labor would come from Mexico by the early 1930s. Mexican field workers first organized the *Confederación de Uniones Obreras Mexicanas* in 1927 (twenty local chapters spread throughout Southern California),[51] and there were a few agricultural strikes in the twenties, with more to come in the next decade. Life and labor at the Rancho evolved into a healthy brand of paternalism, considering the era. Alamitos wages were lower than migrant field workers' and advancement was highly unlikely, but the work was steady. Workers had basic housing (though no indoor plumbing) and plenty of food, and their health and welfare were monitored by Florence Bixby, their concerned patroness, and Fred Bixby, "the Boss."

This is not to say that the people who lived at and worked for Rancho Los Alamitos did not experience the subtle and not-so-subtle attitudes of the era and region, this in a time when Los Angeles would begin to equate the idea of "laborers" with people of Mexican ethnicity[52] and illegally repatriate as many as eleven thousand Mexican nationals during the 1930s.[53] But the Rancho sustained its workers, provided a measure of pride in the place they called home, and softened the effect of the Great Depression to come. José Vasquez, a son of one of the Mexican families living at the ranch, still remembers the advantages of living at Alamitos during hard years: "We had a place to live," he says, "we had food. The Japanese were farming at the time and so generous with their [vegetables]...my father always had a small garden...my mother always had chickens. We didn't know what the Depression was."[54]

The Vasquez children standing in front of their home at Rancho Los Alamitos, July 7, 1944. Girls, left to right: Marguerita, Maura, Socorro, and Catherine. Boys, left to right: Salvador, Ramon, and José

Asunción Vasquez, the wife of ranch worker Jesús Vasquez, standing at home at Alamitos with her children Catherine and Asunción, 1948

Fred Bixby, agribusinessman, ca. 1937

Mr. Bixby's personal saddle horse was a beautiful black Arabian, and he was a real picture of a successful rancher sitting on his silver saddle with a silver bridle on his horse, along with his big hat!

—*Pat O'Sullivan (ranch hand), 1995*

THE MAN OF AFFAIRS

In 1914 Fred and Florence Bixby were humble tourists in Washington, D.C., looking at the White House from afar; eleven years later they were inside shaking hands with President Coolidge. By this time Fred Bixby, an up-and-coming agribusinessman, was no stranger to state or national politics. He was a man at home with California governors and U.S. presidents alike.

Building upon his early partnership in the Enterprise Construction Company in Los Angeles, Fred became an officer and/or director in banking, insurance, warehouse, and family real estate companies.

During the 1920s—a decade in which the population of Long Beach increased 155 percent and Southern California would more than double its starting point of 1,347,050 people[55]—he was president, first of the California Cattlemen's Association, and then of the American National Livestock Association. He lobbied Congress and helped secure legislation to protect cattlemen's profits from middlemen.

When farm prices plummeted during the early twenties, agricultural woes rose to the top of the political agenda. On January 22, 1922, the *New York Times* reported that among the invited representatives, "Fred Bixby of Long Beach, Cal." would be attending the National Agriculture Conference, held by President Warren G. Harding and U.S. Secretary of Agriculture Henry C. Wallace, to speak for 'the range country' on 'conditions confronting farmers'."[56] "Father goes to Washington tomorrow for a conference with the Sec. of Agriculture, Mr. Wallace," Katharine matter-of-factly recorded in her diary on January 16.[57] She also wrote about a memorable evening the following April when her parents hosted a dinner for Henry Wallace at the famed Ambassador Hotel in Los Angeles (with a horse show to follow, of course). There were more events to come. That same year Fred Bixby was appointed a Special Presidential Advisor on Livestock Problems for Calvin Coolidge. Over time, five different governors would appoint him head of the livestock division of the California State Fair, and, in his own right, he established and endowed a Chair for Practical Farming at the University of California, Davis.

Fred Bixby on Chinate, ca. 1920

My dear Frederick,

I am so anxious to have you come East some time for I know you would enjoy it especially Washington. There are so many things to see—Congress, the Capitol, the White House, the government buildings, the Washington Monument, etc.

Father and I went to a reception at the White House last week and shook hands with President and Mrs. Coolidge...the White House is very beautiful, and dignified. Would you like to be President of the United States? I'll vote for you.

Much Love, Mother

Letter from Florence Bixby to her younger son, Frederick, January 28, 1925. Fred Bixby served as a Special Presidential Advisor on Livestock Problems under the Calvin Coolidge administration.

02-12-1928	Expense—People's Anti Single Tax League—$50	
08-22-1928	Reapportionment Campaign Calif Farm—$100	
10-01-1928	Hoover for President—$5,000	

—Fred S. Bixby Cash Book 13, Jan. 1, 1928—Dec. 31, 1929

11-6-1921 Tickets to Washington—Santa Fe R.R.—$508.62

—Fred H. Bixby Cash Book 10, Jan. 1921—Dec. 1923

Thursday, Feb. 1, 1922—National Livestock Convention all day. Father was unanimously re-elected President.

Friday, Apr. 6, 1923—Father had a dinner for Secretary of Agriculture Wallace at the Ambassador. All men but Mother & us. Horse show afterwards.

—Katharine Bixby (Hotchkis) diary

In 1922 Fred Bixby served as a delegate to the National Agriculture Conference held by President Warren G. Harding and U.S. Secretary of Agriculture Henry C. Wallace.

Changing modes of transportation at Rancho Los Alamitos, 1911

A SIGN OF THE TIMES

In retrospect, such agrarian duties and interests seem somehow out of step in the Jazz Age of the Los Angeles region, a fast-growing urban scene more concerned with the gridlocked traffic downtown than rural open space. Over two million people would become Southern Californians during the 1920s, and three-quarters of them chose to live in Los Angeles County.[58] In spite of this, during the early twenties Los Angeles city planners clung to their vision of a *pastoral city*—a new urban metropolis of scattered, self-contained garden communities which would relieve downtown traffic and protect the sunny, low-rise, bucolic landscape.[59] In 1923 the more pragmatic Los Angeles Board of Supervisors established the first regional planning commission (it included forty cities and fifty unincorporated towns) in the U.S. to study traffic:[60] one in seven people in the nation had a car in the mid-twenties; one in four in California; and there was one car for every two and a half people in Los Angeles.[61] Over the course of the decade, four major traffic studies wrestled with the interconnected regional traffic problem, and all went nowhere. (Katharine Bixby's diaries reveal that, like many others in the region, the Bixby family was part of the growing problem: "The whole family in the new Lincoln went down to Coronado," she wrote in 1922. The next year, she revealed that she "Drove...all over—114 miles to Pasadena, Hollywood, Los Angeles."[62] Just like everyone else.)

Times closed in on open space, and Fred Bixby struggled to protect his vested rural interests while also capitalizing on future growth. In 1928 he contributed one hundred dollars to a statewide reapportionment campaign that favored agrarian concerns affecting his far-flung ranches, despite his residency in urban Los Angeles County. Closer to home he reaped income from the real estate developments of the Alamitos Land Company in Long Beach, where times were good and the city's reputation was growing. A promotional piece declared that "Long Beach has few equals in living conditions...a city beautiful, a city of homes and the Atlantic City of the west...noted for its clean, moral conditions."[63] No doubt a 1920 city ordinance defining proper beachwear and behavior helped set the tone as Midwesterners flocked to Iowa-by-the-Sea in the coming decade.[64] Perhaps Fred approved.

The Bixby family car, referred to as "our machine" as was customary at the time, June 1915

My mother Mrs. SPH Bixby purchased a 1906 white steamer from you last fall and a leather top. The cover does not fit. I wish to return it to you and get one that belongs to the top that we have. Another thing about a month ago one of the front openings on our machine snapped in two for no reason whatever. The other day the other one broke on smooth road and the machine was not going over 15 miles an hour at the outside.

—*Letter from Fred Bixby to the White Garage, Long Beach, March 20, 1906.*

2518   A Cozy Bungalow in Winter,
          Long Beach, Cal.

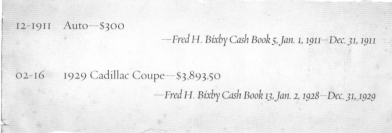

12-1911   Auto—$300
                            —*Fred H. Bixby Cash Book 5, Jan. 1, 1911–Dec. 31, 1911*

02-16   1929 Cadillac Coupe—$3,893.50
                            —*Fred H. Bixby Cash Book 13, Jan. 2, 1928–Dec. 31, 1929*

Thursday, Sept. 7, 1922—The whole family in the new Lincoln went down to Coronado.

Friday, Sept. 8, 1922—Went to Tia Juana in the morning.

Monday, Mar. 19, 1923—Drove the McKenzie's all over—114 miles to Pasadena, Hollywood, Los Angeles.

                            —*Katharine Bixby (Hotchkis) diary*

Prohibition-era Long Beach had discovered the world and in turn had been discovered by the world. The famous, including Herbert Hoover, Babe Ruth, and Charles Lindbergh, dropped by to pay their respects to a city buoyed by good economic times that seemed better every passing year. To celebrate, the city in 1928 put up $650,000 to build, on sixty acres at the west end of Seventh Street, "the Pacific Southwest Exposition," a temporary international city to show "the important relationship" between the American Southwest and the nations bordering the Pacific Ocean.[65] On the night of July 27, Gloria Swanson threw the switch that lit the Moorish splendor of the central quadrangle, with its reflecting pool and the Street of Nations; Clara Bow, Harry Buffum, Upton Sinclair, and president-to-be Herbert Hoover were among those who came to gaze on the glitzy wonder. Within six weeks the lights went out. The site was razed. Omens?

A few of the Belgian tenant farmers enjoying their homemade beer, 1930

One thing we had to do every Saturday morning was make home-made brew. During Prohibition we'd make about thirty-five or forty fifths bottles of beer a week. The men would bring their horses and park them and come in to the ranch back porch—three, four or five men. Everyone would drink a fifth bottle of beer, cellar temperature, not refrigerated. They would drink and discuss what happened during the day and what they were going to do the next day.

—*George Watte (Belgian tenant farmer's son), 1994*

Activities at the beach in Long Beach included a tabernacle meeting on the promenade.

Dear Mr. Bixby,

We hold the same views that you do with regard to Upton Sinclair's candidacy but if he doesn't rent a store from us for his campaign head-quarters, he will rent it from somebody else and we might just as well get the rent as not. I don't see how we are helping him at all and the rent he pays is very welcome. You might just as well start in changing your view on the subject of socialism and communism because it looks like you're going to have to cater to this type for a long time to come; that is, provided you plan on continuing to live in this country.

Yours for the Internacional, comrade,

I. W. [Warren] Hellman

Letter from I. W. Hellman of Wells Fargo Bank to his friend Fred Bixby regarding Upton Sinclair's campaign for governor, May 24 1934.

I was born in Long Beach during the Depression and things were real tight. My father was fortunate in having Fred Bixby's connections to get him a job at a Los Angeles warehouse. Fred Bixby said, "Why don't you save some money and come live on the ranch?" They provided houses for the workers with electricity, running water, all the logs you want to burn, and no rent, so we moved right out here. Mama could walk to work and Dad needed the car to drive to the Los Angeles warehouse. It was good for me because it was the first time I lived in a house with a backyard.

—*John William (secretary's son, Fred Bixby Ranch), 1989*

I started working at the ranch in the autumn in 1936 until the middle of '39. I was a chore boy. I came from Oklahoma. I was one of the "Okies" that came to California.

—*Bob Bonham (ranch hand), 1988*

The stock market crash came a year later, with the Great Depression following close behind. The nation—indeed, the world—suffered gravely in the general economic collapse. Long Beach, with its tourist trade plunging, felt the crippling body blow—then another on March 10 of 1933, when the Newport-Inglewood Fault came unstuck. The 6.4 temblor killed approximately fifty locally and shook down many of the city's structures vaguely anchored in its waterlogged alluvial soil. A little over a year later another shock—this one political—occurred.

Controversial Upton Sinclair, twice the Socialist candidate for governor of California, won the Democratic nomination for governor in August 1934. The polarizing candidate received over two-thirds of his vote from Southern California, and 54 percent from Los Angeles County.[66] Supporters who suffered from the effects of the economic depression rallied around Sinclair's EPIC Campaign (End Poverty in California) and took their arguments from his writings blaming capitalism. Others in the Democratic party kept a safe distance from Sinclair's radical notions and agenda. Franklin Delano Roosevelt, for example, refused to endorse Sinclair. Fred Bixby, though never a fan of Roosevelt, agreed. He wrote I. W. Hellman in San Francisco (a nephew of the original Alamitos partner), demanding to know why Wells Fargo had rented office space to the Sinclair campaign. Hellman answered in the tone of the times: "We hold the same views that you do with regard to Upton Sinclair's candidacy...but we might just as well get the rent as not... You might just as well start in changing your view on the subject of socialism and communism because it looks like you're going to have to cater to this type for a long time to come, provided you plan on continuing to live in this country."[67] The majority of voters agreed with Fred Bixby's view, however. Frank Merriam, a staunch Republican conservative from Long Beach, won the November election.

Paradoxically, the Depression, the quake, and the election did not do Fred Bixby much harm. Being situated on the firmer ground of a hill kept quake damage minimal at the Ranch House. And financially, he found himself spared again. True, his ranches lost money, but thanks to oil royalties he absorbed the red ink without pain—except to his pride.

A temporary outdoor kitchen was set up at Rancho Los Alamitos following the earthquake, March 1933.

Earthquake damage to the Ebell Club in Long Beach

We certainly had some earthquake, and although the walls of my house stood up all right, everything inside was busted up in great shape. All the china, glassware, vases, etc., were thrown into the middle of the floor in each room, bookcases thrown down, furniture moved around three or four feet, and it certainly was a mess.

Letter, Fred Bixby to J. G. Truman, president of the American Shire Horse Association, April 2, 1933.

155

Saturday, Nov II, 1922—Just think, the war ended four years ago!! It seems like yesterday.

—*Katharine Bixby (Hotchkis) Diary*

08-12-1918	Office—War Stamps 10,000 note—$2.00
11-16-1918	Personal—United War Work Fund—$100
01-26-1919	Personal—Belgian Relief Work—$10

—*Fred H. Bixby Cash Book, Jan. 1, 1918—Dec. 31, 1920*

New environmental regulations tarnished the Bixby luck. In 1907, a year before Fred Bixby began leasing government land in Arizona to graze his cattle on, the Arizona Cattle Growers Association had passed a resolution supporting the development of a federal policy to regulate national forests and other public lands,[68] Meanwhile, Bixby obtained his permit to graze cattle on the sixty-thousand-acre Three Bar and I.V. ranches, located in Arizona's Tonto National Forest; in the 1911 directory of the 165-member association, "Fred Bixby of Long Beach" was one of five Californians (all from Southern California) listed. With the outbreak of World War I, the calls to regulate grazing abruptly ended; instead, the financially strapped ranchers were encouraged to overstock their government-permitted ranges to supply meat, and they were allowed to continue the practice through the 1920s to ease their debt.[69]

Extensive grazing on federal lands damaged the soil, plants, streams, and springs of the West and Southwest without check during the twenties. As this overgrazing continued, attitudes changed. Men such as Aldo Leopold, a Forest Service employee often considered the father of wildlife management in the U.S., introduced a "land ethic" into federal policy.[70] The ecological perspective would become the heartbeat of an emerging environmental movement.

The punishing combination of erosion, water pollution, and economic strife resulted in the Taylor Grazing Act of 1934. This law attempted to safeguard public lands by basing grazing permits and the number of livestock allowed on the "carrying capacity" of the range, which took into consideration the condition of the land's water, vegetation, and soil. Inevitably, ranchers' costs increased, public grazing lands were reduced, and permits were revoked to stabilize and restore the land.[71]

Rancher Fred Bixby made his position, as well as his knowledge of the issue, clear. That year he wrote that "the Forest Reserve all over the country is going to force the cattlemen to cut down their numbers, and in the end put us out of the forest. This is especially true where there is some reclamation project within the boundaries of the forest where the cattle might dirty up the water or where somebody might think they would cause some washing or some erosion."[72]

Fred Bixby's ensuing correspondence with the forest supervisor and his ranch foreman weaves a story of emerging environmental policy and hardball politics. In 1934 the Forest Service informed Bixby that he would lose his grazing permit, since deteriorating range vegetation could not support the unauthorized excess cattle on his range. Fred Bixby believed the real problem was public policy: "I think the only way we can ever get the Three Bar and the I.V. back is to throw Mr. Roosevelt out and put in a new Republican president," Fred wrote in 1944. "He will then make a change in the chief of the forest job and the new chief will throw out the fellows in Albuquerque and *then* we may be able to get this range back."[73] The same year, the secretary of the Tonto National Forest Grazing Advisory Board (and a distant cousin of Fred Bixby) added in turn, "It is generally understood that Fred's grazing permits were canceled primarily for political punitive reasons by the Roosevelt administration."[74] Nonetheless, Fred Bixby, a powerful agribusinessman, had met his match.

Fortuitous oil income made up the difference. Fred Bixby's oil income varied from $326,000 in 1932 (when the ranches lost $142,000) to $182,000 in 1939 (when ranch losses had been trimmed to $76,000). What probably pleased him most was the fact that this reduction was brought about while he was adding to the number of properties his companies owned. Some of these additions resulted when friends in rough straits persuaded him to buy into their outfits in order to keep them afloat. He carried several loans as well and, in addition, made many nonranching investments.[75] Life had grown complicated through no asking of his own, and more and more the Los Alamitos Ranch House, parts of it weathered by more than a hundred years of living, served as a refuge from so much pressure and change.

Fred and Florence Bixby at the Moqui Ranch.

The Moqui Ranch in Arizona was also a getaway for the family. Fred Bixby purchased it before his grazing permit to the Three and I.V. Bar Ranch was revoked.

Dear Mr. Bixby,

There is only one trouble in this part of the country, and that is scarcity of money, but I can see that the farmers are feeling better, and I trust that the New Deal will bring back prosperity to all.

Letter from J. G. Truman, president of the American Shire Association, to Fred Bixby, March 13, 1934.

I am again planning to go to the Chicago International and if Landon makes the grade there is quite a possibility that I will be in Chicago at the time of the Meeting. If Roosevelt and his Socialistic advisors go back into power there will be no necessity for me to go east as I will be out of business anyway.

Letter from Fred Bixby to J. G. Truman, president of the American Shire Association, November 3, 1936.

Florence Bixby, 1909

There is helpfulness among peoples. There is the desire to serve, and to co-operate. There is sweetness, and affection and loving kindness. All these things you will find, sometimes hidden, but always there.—*Florence Bixby, 1935*

A PARALLEL LIFE

Florence Green Bixby was a genteel woman by all appearances, but beneath her demeanor she was made of stronger stuff. "Father was the Patron, but [the ranch workers] all came to Mother," remembered her daughter "Sister." "She didn't have a ranch background and some of the things were awfully dangerous that they had to do, but she just knew what to do. She was small and calm and concerned."[76] Florence kept pace with her far-flung husband, but on her terms, in her own interests. She managed and improved the house and environs, not to mention fulfilling the social obligations and civic duties demanded of her. She promoted uncommon causes such as birth control; founded, and for thirty-eight years was president of, the Long Beach Day Nursery; and helped found the Adelaide Tichenor Orthopedic Clinic for Children, for polio victims. She served as a trustee of Scripps College and sat on the boards of various arts, symphony, and museum associations. She filled her home with French Impressionist paintings not yet in keeping

03-22-1930	Children's Hospital Society—$22,000
02-25-1930	Pomona College—$5000
06-07-1930	Ruth Protective Home—$5,000
	—*Fred H. Bixby Ledger 14, 1931-32*
11-28-1930	Day Nursery lot—$4,000
	—*Fred H. Bixby Journal 12, Jan. 1, 1932—Dec. 31, 1937*
05-01-1933	Petra Bosquez—$20; Jesse Munoz—$26.15
	—*Fred H. Bixby Journal 13, Jan. 1, 1932—Dec. 31, 1937*

with popular convention or her family's tastes. In a rare moment of wry frustration, she confided on paper that the general public response to one of her newly designed gardens was much like the response to a painting she had purchased in France, "not [to] be well-considered by all."[77] Though she was surrounded by family and friends, Florence must have sometimes felt alone.

She regularly visited the longtime ranch workers and tenant farmers, supporting their personal and health-care needs and earning respect, appreciation, and gratitude. Together with Fred she checked on the houses of tenant and lease farmers as well as the houses of the Mexican workers on Palo Verde Avenue, just below the Ranch House, to see what needed repairing at company expense. Angie Sisneros Mariscal, wife of a ranch worker, remembered that "Florence used to say, 'Fred doesn't like me to come down here. He says every time I come down here it costs [him] money.'"[78]

Florence Bixby displayed her Impressionist art collection throughout her home, including the Music Room. Left to right: *The Fancy Dress*, 1926, by Frederick Carl Frieseke; *The Water Lilies*, ca. 1903, by Claude Monet; and *Mother About to Wash Her Sleepy Child*, 1880, by Mary Cassatt. Florence bequeathed the two works by Monet and Cassatt to the Los Angeles County Museum of Art. Cristina Klenz Photography, 2009

05-05-1930	Floral Painting—$100
01-22-1931	Childe Hassam—$3,000
06-30-1932	California Institute Guild Associates [LA County Museum of Art]—$1,000

—Fred H. Bixby Ledger 14, 1931-32

THE LOS ANGELES ART ASSOCIATION

hereby certifies that

Mrs. Fred H. Bixby

is a

FOUNDING PATRON

Leader in the cultural life of this community
whose generous cooperation helps to
advance civic art ideals.

1931

President

Florence Bixby served on the board of the Los Angeles County Museum of Art.

Father was the Patron, but they all came to Mother. She didn't have a ranch background and some of the things were awfully dangerous that they had to do, but she just knew what to do. She was small and calm and concerned.

—*Sister (Florence Elizabeth) Bixby Janeway, 1984*

Florence used to say, "Fred doesn't like me to come down here. He says every time I come down here it costs [him] money."
—*Angie Sisneros Mariscal (ranch worker's wife), 1988*

Florence Bixby, 1930

Mother would go down and see the families, see what they needed. The houses weren't very good then, but nobody's house was good then.
—*Sister (Florence Elizabeth) Bixby Janeway, 1985*

02-24-1916   Work Mexican houses—$167.75
—*Fred H. Bixby Cash Book 8, Jan. 1, 1915–Dec. 1917*

A ranch worker's home at Rancho Los Alamitos, ca. 1954

In 1936 a small cluster of homes was built for the families of the Mexican ranch workers on the road leading up the hill to the Rancho. Today the road is known as Palo Verde.

The Sisneros children in front of their Alamitos home, ca. 1940

We had four children—Martha, Tom, Virginia, and Frederick. Mrs. Bixby paid for all of them, paid the hospital. My husband, Joe, was a gardener, then later became chauffeur. The workers that had families lived down below the hill. There were quite a few people, we all lived like in a circle just below Palo Verde. Mr. Bixby used to call it Little Mexico.—*Angie Sisneros Mariscal (ranch worker's wife), 1988*

The first house we lived in was just two bedrooms, nice kitchen, no bathroom. Rain or shine or muddy we had to walk all the way down to the bathroom. There were two, one for the men and one for the women. In the late or middle thirties they started building new houses in a row for the ones that stayed here.

—*Antonia Machuca Castillo (ranch worker's daughter), 1998*

When they had the roundups we used to stay indoors because they used to come up Palo Verde and the cattle would wander right through the homes. Sometimes we had fences but that didn't make any difference.

—*Maura Vasquez Castillo (ranch worker's daughter), 2000*

By 1948 the houses of the Mexican families at Rancho Los Alamitos lined the road up the hill.

Children of the Alamitos ranch workers

The Lerno family, Belgian tenant farmers, at Rancho Los Alamitos, 1938

"We moved there in 1926. I was five years old and could speak only Flemish. They let me go to the Bixby School at Stearns and Palo Verde—one acre fenced off with barbed wire to keep the cattle out. A lot of the Mexican kids couldn't afford shoes so they came barefooted. That's what we wanted to do. Mom finally consented. Our feet got so tough that we could walk across alfalfa stubble fields.

My dad was a believer in using kids to work, even at age ten. He lowered some of the equipment seats so I was able to reach the pedals and handle a team and mow hay. During cutting time I would work for an hour cutting hay and then come in and eat and go to school."

—*Walter Vlasschaert (Belgian tenant farmer's son), 2002*

Mrs. Bixby would come right to the house. The house we lived in was board and batten, nothing fancy, and she would stop in and visit with Mom and ask if anything needed painting.

—*Albert Cosyns (Belgian tenant farmer's son), 1991*

My sister was poisoned, I think from polluted water. Anyway she got extremely sick, needed medication and treatment. Mrs. Bixby used to come over to the house and help my mother with my sister and saw that she had the proper care because my mother didn't speak any English.

—*Eme Otte (Belgian tenant farmer's son), 1987*

07-13   ½ Cost painting tenants place—$24

—*Fred H. Bixby Ledger 14, 1931-32*

In the company of her family, Florence Bixby found a certain comfort and refuge from the rough-and-ready world of the working ranch. Author Sarah Bixby Smith, Fred Bixby's cousin, and her husband, Paul Jordan-Smith (literary editor of the *Los Angeles Times*), were part of the intelligentsia of Los Angeles, and their home in Claremont, and subsequently Los Angeles, was filled with luminaries—writers, artists, and photographers—and avant-garde thinking. Florence's association with Sarah led to Florence's appointment as a trustee of Scripps College and no doubt also influenced her forward-thinking views on social issues, encouraged her writing, and helped her to cultivate a taste for art and design.

The Bixby School, established for the Alamitos tenant and ranch worker children, ca. 1930

We had one teacher for all eight grades and two three-holers down the boardwalk. I went to school with all the Bixby hired hands. The Sisneros, the Perezes—we all grew up together.

—*Albert Cosyns (Belgian tenant farmer's son), 1991*

Children of Belgian tenant farmers at Alamitos, 1921. Walter de Brouwer is holding Walter Vlasschaert.

The Bixby children, August 1913 Katharine Bixby's notation reads, "The day before I went to boarding school for first time."

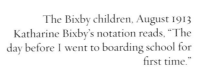

A signed portrait of Sarah Bixby Smith, ca. 1915–1925, by Edward Weston. Courtesy of Rancho Los Cerritos Historic Site, Long Beach, California

Sarah Bixby Smith, Los Angeles, ca. 1920s. Photograph by Edward Curtis, courtesy of Rancho Los Cerritos Historic Site, Long Beach, California

Florence's sister Leslie Green Huntington was married to wealthy Howard Huntington, relative of railroad magnate Collis P. Huntington and son of Henry E. Huntington. "Took Grannie and went to call on Mrs. H. E. Huntington. Saw the wonderful Gainsborough's "Blue Boy"—the most glorious painting I have ever seen,"[79] raved Florence's daughter Katharine in 1922. Fred's sister, Susanna, was married to the Huntingtons' doctor, Ernest Bryant, and the family connections offered marvelous opportunities which helped Florence create a remarkable world of grace and style at the ranch.

A RHYTHM OF ITS OWN

In 1906 Florence and Fred revived the Christmas parties that Susan had not the heart to carry on after John's death. Fred bought a big evergreen in Long Beach and put it up in the parlor, lopping off the top so the branches of the tree brushed flat against the ceiling. With the children helping, or thinking they were, Florence and Fred hung ornaments and clipped on candles and invited the ranch workers and tenants and their wives and children to a Christmas Eve celebration as in bygone days. With his long cigar cocked as usual in one corner of his mouth, Fred ladled out punch from a cut-glass bowl and told jokes, some of which Florence probably found inappropriate. Gifts were passed around.[80]

Sister remembered that it took two days to ride to all of the houses, getting "the names and ages of the invitees, including the families of the Japanese lease farmers who often came in traditional dress."[81] As the Christmas Eve parties continued, the family traditions grew—special ways of preparing presents, adding magicians, puppet shows, or clowns as entertainment, and singling out one of the ranch hands as the recipient of a joke gift. The real presents followed, carefully suited to the age and sex of the steadily enlarging family around the tree—that is, most of the time. Over sixty years later, Eme Otte, the son of a Belgian tenant farmer, remembered the year when, much to his youthful dismay, the Bixby girls "goofed up...they looked at my name as being a girl, Eme, so I got a set of pearl beads that Christmas."[82]

It would have been remarkable if, in fact, Eme's unwanted set of pearls was the only mistake made over the years. "Just began my Christmas shopping. Bought 1008 toys in L.B.," Katharine wrote in her diary

Children of the Alamitos ranch workers and tenant farmers at the Bixby School, ca. 1917

on December 8, 1922, adding several weeks later, "Wrapped and tagged presents all evening till about 1:00. The list of tenants is enormous this year. It's an awful task to get two suitable presents for each child."[83] But with the Bixby children marrying and scattering—and John, the first boy, dying in an automobile accident in 1929—the celebrations ended in 1930 with a bang, not a whimper: nearly three hundred members of the "extended family" somehow crowded into the house for that last holiday party.

Two of the Belgian tenant farmers' children and their grandmother at Alamitos, 1928

At Los Alamitos Rancho, Mr. and Mrs. Fred Bixby will give their usual Christmas tree and entertainment to the employees of the ranch and their families. There are more than one hundred of these and all are remembered with gifts. On Christmas day a family dinner will be given. —Long Beach Daily Telegram, *December 23, 1917*

Friday, Dec. 8, 1922—Just began my Christmas shopping. Bought 1008 toys in L.B.

Saturday, Dec. 12, 1922—Busy all day long getting the house ready. Loads of holly & the house looked so nice. 198 people at the tree. Sleight of hand man & an accordion player to entertain us.

Friday, Dec. 22, 1922—Shopped all afternoon with Sis. Wrapped and tagged presents all evening till about 1:00. The list of tenants is enormous this year. It's an awful task to get two suitable presents for each child.

—Katharine Bixby (Hotchkis) diary

02-06-1930   Xmas tree etc.—$87.25

—Fred H. Bixby Ledger 14, 1931-32

Christmas we had a party for the ranch people. We'd ride around to each of the tenants' houses. It took two days because of the horses, and the cattle too, to get the names and ages of the people. They were all invited. The Japanese tenants would come in costume quite often.

—Sister (Florence Elizabeth) Bixby Janeway, 1982

The June Party, 1915

Wednesday, June 18, 1922—The day of the June Party. 226 people here. It was a lovely sight & everyone seemed to have a good time. Jumping in the hay, hay rides, goat rides, horse-back rides, popcorn balls, watermelon, cantaloupes, dancing, bridge. This was the ninth party we have given of this type. It really is most unique.

—Katharine Bixby (Hotchkis) diary

To Mr. Frd. H. Bixby Esq

How-dy-do old kid—howdy-do? Your Mother, the girls are working themselves to death over the June Party that comes off tomorrow. Sorry you are not going to be here but I am glad you are up in the Yosemite, that is very beautiful up there and will never forget it as long as you live. Just think of the thousands of people that never get a chance to see a thing of that kind.

Everybody sends love, Father

Letter from Fred Bixby to his young son Frederick, June 17, 1922.

The first children's party June 21, 1913

The June Party, 1913. The annual June Party celebrated country living in increasingly urban times.

The seasonal celebrations at Rancho Los Alamitos, perhaps not dissimilar to the ancestral days in the village of Povuu'ngna, had a rhythm and ritual of their own. June parties were held annually from 1913 through 1925 for the Bixby children and their numerous relatives and friends: "The day of June Party," wrote Katharine in her diary on June 28, 1922, "226 people here. Jumping in the hay, hay rides, goat rides, horse-back rides, popcorn balls, watermelon, cantaloupes, dancing, bridge. This was the ninth party we have given of this type. It really is most unique."[84] The guests thought so, too. Most small fry and their parents came from the cities—Los Angeles, Pasadena, Long Beach. The invitation gave streetcar directions but also welcomed anyone driving their own "Rolls Royce or Ford."[85] And so the city slickers arrived eager to be entertained with country pageantry. Cages holding baby chicks, ducklings, rabbits, and guinea pigs decorated the tables on the front lawn. Larger animals were parked nearby. There were rides on Shetland ponies and gentle horses, or in a wagon drawn by a team of Fred's huge, feather-footed Shires.

This year's June Party was celebrated in July.

Oh Boy! The Party's on again!

When?

Wednesday, July 2nd 1920

Where?

Rancho. Los Alamitos,
Long Beach

Same old car will leave
Pacific Electric Building
From gate 10, at 11:30

Same old lunch will be served
at one o'clock

Same old stunts will take place
in the p. m.

Same old hostess,
Mrs. Fred Hathaway Bixby,
assisted by
Katharine, Elizabeth, Deborah,
John and Frederick
and

Mr. Fred Hathaway Bixby

If you are coming in your own machine
(either Ford or Rolls-Royce)
kindly SAY SO.

The Bixby children, 1911

The Bixby children celebrating with their grandfather, July 4, 1913

On the Fourth of July when all of Fred Bixby's grandchildren were here during the summer, he would invite all the families from down below to come and have a big party with fireworks. They used to have *tons* of fireworks and popcorn balls, beer for the men. There was a big place where we all would sit out by the palm trees facing the tennis court and it was a couple of hours of just fireworks and socializing.

—*José Vasquez (ranch hand's son), 2001*

Dear Frederick,

Your letters sound a little homesick—cut that homesick stuff out and get in and enjoy yourself. The 4th of July Aunt Sue gives a picnic on the beach and we go up to the Cojo on the 5th of July to stay for several days—maybe a week. Well have a good time. We'll be waiting for you when you come home.

—*Your affectionate Father*

Letter from Fred Bixby to his son Frederick, July 2, 1922.

John and Frederick Bixby, December 1914

Left to right: Deborah, Sister, and Katharine Bixby at the beach, 1912

Saturday, July 1, 1922—Another lovely day on the ranch. I wish they would happen more often.

—*Katharine Bixby (Hotchkis) diary*

The Bixby children riding with their cousin Elizabeth Huntington, August 1914

Young Frederick Bixby, unfortunately known as "Icky," with his cousin, 1919

The Bixby children, 1911

The Bixby children and their cousins at the beach, ca. 1920

Often there would be gathered at the Alamitos, in addition to the children who belonged, half a dozen cousins with their friends. The house was elastic.

—*Sarah Bixby Smith,* Adobe Days

TOWN, GOWN, AND COUNTRY

The blending of city and country life came naturally to the daughters of Florence and Fred—Katharine, Sister (Florence Elizabeth), and Deborah. Florence, well aware of the social obligations that lay ahead, quietly counterbalanced their rugged life as cowhands. She wanted them to be able to take their places in the social world. They learned to play musical instruments, handle teacups, and push their spoons away from themselves when eating soup.

By 1921 Florence felt appropriate suitors should be encouraged to come around. After all, Katharine, twenty-two, had just graduated from Vassar; Sister was twenty-one; Deborah, seventeen. So, in spite of Fred's grumbling, she had a tennis court built at one side of the expanding house, where the old house from the bluff had stood. (During the twenties most tennis courts were located in private clubs, but Los Angeles and surrounding cities began building public courts during that decade.)[86] She arranged the small music room so dancing parties could be held. She had one of its windows changed to French doors and a special canvas cut so it could be laid down on the cement patio outside, for dancing beside the Spanish fountain with its goldfish. Cornmeal gave the canvas the necessary slickness; lights in a big, feathery pepper tree provided illumination. The imported band grouped around the piano; the music flowed through open doors and windows; and dancing as well as tennis became a part, for at least a little while, of the children's gatherings.

The energy with which the girls melded lifeways is astounding, and Fred Bixby's "cowgirls" reveled in the Jazz Age scene. On many occasions after she had graduated from Vassar (Deborah also attended Vassar and UCLA, while Sister stayed closer to home), Katharine arose before six, worked cattle most of the day, changed from split skirt and riding habit

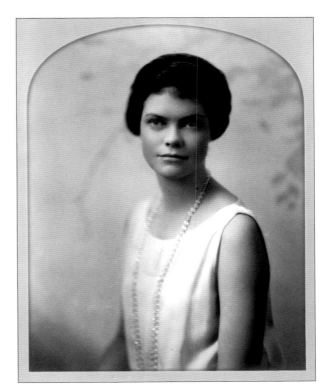

Katharine Bixby, 1924

Tuesday, Feb. 10, 1923—Went up to Los Angeles to the Ambassador. Packed, jammed with seething humanity. Very good time.

—*Katharine Bixby (Hotchkis) diary*

into a party dress, and drove to Hollywood for a night out at the theater, symphony, opera, or a club. "Went up to Los Angeles to the Ambassador. Packed, jammed with seething humanity. Very good time,"[87] Katharine secretly told her diary on February 10, 1923.

Father never wore sports clothes. Played tennis in his suit and his boots, the few times he played. He was very good at tennis. He used to play in college. That's how Mother was able to get the tennis court put in, by reminding him what a good tennis player he was.

—*Katharine Bixby Hotchkis, 1975*

The Cactus Garden and tennis court, 1924

The front lawn and tennis court at Rancho Los Alamitos, 1931. *Phoenix canariensis*, the regional icon, lined the front drive.

Dear Icky,

How are you you old skunk-bunny? Aren't you glad I mean sorry, to be away from your three lovely beautiful delightful, sweet, wonderful sisters? The tennis rackets have just been restrung and so we will be able to play very wonderfully. I'm going to beat you when you get back, unless you become a champion.

Letter from Deborah Bixby to her younger brother Frederick, July 11, 1922.

The Alamitos girls today have always been horse-women with their father, and can handle cattle better than most men; and then they can lay aside their ranch togs and don a cap and gown and hold their own in a college, or in filmy dress and silver shoes, grace a city dance—competent and attractive daughters of California.

—*Sarah Bixby Smith,* Adobe Days

K. on 'Chinata' 1918

Katharine Bixby, 1918

Tuesday, Oct. 3, 1922—Up at 5.30. Worked cattle till about 11.00. Two trips to L.B. & back. Visited Day Nursery. L.A. for music lesson. Orphans Home arranging books till 4:45. Call on Wards. Drove home again. Changed. Supper. College Women's Club till 11:00. I'm on the hospitality committee & Ma is Pres. Bed by 12:00!!!!!!!!

—*Katharine Bixby (Hotchkis) diary*

Sister Bixby, ca. 1916

Sister Bixby, ca. 1920

10-24-1921   Tournament of Roses Box—$1320
—*Fred H. Bixby Cash Book 10, Jan. 1921—Dec. 1923*

Deborah Bixby, ca. 1924

Deborah Bixby, 1916

The Cocoanut Grove nightclub at the Ambassador Hotel on Wilshire Avenue was the place to be in the Roaring Twenties. The palatial hotel was designed by architect Myron Hunt, of Rose Bowl fame, and there you could find the rich, glamorous, and powerful, including Gloria Swanson, Charlie Chaplin, Rudolph Valentino, and Louis B. Mayer of Hollywood, by now the home of the nation's fifth-largest industry.[88] Katharine, Deborah, and Sister danced until one or two in the morning, drove home, tumbled into bed, and were ready to swing aboard a horse early the next morning[89]—although Sister, the true working cowgirl of the three, once confessed to her little brother "Icky" (Frederick), "What a life? Once in a while it is lots of fun but not every night for me!"[90]

The Bixby daughters met friends for lunch and dinner at the old-line clubs of Los Angeles—the Wilshire, University, Los Angeles, and California—all established in a more inclusive era. The roster of the California Club (founded in 1887), for example, listed the names of Californios, as well as members of the early Jewish community, including Alamitos partner I. W. Hellman. But the older clubs became more exclusive, like the hundred or so new ones that were created during the 1920s, and the clubs of the Los Angeles region soon reflected the hardening status quo of America—restriction by race, creed, income, and gender.[91]

The times, good and bad, did not last, of course. Though Sister stayed home, working on the Alamitos ranch until she was forty-two, the other two girls married in their early twenties and left. Most devastating was the unexpected death of John, Fred and Florence's favorite child, at age twenty-three. The remaining son, Frederick, never a favorite of his father and out of step with the rest of the family, went his own way.

Without all the children the house wasn't exactly lonely—there were always guests, it seemed, but it was very different. Florence consoled herself with the thought they would soon be returning with their own children, and in 1926 she added a partial second story, containing bedrooms and bath, to the old adobe section of the house. The Ranch House, along with the adjacent Old Garden, redesigned by Paul Howard in 1921, suggested the influence of the Mission Revival era and was perfect for the quintessential garden patio lifestyle of the region.

John T. Bixby at Thacher School, 1925

Death claimed the scion of one of Southern California's most prominent families.

—*Long Beach Press-Telegram, 1929*

Shortly before Grandfather [John Bixby] died, he set up [a billiard table] in the parlor so Grandmother turned the dining room into the parlor, the kitchen into the dining room and pushed the kitchen out into the Stearns' bunkhouse. The first thing Mother [Florence Bixby] did when she arrived on the scene was to have a huge skylight cut into the roof of the parlor which remains the Library. To accommodate their growing family Father added another bedroom to Grandmother's wing.
—*Katharine Bixby Hotchkis, 1968*

Back Patio and Ranch House with the second-floor addition, 1928. Photograph by Albert E. Cawood.

1911 Icky

Fred, Florence, and young Fred walking in the Back Patio at Los Alamitos, 1911. The second-floor addition to the Ranch House has not yet been built.

Dearest Frederick,

I hate to tell you, but I am having your room re-papered! You know, Mother's always doing something to the home!

Letter from Florence Bixby to her son Frederick, March 2, 1925.

12-15-1911	Long Beach Paper & Paint Co.—$8 expense
01-29-1921	Cleaning floors—Nat. Hardwood Co.—$113.75
	—Fred H. Bixby Cash Book 5, Jan. 2, 1911—Dec. 31, 1912
11-30-1928	Improvements to house—old adobe $1,044.80
	—Fred H. Bixby Ledger, Jan. 1, 1927—Dec. 31, 1929

EVERLASTING HEART

Perhaps more than any other member of the family, Florence felt a sense of life's continuities, both past and future, in the hilltop house that was so different from the Bay Area she had known as a girl. In 1936 she incorporated the sentiments into an essay. She called it "The Old Room," by which she meant the library, the center of so much of the family's life after the rush of the day's work was over, and her favorite room. "It was the feeling of the life that had been lived here before," she wrote, "a thousand other human influences...the continuity of life...as though a great river were flowing past."[92] She added that the old room contained a "beautiful piece of Indian bead work of curious shape and pattern" that had once belonged to Susan Bixby and now hung in the window alcove of Florence's library.

Florence Bixby with Katharine and Sister, ca. 1902

Dear Icky,

Last night we looked over the planned trip for Europe...I think you are right about Paris not being typical of France. But I'm anxious to go anyway, because it is so much talked of. It must be very Americanized...Mother wants to drive a lot in a machine, so we will get a good idea of the country. Since we will have to car about and hit the usual places, we will be branded tourists immediately. Mother doesn't think we can find time for Spain, which is my favorite place to go...Father wants to go there, too, since he is being forced to go at all.

Good night, Sister

Letter from Sister Bixby to her brother Frederick, May 5, 1926.

My dear Frederick,

I am trying to read about England and France, so that I shall know a lot about it when we arrive. But there is so much to know. So much history behind everything we shall see that I wish I had begun to read and study years ago...

Letter from Florence Bixby to her son Frederick, May 22, 1928.

Florence Bixby with her three daughters and son John, ca. 1911

Katharine (left) and Sister, 1903

Originally the room had been her mother-in-law's "new" parlor, dark and gloomy because of its inside location. One of Florence's first remodeling jobs after moving in was brightening it by having a big skylight cut in the roof. Then she filled the room with books: complete sets of Thackeray, Dickens, Dumas, Thomas Hardy, Mark Twain, and a long list of Victorian and German poets whose works she cherished.[93]

It was the room where Fred would drop into his father's old Turkish-style chair after dinner with a deep sigh of contentment, scatter cigar ashes over the rug without regard, and talk over the day's events. In an era when there was no television, it was the place for stories going back in time—stories about scar-faced Abel Stearns, who bridged Hispanic and American ways, of old Manuel Nieto and his Spanish grant, and of the people of Povuu'ngna before.

More than Susan, Florence Bixby accented her home with Native American collectables. Living on a ranch, she and her family naturally identified with the American West, and doing so was fashionable: early twentieth-century promoters—the Atchison, Topeka and Santa Fe Railroad; Fred Harvey, who developed cultural tourism and native-crafted merchandise; and organizers of the international expositions and fairs—had developed iconic Western themes and energetically popularized them. The Bixbys had attended the Panama-Pacific and Panama-California Expositions; they visited resorts at Tahoe and Yosemite and traveled to ranches in Paso Robles and Arizona. Their excursions offered ample opportunity to collect Native American cultural objects, including new pieces made for the tourist trade—baskets, pottery, rugs, and more.[94]

The Ranch House library, 2009. The library is filled with Florence Bixby's books. Cristina Klenz Photography

05-17-1915—Books of poetry—$32

—*Fred H. Bixby Cash Book 8, Jan. 1, 1915—Dec. 1917*

Sikyatki Revival Olla by Frog Woman. The style of this wide-mouth pot collected by Florence Bixby is based on the revival of prehistoric Sikyatki polychrome begun by famed Hano village potter Namepeyo around 1900. Namepeyo created her work for the tourist trade and demonstrated pottery making for the Fred Harvey Company at the Hop House (Grand Canyon), and at the U.S. Land and Irrigation Exhibition in Chicago in 1910. Cristina Klenz Photography (information courtesy of Pamela Young Lee, Curator, Rancho Los Alamitos Foundation)

The popular turn-of-the-century Arts and Crafts movement emphasized hand-crafted furnishings and the use of Native American artifacts in home decor; its Southern California expression was called the Arroyo Seco Movement, with its distinct Southwestern flavor coming from native and Latin culture, and was promoted by Charles Fletcher Lummis. Florence eagerly followed the trend. She covered the floors of her home with Navajo rugs from Arizona and displayed baskets and pottery on her bookshelves and hearths throughout the house, where she also tucked objects carved from wood and horn. In time the Klamath and Tlingit peoples of the Northwest; the Yokuts and Hupa of Central and Northern California; the Paiute and Chemehuevi of the Great Basin; and the Tohono O'odham (Papago), Akimel O'odham (Pima), and Apache tribes of the Southwest were all represented in her collections.[95]

And what of the people of Povuu'ngna? In 1822 Father Gerónimo Boscana had written *Chinigchinich*, offering the first in-depth description of Tongva culture. Little less than a century later, Fred and Florence Bixby would partially fund a new edition published by the Fine Arts Press in Santa Ana. The 1933 edition contained an original series of color woodcuts as well as annotations by ethnologist and linguist John P. Harrington, from the Smithsonian Institution, who had interviewed Tongva people and local landowners in the early twentieth century. Among those Harrington interviewed was Fred Bixby, who recalled the "jungle of small cottonwoods" at Alamitos.[96]

Dear Mrs. Isles,

The first thing of interest happened on the Fourth of July...went for a motor-boat ride on the lake...The next morning we all went to Truckee...a little town about fifteen miles from the Tavern [Resort]. It is made up chiefly of saloons and drunken men, but it is very interesting...[Thursday] afternoon we rode over to an Indian Basketry. We bought a pretty basket for Mother. Her birthday is the eighteenth of this month. We saw a squaw there that wove baskets....Her name is Dat-so-la-lee....Tuesday Jessie, Sister, Elizabeth, and I went around the lake on the steamer that goes around every day...When the steamer stopped at Tallac, a town on the lake, it staid half an hour. We got off and walked around. There were lots of Indian squaws with their papooses [sic], and Indian men with baskets, and bows and arrows to sell. I tried to take a picture of some squaws and their papooses, but as soon as they saw my Kodak directed towards them they put a shawl over their faces, or turned their back, or hid behind their papooses. I finally did get one picture.

Letter from Katharine Bixby (Hotchkis) to Elin Engblom Isles, wife of Rancho Los Alamitos foreman Frank Barneigh Isles Sr., July 15, 1912. That year Katharine and Sister vacationed at Lake Tahoe with Aunt Lel (Leslie) and Uncle Howard Huntington and their cousins Elizabeth, Margaret, and Harriet. (Harriet Doerr would become the award-winning author of Stones for Ibarra*). Katharine's letter refers to Florence Bixby's interest in collecting Indian goods, as was common in the era, although her youthful observations also reflected the cultural biases of the time. The baskets of Dat-So-La-Lee (ca. 1829–1925), a celebrated Washoe basket weaver, commanded thousands of dollars during the 1920s. From 1895 to 1928 she and her husband stayed in a summer house near Tahoe Tavern, the elegant resort where the Bixby girls vacationed. (Information courtesy of Pamela Young Lee, Curator, Rancho Los Alamitos Foundation.)*

06-23-1906—Cleaning Indian blankets—$6.00

—*Fred H. Bixby Ledger, 1906*

04-05-1930   Indian Board of Cooperation—$1,000

—*Fred H. Bixby Journal 12, Jan. 3, 1930–Dec. 31, 1931*

Donations: Presbyterian Indian Mission—$892

—*Fred H. Bixby Cash Book 13, Jan. 1, 1928–Dec. 31, 1929*

Fred and Florence Bixby demonstrated an ongoing interest in Native American culture. Like many in the era they collected "artifacts," but they also contributed to Native American advocacy groups.

"The Ascension of Chinigchinich into the Heaven of Stars," by Jean Goodwin. The woodcut illustration is from the 1933 edition of *Chinigchinich* by Father Gerónimo Boscana, published by the Fine Arts Press in Santa Ana.

The Geranium Walk, 1928. The Geranium Walk was designed by renowned designer Florence Yoch around 1922. Photograph by Albert E. Cawood

You'll see the old give way to the new. You'll see new life, new thoughts, new ideas replacing the worn-out ones. But you'll never find anything to replace the beauty of this world, the beauty of nature, the beauty of spiritual things.—*Florence Bixby, 1928*

Fred and Florence Bixby understood that the significance of Povuu'ngna reached beyond the trade in decorative native-made objects. In 1929 and 1930 they made substantial donations to the Presbyterian Indian Mission and the Indian Board of Cooperation, a Northern California–based native advocacy group. Groups across the country had begun advancing the causes of American Indians in the early twentieth century, including the powerful Mission Indian Federation of Southern California, which strove to "end Mission Indian Agency abuse and paternalism and to bring equal rights, justice, and 'home rule' for southern California Indians."[97] They lobbied to regain the land of the native people; to achieve the U.S. citizenship denied Indians; to further basic educational opportunities, including the right to attend public school; to improve the general welfare and living conditions of native people; and to receive compensation for the unfulfilled treaty terms of 1852.[98]

In 1917 the Supreme Court of California ruled that Indians were citizens. Seven years later the U.S. finally granted citizenship to all native people. And in 1927 the State of California authorized lawsuits and monetary claims against the federal government on behalf of California Indians affected by the unratified treaties. The Tongva were included in the lawsuit and, like other native people, required to enroll and indicate their tribal affiliation to file an individual treaty claim. But unlike many native people in California (and like many others), the Tongva were not as a whole recognized by the government as a tribe.[99] (Though groups of Tongva descendants are still struggling for federal recognition and the rights and advantages of that designation, the state of California officially acknowledged the Gabrielinos' status as the aboriginal tribe of the Los Angeles Basin in 1994.[100])

Florence Bixby was artistic and had talent, but she had the best of guidance and help. These are beautifully designed gardens, they didn't just happen. These are the gardens of a city woman. There's nothing countrified about them. They're very sophisticated. —*Virginia Russell, landscape designer, 1986*

08-11-1923—Garden lights—$19.23
—*Fred H. Bixby Cash Book 10, Jan 1921—Dec 1923*

12-10-1908   Improvement Account Alamitos
                    Nursery—$160.25; Long Beach
                    Nurseries account—$2.50
—*Fred H. Bixby Ledger 3, April—Dec 1907*

The Back Patio was designed by Paul Howard in 1921 to separate the Ranch House from the barnyard, but the nearby Big Red Barn still loomed over all.

05-03-1921   House—cement wall—Paul J. Howard—$344.43
—*Fred H. Bixby Cash Book 10, Jan 1921—Dec 1923*

Florence's sense of life's continuities also helped guide the creation of her magnificent gardens. She began building on the foundations Susan, her mother-in-law, had planted. Gradually Florence circled the house, planning alone at first and later employing notable landscape architects such as Paul Howard and Florence Yoch (Yoch also designed for Hollywood, including the movie sets for *Gone with the Wind* and *Romeo and Juliet*), and noted botanist William Hertrich, the landscape designer of the Huntington Estate.

Sun., May 8, 1927

Up this morning on Sunday to the garden to irrigate having last night told the gardener that I would water certain portions, thinking erroneously that the then overcast heavens would doubtless, the following morning, send a deluge of rain upon the land. Did irrigate for several hours, having care for my recently manicured nails, and musing, meanwhile, upon the peculiar providence that causes so delightful a pastime as gardening to be accompanied by so much dirt. And then to my desk. Lord, how one's bills do rise, although as I look around upon new walls and new plants, I cannot fail but see the reason. How much money a woman should spend upon her garden? As much as she can lay hand on. —*Florence Bixby*

They had started out, I think, being ranch hands, and then they were relegated to just the gardens. These men had almost a pride of ownership. They were "their" gardens and they worked, really worked, and the gardens were in good shape.

—*Nerine Salzer (ranch bookkeeper's wife), 1978*

03-18-1927	Oil—Marland Oil Co.—$42,344.89; Oil—Marland Oil Co.—$75,906.12

—*Fred H. Bixby Cash Book 12, Oct. 20, 1924–Dec. 31, 1927*

Florence Bixby directing ranch worker Joe Sisneros in the garden, 1938.

In 1926, flush with revenue from the Seal Beach oil strike, Florence Bixby hired the Olmsted Brothers of Brookline, Massachusetts, to design a series of small gardens which would envelop the hilltop in a simple, tranquil green oasis suiting the working ranch. The nationally renowned firm designed the Secret Garden adjacent to the Ranch House, a place where Florence might indulge her need for a "secret place" to read and write. The nearby formal Rose Garden, Olive Patio, and Oleander Walk offered grand views south to the ocean and shady walkways leading to a small Cypress Patio and Italianate Cutting Garden. The more playful Friendly Garden displayed the cuttings and plants given to Florence by her friends and family and led to the stately Jacaranda Walk, where panoramic views to the east looked over the fields below and on to the foothills and mountains laying north. In turn, the Cactus and Native Gardens suggested the native environment, an idealized portrait of the California landscape. In keeping with the lush greening of the hilltop, the Olmsted Brothers designed an elegant yet simple drive leading to the Ranch House, capturing the natural elegance of the hilltop setting.

The Cypress Patio, 1928. The family's 1926 trip to Europe inspired the Cypress Patio, which was designed by the Olmsted Brothers to serve as the backdrop for an eighteenth-century Italian sculpture titled *Springtime*. Photograph by Albert E. Cawood

Fred and Florence Bixby's grandchildren in front of the Big Red Barn, 1943. As the photo reveals, Florence Bixby planted trees, plants, and vines throughout the barnyard as well as in her gardens.

My dear Mrs. Bixby,

The idea of planting these cypresses is to have them as soon as possible grow closely together and make a perfectly solid wall of green. The East has been very beautiful this year on account of so much rain and now the fall coloring is just starting; in places, it is quite gorgeous. I wish that it were possible to tie together some of these beauties with those of the California country.

Letter from J. Frederick Dawes, Olmsted Brothers, to Florence Bixby, October 11, 1927.

She was always out in the garden. She directed the gardeners. It would have to be done the way she wanted it. Mrs. Bixby didn't believe in having her bushes trimmed a lot, just a little bit. She wanted them to grow naturally. They would keep it up, but they worked all day every day, six days a week.

—*Angie Sisneros Mariscal (ranch worker's wife), 1988*

The Rose Garden, 1928. Designed by the Olmsted Brothers in 1927, the Rose Garden features a view out to the Pacific Ocean. Photograph by Albert E. Cawood

The Jacaranda Walk, 1928. When the Olmsted Brothers designed the Jacaranda Walk in 1927, the viewshed swept over the fields to the foothills and mountains in the north. Once called the Adobe Terrace because of the soil composition, the Jacaranda Walk still reveals the surface shells of the Povuu'ngna midden. Photograph by Albert E. Cawood

Dear Mrs. Bixby,

I enclose herewith two prints, one showing the arrangement for the arbor on the adobe terrace. I changed the location of the posts in order to give a larger space looking from the tennis court toward the mountains.

Letter from J. Frederick Dawes, Olmsted Brothers, to Florence Bixby regarding the Jacaranda Walk, February 11, 1928.

I called on Mrs. Bixby. She wanted to have us make a little plan for the end of the Rose Garden. Our original plan showed a small semi-circular and a few steps below the Rose Garden proper. She never put this in because she did not like it and she wanted to know if I still thought that something ought to be developed at this end, and I told her it did need something there because the Rose Garden looked decidedly as though it was chopped off before it was finished.

Office memo from J. Frederick Dawes, Olmsted Brothers, March 26, 1931.

Dear Mrs. Bixby,

I understand that you would like to build the path connecting the Rose Garden with the lower end of the long Terrace. I would be inclined to make the entire walk either of grass or brick. I think we all sort of hesitate in California about building the walks of grass on account of the amount of the watering that will be required.

Letter from J. Frederick Dawes, Olmsted Brothers, to Florence Bixby, August 11, 1927.

The Friendly Garden, 1928. This playful garden is attributed to the Olmsted Brothers and was designed to grow the cuttings and plants received from friends and family. The sculpture in the center of the garden was created by Harriet Frismuth. Photograph by Albert E. Cawood

Oleander Walk, 1928. The Oleander Walk was designed in 1927 by the Olmsted Brothers to screen out the growing urban scene. Photograph by Albert E. Cawood

Dear Mother,

How is your garden now? Are you still extending it? Are there any more additions to the Friendly Garden? I think that the garden makes the place. At least when I think of home I think of the garden.

— *Letter from Frederick Bixby to his mother, May 22, 1928.*

12-17-1928   Photos—Albert E. Cawood—$180

— *Fred H. Bixby Cash Book 13, Jan. 1, 1928–Dec. 31, 1929*

A portion of Rancho Santa Ana Botanic Garden site and the Administration Building, August 3, 1933

Rancho Santa Ana Botanic Garden

of the

NATIVE PLANTS OF CALIFORNIA
HERBARIUM
BOTANICAL LIBRARY

Santa Ana Cañon, Orange County, California

In 1927, as Florence Bixby developed the gardens at Rancho Los Alamitos, her sister-in-law Susanna Bixby Bryant founded her own superb garden as a memorial to her father, John Bixby. Today the Rancho Santa Ana Botanic Garden is the largest botanic garden dedicated exclusively to California's native plants.

PURPOSES...to assemble in one accessible locality, our native California plants which grow wild in such riotous profusion throughout the length and breadth of the State of California.

—*Susanna Bixby Bryant, founder, Rancho Santa Ana Botanic Garden, 1927*

07-13-1928   Personal—Calif. Botanical Garden—$1,000
—*Fred H. Bixby Cash Book 13, Jan. 1, 1928—Dec. 31, 1929*

08-1-1932   Personal—Calif. Council for Protection of Roadside Beauty—$10
—*Fred H. Bixby Cash Book 15, Jan. 1932—Dec. 1937*

Florence's correspondence with J. Frederick Dawes in the Olmsted firm's local Palos Verdes office reveals the collaboration that produced the restrained elegance of the ranch gardens, so in keeping with the nature of the place (in contrast with the flamboyant estate gardens of the era), as well as the firm's attention to the environmental design. "I think we all sort of hesitate in California about building the walks of grass on account of the amount of the watering that will be required,"[101] wrote Dawes as he developed the new Oleander Walk for the Rancho gardens. The walkway would be made of brick, but the gardens depended on the old springs of Povuu'ngna—"the most famous in the region, the only spring on the inland side of Alamitos Bay," said Fred Bixby proudly in his interview with John P. Harrington.[102]

Florence's style ran from displays of native growth to the formal plantings then popular for showing off the possibilities inherent in soil, sunlight, and the nurturing climate of Southern California. The gardens could be a refuge as well. Throughout each separate "outdoor room"—and not just in the Secret Garden that Florence had placed where Fred's huge water tank had once stood—runs the feeling that here is where her heart truly was. Her careful effort would receive recognition in the future: in 1981 Rancho Los Alamitos would be listed on the National Register of Historic Places, in part for the cultural significance of Florence Bixby's gardens.

Florence was among the Olmsted Brothers' many clients in California during the 1920s and 1930s. The year after the firm completed its final design for the ranch, Frederick Law Olmsted Jr. finished his survey of potential state parklands, and in a bow to California car culture all the proposed land was near scenic, coastal Highway 1.[103] Not long after, Florence Bixby made a small donation to the California Council for Protection of Roadside Beauty, an action no doubt influenced by the Olmsted survey.

LOOKING OUT, LOOKING IN

From 1921 until 1952 the Alamitos ranch was an anachronism supported largely by income generated from an industrial product, and Fred knew it. But he also depended on the other great natural asset of Alamitos—water. In 1914 he confidently reported, "The artesian wells are not affected by the flood or surface water. Our wells are nearly 1000 feet down and are not affected by dry years either."[104] Not everyone was so lucky. By the turn of the century, some 40 percent of Californians lived in the San Francisco Bay Area or greater Los Angeles, and their future depended on acquiring new sources of water.[105] The City of Long Beach, for example, bought out the local water systems in 1911, including the old Alamitos Water Company established for John Bixby's development.[106] Twenty years later, burgeoning Long Beach, unable to meet demands for water with its own artesian wells, followed the lead of a dozen other Los Angeles Basin municipalities and joined the gargantuan Metropolitan Water District of Southern California, the overseer of the Colorado Aqueduct and the distribution of water throughout the L.A. Basin.[107] How quickly times were changing.

The two water tanks on the Alamitos hilltop, April 1914. In 1927 the tank at the back of the Ranch House was removed, making way for the secluded, walled Secret Garden designed by the Olmsted Brothers.

Fred Bixby driving a water wagon at Rancho Los Alamitos, ca. 1907

Ranch hand Robert Crawford driving a water wagon at Rancho Los Alamitos, 1937

I drove horses for the team that pulled the sprinkling tank that watered down things around the headquarters every weekend.

—*Robert T. Crawford (ranch hand), 1994*

Mr. Bixby has a flowing well on the ranch which yields 500 inches of water for irrigating purposes. —*unidentified Long Beach newspaper, February 10, 1905*

The artesian wells are not affected by the flood or surface water. Our wells are nearly 1000 feet down and are not affected by dry years either.

—*Fred Bixby, Long Beach Evening Express, Sept. 23, 1914*

They had a pump at the artesian well that would push the water up here, a lot of pressure. The water tank was huge and always filled up. It provided all the water for the ranch here and the houses down below. Every once in a while the pump would stop.

—*José Vasquez (ranch hand's son), 2000*

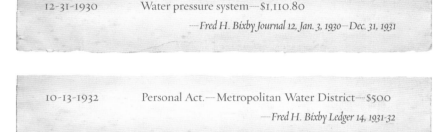

12-31-1930   Water pressure system—$1,110.80
—*Fred H. Bixby Journal 12, Jan. 3, 1930—Dec. 31, 1931*

10-13-1932   Personal Act.—Metropolitan Water District—$500
—*Fred H. Bixby Ledger 14, 1931-32*

A deepening interdependence, rather than self-sufficiency, was the growing order of society. Sooner or later Rancho Los Alamitos would have to face that future, although in 1930 the ranch's immediate environs looked much as they had for the past century. In 1932 Fred Bixby paid the Metropolitan Water District five hundred dollars, although his ledgers don't tell us why. It seems unlikely, but perhaps he suspected that his own supply of water would not last forever.

Could Fred protect the things he loved—the house, with its quiet, elegant gardens, the barns, ample pasturage for a couple of milk cows and some of his beloved horses (the others could range at the Cojo), space for vegetable gardens and grain fields? In short, could he provide himself, his wife, his children, and even his grandchildren with a haven to which they could turn when they needed relief from the rapidly urbanizing southern coast of Los Angeles County? The daughter of a ranch worker nostalgically summarized the appeal of the Rancho years later: "I remember the fields and being able to run and play, making our own kites. We'd get our gunny sack full of hay and slide down the hill. Maybe we'd go to the orchards and pick some fruit, or be by the horses...I think we realized what we had there, what a great opportunity we had to be out in the open space."[108]

In 1931, with those ideals in mind, Fred put 148 acres, the house at their heart, under an umbrella he named the Home Property Trust. He designated himself, Florence, and his four surviving children as trustees of the unit and deeded the rest of Rancho Los Alamitos' thousands of acres and those of the other properties he owned to the Fred H. Bixby Company. Funds for maintaining the trust property were to come from renting office space in the ranch buildings to the Fred H. Bixby Company and from farming operations on Home Property Trust land.[109]

The strangulation of the ranch that Fred had dreaded came slowly, trailing the military buildup in Long Beach, home port of the Pacific Fleet. Japan's imperial adventures in the Far East alarmed American military strategists for years before the actual onset of World War II. In 1935 the U.S. Navy leased acres on Terminal Island for what would be Terminal Island Naval Air Station. In 1940, much closer to Fred Bixby's pastoral Eden, the U.S. Army presence was enlarged at Daugherty Field to prepare a headquarters for its Air Transport Command's Ferrying Division. To ferry what? Airplanes—many thousands of them.

On November 22, 1940, Donald Douglas turned over the first spadeful of earth for a two-hundred-acre aircraft plant between Lakewood Avenue and Cherry Avenue that would become a fixture in President Roosevelt's "Arsenal of Democracy." A world getting ready for war was closing in.

Aerial view of the 148-acre Bixby Home Property Trust and the encroaching urban scene, 1960

12-30-1931	Improvements Bixby Home Prop—$17,906.95
	—Fred H. Bixby Journal 12, Jan. 3, 1930—Dec. 31, 1931

I remember the fields and being able to run and play, making our own kites. We'd get our gunny sack full of hay and slide down the hill. Maybe we'd go to the orchards and pick some fruit, or be by the horses. I think we realized what we had there, what a great opportunity we had to be out in the open space.

—*Virginia Sisneros Le Gaspi (ranch worker's daughter), 1988*

Rancho Los Alamitos, 1947. A portion of Rancho Los Alamitos was condemned to build the naval hospital visible at upper left. The line of California pepper trees leading from the hilltop ranch was planted by John and Susan Bixby in the nineteenth century. The housing for the Mexican ranch worker families appears below the trees.

Sept. 6-7-8—They have word and orders from Washington and are taking the heart of the Alamitos for Navy Hospital location.—RATS!!!

—*Fred H. Bixby Cojo Diary, 1941-42*

In 1941, just before Pearl Harbor, the U.S. government condemned 84.2 acres of Rancho Los Alamitos' best barley land for a munitions dump and naval hospital. Fred vented to his diary, "They have word and order from Washington and are taking the heart of the Alamitos for Navy Hospital location—*rats!!!*"[110]

On February 19, 1942, Executive Order 9066 consigned ninety-three thousand Japanese Americans throughout California—including the Japanese tenant farmers and their families who lived at Rancho Los Alamitos—to inland relocation camps across the West. John Bixby had hired Japanese workers during the early 1880s, when there were few Japanese immigrants in California. Their numbers increased in the 1890s,[111] and by 1909 almost half of California's farmworkers were Japanese.[112] As their numbers grew, so did anti-Japanese sentiment, supported with the same arguments that had been used against Chinese immigrants decades before: their cheap labor was perceived as taking away jobs from other Americans. Moreover, Japanese lease farmers were "unfairly"—and successfully—competing against small-scale farmers.[113]

In 1900, 481 Japanese people lived in Southern California,[114] several at Rancho Los Alamitos. In 1905 a Long Beach newspaper reported that Fred Bixby had "a large tract of peat land as yet uncultivated" and he "recently leased this to some Japanese who will experiment this year in raising celery.[115] He was not the only one to do so. In two years' time, Japanese farmers would own 2,442 acres in the state and lease 54,830 more.[116] Anti-Japanese sentiment grew to hysteria as their acreage increased. Repeated pressure from the state of California—as in the case of the Chinese Exclusion Act of 1882—led to the federal Alien Land Law of 1913, which prohibited immigrants not eligible for citizenship from owning land. Nor could they lease land for more than three years. Though it didn't explicitly state as much, the law took cruel aim at Japanese Americans: Asians were denied citizenship under the Naturalization Act of 1870, so the law meant that no Asian immigrant could own land.[117] As a result, many first-generation Japanese Americans purchased land in the names of their American-born children. In the aftermath of World War II, the state of California, with financial backing from the legislature, aggressively attempted to confiscate these properties fourteen times between 1944 and 1948. A Japanese American family from San Diego filed a lawsuit protesting the confiscation of their land; they prevailed in the California supreme court, and the decision was upheld in the U.S. Supreme Court in 1948. That year California halted all confiscation proceedings. Though the Alien Land Law was no longer a legal reality,[118] it remains a devastating and shameful cultural memory.

We do not know Fred Bixby's views on the law, but in 1915 he received rental income from at least four Japanese farmers. During the Depression years of 1929 through 1931 he made improvements to "Jap House #1, #2, #3, #4," located south of the hilltop, as well as to the "Vegetable Wash House" in "Little Tokyo," as the area became known at the ranch. By all accounts, the Japanese lease farmers at Alamitos were integrated into the family of workers at the ranch. They gave their farmed vegetables to other ranch worker families during the Depression, and their children played with the children of the Mexican and Belgian tenant farmers. Ray Rodriguez, whose father leased land nearby, remembers the lasting childhood friendships: "I would come out to [Alamitos to] visit my cousin or one of the Sisneros kids," he says, "...and wander down the hill and visit with the Japanese kids, like Sakia Ogata, or I would go out to Albert Cosyns's farm....If a kid had to work we'd pitch in and help him...there was a real camaraderie....I spent more time

[Fred] Bixby has 7500 acres in all—alfalfa, barley, and beets. His rent from his pasture lands brings him about $500 per month. Mr. Bixby has a large tract of peat land as yet uncultivated. He has recently leased this to some Japanese who will experiment this year in raising celery.

—*unidentified Long Beach newspaper, February 10, 1905*

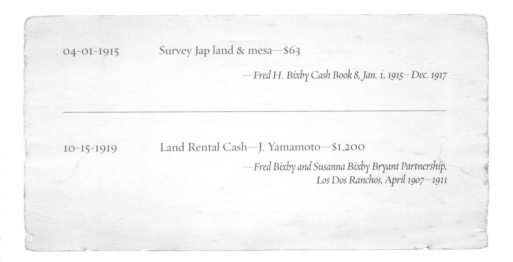

04-01-1915   Survey Jap land & mesa—$63

—*Fred H. Bixby Cash Book 8, Jan. 1, 1915—Dec. 1917*

10-15-1919   Land Rental Cash—J. Yamamoto—$1,200

—*Fred Bixby and Susanna Bixby Bryant Partnership, Los Dos Ranchos, April 1907—1911*

A page from one of John Bixby's ledgers shows that he hired "Japaneese" workers at Alamitos as early as 1881.

The Mexican families lived north, down over that hill on Palo Verde. The Belgians were tenants scattered on the acreage mostly to the east. South was across Seventh Street. That's where the Japanese tenants had beautiful peat land, kinda moist and black and very rich and they raised celery and vegetables.

—*Sister (Florence Elizabeth) Bixby Janeway, 1984*

with the Belgians and Japanese kids than I did with the Mexicans."[119] Along with the ranch worker and tenant families, the Japanese farmers attended the Bixbys' annual Christmas party. They socialized with Japanese families in Seal Beach and supported a Japanese school and the organization of a formal men's group, which attracted the unwanted attention of the FBI.

When Executive Order 9066 was issued in 1942 the Japanese families at Alamitos had to evacuate, despite the efforts of Fred and Florence Bixby: "Mr. and Mrs. Bixby went to all lengths to help us from evacuation but to no avail," recalled Mrs. Chiyo [Kawanami] Ohira much later. "Government order, nothing could be done."[120] The Japanese lease farmers at Alamitos lost their homes, their assets, and years of proud accomplishment. They would not return to the Rancho for several more decades.

After the December 7 attack at Pearl Harbor, the population of Long Beach swelled beyond its seams. Some fifty thousand service personnel called the city a temporary home at any given time, some going out to, some coming back from, the Pacific theater of operations. Also arriving en masse were defense workers—many of them blacks and Mexican Americans and women previously denied such employment—to build planes at the Douglas Aircraft plant or, later, repair damaged warships at the Long Beach Naval Shipyards.

Farmed and raised family, worked from sun up to sun down since early 1900s. Children all went to grammar school, Junior Hi and High school plus Japanese school two days a week after public school, and on Saturday—whole day of Japanese school. Sunday was our free day but our parents toiled on the farm harvesting vegetables for Monday morning market....The families remained until April of 1942 when we were ordered to evacuate by the government at the outbreak of war. Because our parents were affiliated with the Japanese school, our fathers were taken into custody by the FBI. With the help of Mr. Bixby we learned of their whereabouts. We were separated from our fathers when we finally evacuated, but rejoined with families about a year later at the relocation camp. We lost everything from household belongings, automobiles, farm equipment and crops.... Mr. and Mrs. Bixby went to all lengths to help us from evacuation but to no avail. Government order, nothing could be done.

—*Mrs. Chiyo (Kawanami) Ohira (Japanese lease farmer's daughter), 1998*

Shipbuilding in Long Beach Harbor.

| 10-31-1919 | W. Yasumoto—rent 1919—$262; T. Kawanami rent 1919—$1,000; S. Shigetomi rent 1919—$935.80; Y. Mizuno rent 1919—$1,000 |

—*Fred H. Bixby Journal 8, Jan. 3, 1917—Dec. 31, 1919*

09-04-1929	Lights; Jap house #3—$33.93
09-25-1929	Jap house #2—$700
10-31-1929	Improvement labor—Jap barn #1—$138.87
12-16-1929	Bath tub—Jap house #3—$43.30

—*Fred H. Bixby Cash Book 13, Jan. 1, 1928—Dec. 31, 1929*

| 01-03-1930 | Jap garage—$22; Jap wash house—$27.77 |

—*Fred H. Bixby Journal 12, Jan. 3, 1930—Dec. 31, 1931*

01-07-1930	Nails—Jap house #3
04-01-1930	Improvement—Jap veg wash house—$30
04-01-1930	Improvement labor—Jap garage—$26
11-06-1931	Jap house #4—painting & plumbing—$49.61

—*Fred H. Bixby Cash Book 14, Jan. 1, 1930—Dec. 31, 1931*

Left: Antonia Machuca Castillo and Tom Sisneros, the children of Alamitos ranch hands, ca. 1945

I am so burnt up over the apparent inability of the Federal Government to do anything about anything that has to do with the part of the United States west of the Mississippi. You have heard about the forgotten man, or the man without a country. Well, we in California are certainly in the same fix he was in. —*Fred Bixby to Governor Earl Warren, March 22, 1943*

I think Governor Warren has the right idea about this farm labor problem. I think the War Labor Board, or the OPA, or some other federal alphabetical committee, is really doing nothing about it, and I think the state will have to if we expect to produce anything like our normal production of food commodities....Mexican farm labor from farming communities in Mexico are more than anxious to come up here and to work in the United States. They are, however, so handicapped and so frightened by what they have to go through at the border that they are afraid to even try to come into the country....I don't know of any better source of supply as far as farm labor is concerned than Mexico although we certainly could use some Chinamen. This idea of bringing in Chinamen, however, would be against the law, according to the Chinese Exclusion Act.

Letter from Fred Bixby to Frank P. Doherty, president of the Los Angeles Chamber of Commerce, March 22, 1943

UNITED STATES
DEPARTMENT OF JUSTICE

IMMIGRATION
AND
NATURALIZATION
SERVICE
DUPLICATE
Alien Registration
Receipt Card

Registration Number
A-2 433 447

FORM I-151 (1-14-49)   16—48499-3

As if losing land to the government and intense urbanization were not enough, Fred Bixby, like all ranchers and growers in California, suffered from an unprecedented farm labor shortage during the war.[121] Sons of the Alamitos ranch workers and tenant farmers had enlisted, and immigration from Mexico had dropped. (Mexico had been excluded from the U.S. immigration quotas following World War I, and though Mexican immigration to the U.S. increased during the 1920s, it declined during the Depression years.[122]) In the spring of 1942, California growers predicted a shortage of labor for the fall harvest and called for forty thousand to one hundred thousand Mexican farmworkers to be imported.[123] During World War I, private contractors had supplied farmers with seasonal workers from Mexico, but in 1942 the United States government created the Bracero program under the Department of Labor to accomplish this. During World War II only sixty-two thousand farmworkers were recruited from Mexico, but by 1964, when the Bracero program ended, 4.6 million temporary farmworkers from Mexico would be admitted to the U.S.[124]

Facing his own wartime dilemma, on March 22, 1943, Fred Bixby wrote the head of the Los Angeles Chamber of Commerce, assessing the farm labor problem and acknowledging the ironies of decisions from the past:

> Mexican farm labor from farming communities in Mexico are more than anxious to come up here and to work in the United States. They are, however, so handicapped and so frightened by what they have to go through at the border that they are afraid to even try to come into the country…I don't know of any better source of supply as far as farm labor is concerned than Mexico although we certainly could use some Chinamen. The idea of bringing in Chinamen, however, would be against the law, according to the Chinese Exclusion Act.[125]

The same frustrating day, he turned to his political ally California Governor Earl Warren, writing: "I am so burnt up over the apparent inability of the Federal Government to do anything about anything that has to do with the part of the United States west of the Mississippi…you have heard about the forgotten man, or the man without a country. Well, we in California are certainly in the same fix he was in."[126]

The remaining acreage of Rancho Los Alamitos, 1964. California State University, Long Beach, was built on the site of Rancho Los Alamitos and Povuu'ngna.

I don't see Long Beach, Cal State Long Beach, Rancho Los Alamitos—maybe a little bit—I see Povuu'ngna.

—*Cindi Alvitre, Tongva, 2005*

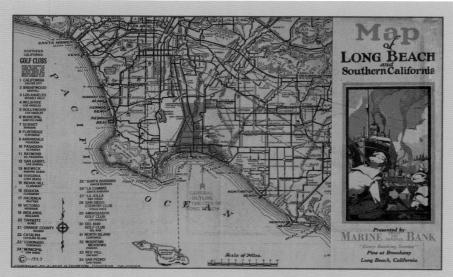

The street map of Long Beach published in 1923 by the Marine and Trust Savings Bank suggests the increasing congestion throughout Long Beach and Southern California.

The two boys to whom I have given this letter are the sons of one of the tenants of mine that has been farming for me for the last thirty years here on the Alamitos Ranch. They are applying for some of the land the government is handing out to the former members of the Armed Forces in World War II. They are farmer's sons and are good straight young fellows. Anything you can do to help them get a good piece of land will be very much appreciated.

Letter from Fred Bixby to Mr. Liskey, December 16, 1947.

In regard to this college site which the City of Long Beach has purchased and which they are planning to give to the state. Could this college site out here be called Los Alamitos Mesa State College? This particular area from the time I can remember has always been known as the Los Alamitos Mesa and it would be a most appropriate name to pass on to posterity.

Letter from Fred Bixby to Sam Vickers, Long Beach City Manager, March 27, 1951

The war effort was not alone in making demands on Fred Bixby's precious land. By 1944, 283.5 acres of ranchland bordering the Home Trust were condemned for the establishment of a state college. Fred Bixby attempted to salvage a bit of history and a longstanding identity when, in a letter to the city manager, he recommended that the college be named Los Alamitos Mesa State College: "This particular area from the time I can remember has always been known as the Los Alamitos Mesa and it would be a most appropriate name to pass on to posterity."[127] He would lose this battle, too, and the college was christened Long Beach State College (now California State University, Long Beach).

A welcome end to the war of wars did not mean relief for Fred H. Bixby, besieged rancher. Those who had come West on their way to fight for their country, or to make and fix the weapons used in the fight, decided they liked the climate, the open space, the lifestyle. Others who came and returned settled into what a new state freeway system made possible—strings of clean new satellite communities rather derisively

Fred Bixby indicated that one of his favorite structures on the estate was its big barn. It had at one time housed Southern Pacific rolling stock in Wilmington and was moved to its present site when John Bixby moved there.

—Long Beach Press Telegram, *May 17, 1952*

The Big Red Barn, the symbol of Rancho Los Alamitos, burned down in 1947

branded "slurburbia." These, in turn, created a need for more schools, flood control channels, freeways.[128] At the ranch, the diminishments continued. It was the pattern, though not the details, Fred Bixby had foreseen twenty years before.

As if in response to the relentless encroachment, the Red Barn caught fire one September afternoon in 1947 while Fred and Florence were at the Cojo. The bookkeeper rushed to call the volunteer fire department in the town of Los Alamitos. Meanwhile, the wife of the commandant of the naval hospital on the old barley field saw the smoke and sounded an alarm, and military equipment hurried to the scene. Horses plunged wildly. Flames and black smoke from more than a hundred tons of hay filled the sky. Fred and Florence, summoned from the Cojo, arrived too late to see more than the mop-up and to help serve coffee to the exhausted firemen. Though several structures had been damaged, only the barn was gone—completely gone except for some distinctive old square nails the night watchman, Pete Nissen, picked up out of the cooling ashes.[129]

In 1947 a *fire* started in the big red barn. Though most of the corrals, barns and shed were badly damaged, they were not a complete loss. But there was nothing left of the beautiful big red barn. Up on the hill against the horizon, it had been a landmark for seventy years and a backdrop of continuity for four generations. Now there was just a mammoth heap of ashes. Mother had pepper trees planted in the emptiness, and nothing was ever the same again.

—*Katharine Bixby Hotchkis, 1967*

Rancho Los Alamitos, 1948. After the fire Florence Bixby planted California pepper trees in the footprint of the Big Red Barn (center of photo).

07-1930	Big old barn—$405.30
07-1930	Blacksmith shop—$46.20; granary—$40.60; big corral shed & chutes—$364.70; stallion [barn]—$791.70; chicken house & corral—$29.40; pigeon house & corral—$85.40

—*Fred H. Bixby Ledger 14, 1931-32*

Fred Bixbys to Note 50th Anniversary

Friends of Mr. and Mrs. Fred H. Bixby this afternoon will drive along the winding road, flanked by red and white oleanders, leading from E. Seventh St. to the spacious rambling part-adobe Bixby home. Guests will include relatives, old-time friends, employees, former employees and tenants. Mrs. Bixby will wear her wedding dress of white satin with a full skirt, boned bodice and tulle sleeves.

—Long Beach Press Telegram, *August 1948*

Fred and Florence Bixby and their grandchildren at the thirty-fifth wedding anniversary celebration, 1938

Fred and Florence Bixby celebrating their fiftieth wedding anniversary at Rancho Los Alamitos, 1948

Almost exactly a year later, more than a thousand guests gathered on the Rancho's front lawn to celebrate Fred and Florence's golden wedding anniversary. During the ceremonies, Pete Nissen stepped up and presented the couple with the square nails he had found and carefully gilded. But the loss could not be mitigated. "It had been a landmark for seventy years and a backdrop of continuity for our generations. Now there was just a mammoth heap of ashes. Mother had pepper trees planted in the emptiness, and nothing was ever the same again,[130] said Katharine Bixby Hotchkis in 1967.

1898   1938

Mr. and Mrs. Fred Hathaway Bixby

At Home

on Sunday, the twenty-eighth of August

from four until seven

Rancho Los Ala...

Long Beach...

1898   1948

Mr. and Mrs. Fred Hathaway Bixby

At Home

on the Fiftieth Anniversary of their marriage

Sunday, the twenty-ninth of August

from four until seven o'clock

Rancho Los Alamitos

6511 East Seventh Street

Long Beach, California

Kindly omit gifts   Please reply

You have made us very happy with your beautiful plaque of appreciation on our Golden Wedding anniversary. No present of gold or of silver would have pleased us more. Many of you have been our neighbors for a great many years and we have always been friends. We have known your children and now we are beginning to know your children's children. It has been a fine relationship and we hope that it will always continue in that way.

—*Florence Bixby to the Belgian tenant families, September 1948*

Always keep your position as the head of the house (I always have for thirty-seven years and three times a day brought the subject to the attention of Mrs. Bixby). This is a rather advisable attitude to take, but have been unable to decide as to whether this constant talking about it gets you anywhere or not.

Letter from Fred Bixby to I. W. [Warren] Hellman, 1935, offering advice on his friend's upcoming marriage.

It was a very empty land, empty of people and town, of trees and cultivated fields.

—*Sarah Bixby Smith,* Adobe Days

Fred Bixby died in 1952 believing that he had saved those timeless things that mattered most to him. Florence died at Alamitos in 1961. Outside the ranch, the frenetic pace of growth roared on, lifting Los Angeles County's population above the seven million mark—in 1962, California would surpass New York to become the most populous state in the union. Inside the ranch the Povuu'ngna spring, giver of life going back to the people of Chinigchinich, became brackish and unusable, as did the artesian wells that had once nourished Florence Bixby's gardens. In 1956 the ranch paid its first water bill to an outside source and three years later the City of Long Beach spread its jurisdiction across the remaining acres of the ranch. In 1968, the seven and a half remaining acres of Manuel Nieto's original three-hundred-thousand-acre Spanish grant were deeded to the City of Long Beach. Soon concentric rings of a private residential community circled the Rancho—but the name of one street in the subdivision, it is good to note, is Shire.

About five miles easterly from Long Beach, near the center of the great Alamitos tract stands the Alamitos ranch house and its belongings—a kingdom within a kingdom. The residence commands an unrivaled view, the blue sea and winding Bay in one hand and the ever green meadows, the groves, villages and mountains on the other. Below the house, among a romantic background of trees, is a wind mill, and a wonderful natural spring whose cool, bubbling waters are forced upward for domestics by means of a hydraulic ram.

—Long Beach Journal, *1888 (Amos Bixby, brother of Jotham Bixby and a cousin of John Bixby, cofounded this weekly paper.)*

Rancho Los Alamitos is in the center of this 1988 aerial view, but barely visible in the contemporary scene.

NOTES

INTRODUCTION

1.   Interview with Cindi Alvitre, May 16, 2006 (Rancho Los Alamitos Foundation Archives).

ONE: PUVUU'NGNA

1.   William McCawley, *The First Angelinos: The Gabrielino Indians of Los Angeles*, p. 3.

2.   William McCawley, *Povuu'ngna: The Village at the Center of the World*, pp. 2–3.

3.   McCawley, *First Angelinos*, p. 9.

4.   Ibid., p. 172.

5.   Father Gerónimo Boscana, *Chinigchinich: A Revised and Annotated Version...*, pp, 31–33.

6.   Interview with the Ti'at Society, Rancho Los Alamitos, October 15, 2009 (transcript in the Rancho Los Alamitos Foundation Archives); Claudia Jurmain and William McCawley, *O, My Ancestor: Recognition and Renewal for the Gabrielino-Tongva People of the Los Angeles Area*, p. 128.

7.   Jurmain and McCawley. *O, My Ancestor*, p. 103.

8.   McCawley, *Povuu'ngna*, p. 2.

9.   Ibid.

10.   Ibid., p. 4.

11.   McCawley, *First Angelinos*, p. 112.

12.   William McCawley, "From Village to City: Identity in a Changing World," p. 37.

13.   McCawley, *First Angelinos*, p. 110.

14.   Ibid. pp. 25–26.

15.   Ibid., pp. 129–130.

16.   Interview with Anthony Morales (Kimberly Morales Johnson and Andrew Morales also present), June 7, 2006 (transcript in the Rancho Los Alamitos Foundation Archives); Jurmain and McCawley, *O, My Ancestor*, p. 287.

17.   Randall Milliken and William R. Hildebrandt, *Assessment of Archaeological Resources at the Rancho Los Alamitos Historic Ranch and Gardens*, pp. 33–34.

18.   Jurmain and McCawley, *O, My Ancestor*, p. 116.

19.   McCawley, *Povuu'ngna*, p. 6.

20.   Jurmain and McCawley, *O, My Ancestor*, p. 107.

21.   Jurmain and McCawley, *O, My Ancestor*, p. xv; Milliken and Hildebrandt, *Assessment*, p. 50.

22.   Jurmain and McCawley, *O, My Ancestor*, pp. 107–108.

23.   McCawley, *First Angelinos*, pp. 29–30.

24.   Ibid.

25.   Ibid., pp. 11–13.

26.   McCawley, "From Village to City," pp. 41–42.

27.   McCawley, *First Angelinos*, p. 89.

28.   McCawley, *Povuu'ngna*. p. 12.

29.   Ibid.

30.   McCawley, *First Angelinos*, p. 179.

31. McCawley, *Povuu'ngna*, p. 12.

32. McCawley, *First Angelinos*, p. 4.

TWO: BROWN ROBES AND LEATHERJACKETS

1. Steven W. Hackel, *Children of Coyote, Missionaries of Saint Francis: Indian-Spanish Relations in Colonial California 1769–1850*, p. 44.

2. Claudia Jurmain and William McCawley, *O, My Ancestor: Recognition and Renewal for the Gabrielino-Tongva People of the Los Angeles Area*, p. 13.

3. William McCawley, *Povuu'ngna: The Village at the Center of the World*, pp. 17, 18.

4. Jurmain and McCawley, *O, My Ancestor*, p. 17.

5. Ibid., p. 13.

6. George Harwood Phillips, *Chiefs and Challengers*, p. 22.

7. Jurmain and McCawley, *O, My Ancestor*, p. 108.

8. Ibid., p. 17.

9. Hackel, *Children of Coyote*, p. 92.

10. McCawley, *Povuu'ngna*, p. 18.

11. George Harwood Phillips, "Indians in Los Angeles, 1781–1875: Economic Integration, Social Disintegration," p. 448.

12. Jurmain and McCawley, *O, My Ancestor*, p. 17.

13. Ibid., p. 17; Hackel, *Children of Coyote*, p. 202.

14. Ibid., p. 281.

15. Lisbeth Haas, *Conquests and Historical Identities in California*, p. 24.

16. Jurmain and McCawley, *O, My Ancestor*, p. 16

17. Ibid.

18. Ibid., p. 13.

19. Hackel, *Children of Coyote*, p. 146

20. Ibid., pp. 163–164.

21. Ibid., p. 281.

22. Ibid., p. 286

23. Jurmain and McCawley, *O, My Ancestor*, p. 17.

24. Janice Ramos, in Interview with the Ti'at Society, October 15, 2005 (transcript in the Rancho Los Alamitos Foundation Archives).

25. David Lavender, *Los Angeles Two Hundred*, p. 22.

26. Loretta Berner, "Dos Ranchos: Rancho Los Alamitos and Rancho Los Cerritos," pp. 12–14: Espediente No. 103—Petition to Governor Fages from Manuel Nieto requesting La Zanja, Spanish-Mexican Land Grant Records (translated copy in Rancho Los Alamitos Foundation Archives); Espediente No 103—Governor Fages grants La Zanja to Nieto, Spanish-Mexican Land Grant Records (translated copy in Rancho Los Alamitos Foundation Archives).

27. James J. Rawls and Walton Bean, *California: An Interpretive History*, p. 52.

28. Cleland, *The Cattle on a Thousand Hills*, pp. 8–9; Berner, "Dos Ranchos," p. 11 and N1.18; U.S. Land Commission Hearing Cases 404, Abel Stearns claimant for the place named Los Alamitos (copy in Rancho Los Alamitos Foundation Archives).

29. Berner, "Dos Ranchos," p. 11 and N1.18; Cleland, *Cattle*, pp. 12–15.

30. Phillips, "Indians in Los Angeles," p. 431.

31. The descriptions of La Zanja seem to place the property northeast of Rancho Los Alamitos, possibly between the San Gabriel Mission and the Spanish-period Rancho Encino. Berner, "Dos Ranchos," p. 13.

32. Berner, "Dos Ranchos," pp. 14–15: Espediente No. 103—Nieto to Fages.

33. Ibid.: Espediente No. 103—Pedro Fages declines Nieto's petition, instructs him to proceed to Los Coyotes, Spanish-Mexican Land Grant Records (translated copy in Rancho Los Alamitos Foundation Archives).

34. Jurmain and McCawley, *O, My Ancestor*, p. 241.

35. Cleland, *Cattle*, pp. 14, 285-N35. Permission for Verdugo to use the land known as La Zanja de Zacamutin was granted at the end of 1794. Later correspondence between the priests of San Gabriel and Crown officials indicated that the land to which Verdugo retired and which became known as Rancho San Rafael was Nieto's original 1784 land concession.

36. Jurmain and McCawley, *O, My Ancestor*, p. 13.

37. Berner, "Dos Ranchos," p. 19.

38. Hackel, *Children of Coyote*, p. 275.

39. Berner, "Dos Ranchos," pp. 18–33: Espediente No. 104—Nieto complaint to Governor Borica regarding Mission San Gabriel, Spanish-Mexican Land Grant Records (translated copy in Rancho Los Alamitos Foundation Archives).

40. Ibid.: Espediente No. 103—Governor Borica divides Los Coyotes between

Nieto and Mission San Gabriel, Spanish-Mexican Land Grant Records (translated copy in Rancho Los Alamitos Foundation Archives).

41. Ibid., pp. 15–16.
42. Jurmain and McCawley, *O, My Ancestor,* p. 13.
43. Douglas Monroy, *Thrown Among Strangers,* p. 117.
44. Phillips, *Chiefs and Challengers,* p. 33.
45. Monroy, *Strangers,* p. 67.
46. Hackel, *Children of Coyote,* p. 281.
47. Ibid.
48. Monroy, *Strangers,* p. 116
49. Phillips, "Indians in Los Angeles," p. 433.
50. Hackel, *Children of Coyote,* p. 311.
51. Monroy, *Strangers,* p. 112.
52. Hackel, *Children of Coyote,* p. 311.
53. Phillips, "Indians in Los Angeles," p. 433.
54. Ibid.
55. Jurmain and McCawley, *O, My Ancestor,* p. 20.
56. Cleland, *Cattle,* pp. 7–8.
57. Berner, "Dos Ranchos," p. 33; Cleland, *Cattle,* p. 8.
58. "Rancho Los Alamitos Historic Structures Report," p. 28.
59. Monroy, *Strangers,* p. 122.
60. Haas, *Conquests,* p. 30.
61. Ibid., pp. 32–33.
62. Ibid., p. 33; Hackel, *Children of Coyote,* pp. 376–377, 381–382.
63. Monroy, *Strangers,* p. 29; Doris Marion Wright, *A Yankee in California: Abel Stearns, 1798–1848,* pp. 45–46.
64. Monroy, *Strangers,* p. 122.
65. Berner, "Dos Ranchos," p. 43.
66. Ibid., p. 48: Espediente No. 103—Request and permission to divide Los Coyotes, Spanish-Mexican Land Grant Records (translated copy in Rancho Los Alamitos Foundation Archives).
67. Ibid., p. 52.
68. Ibid., pp. 51–52: Espediente No. 57, Spanish-Mexican Land Grant Records (translated copy in Rancho Los Alamitos Foundation Archives).
69. Ibid., pp. 52, 53: Espediente No. 57.
70. Ibid., p. 54: Espediente No. 57.
71. Ibid., p. 56.
72. Ibid., pp. 49–50: Espediente No. 103.
73. Ibid., p. 57.
74. Ibid., pp. 60–61.
75. Haas, *Conquests,* pp. 3–4, 33.
76. Hackel, *Children of Coyote,* p. 386.
77. Rawls and Bean, *California,* p. 50; Haas, *Conquests,* p. 34.
78. Jurmain and McCawley, *O, My Ancestor,* p. 114.
79. Ibid.
80. Ibid., p. 275.

THREE: THE CATTLE ON THE GOLDEN HILLS

1. Robert Glass Cleland, *The Cattle on a Thousand Hills,* pp. 19–20.
2. Doris Marion Wright, *A Yankee in Mexican California: Abel Stearns, 1798–1848,* pp. 3–9.
3. Ibid., p. 11.
4. Lisbeth Haas, *Conquests and Historical Identities in California 1769–1936,* p. 34.
5. Wright, *Yankee,* pp. 14–17.
6. Walton Bean and James J. Rawls, *California: An Interpretive History,* pp. 49
7. Wright, *Yankee,* pp. 19–25.
8. Ibid., pp. 26–27.
9. Bean and Rawls, *California,* p. 49.
10. Wright, *Yankee,* pp. 27–28.
11. Ibid., pp. 29–30.
12. Douglas Monroy, *Thrown Among Strangers,* p. 156.
13. Wright, *Yankee,* pp. 29–30.
14. Monroy, *Strangers,* p. 156.
15. Wright, *Yankee,* p. 66 ("Diseño de los parages llamados St. Gertrudes, Coyotes, Bolsas, Alamitos y Sierritos").
16. George Harwood Phillips, "Indians in Los Angeles, 1781–1875: Economic Integration, Social Disintegration," p. 436.
17. Wright, *Yankee,* pp. 54–58.
18. Ibid., p. 16.

19. Monroy, *Strangers*, p. 159.

20. Wright, *Yankee*, pp. 68–70.

21. Ibid., pp. 76–78.

22. Ibid., pp. 80–83.

23. Cleland, *Cattle*, pp. 190–193. According to Cleland, Stearns's statements about what was on Rancho Los Alamitos at the time of his purchase vary markedly. It is not clear exactly what improvements and stock Stearns obtained in addition to the land.

24. Monroy, *Strangers*, p. 160; Cleland, *Cattle*, p. 189.

25. Monroy, *Strangers*, p. 162.

26. Kevin Starr, *Inventing the Dream: California through the Progressive Era*, p. 19.

27. Wright, *Yankee*, pp. 84–90.

28. Ibid., p. 90

29. Cleland, *Cattle*, p. 192–193; Loretta Berner, "Dos Ranchos: Rancho Los Alamitos and Rancho Los Cerritos," p. 86.

30. "Rancho Los Alamitos Historic Structures Report," p. 33.

31. Claudia Jurmain, *Planting Perspectives*, p. 62.

32. Berner, "Dos Ranchos," p. 67.

33. James J. Rawls and Walton Bean, *California, An Interpretive History*, pp. 71–73; Wright, *Yankee*, pp. 121–134.

34. Berner, "Dos Ranchos," p. 69; Sarah Bixby Smith, *Adobe Days*, pp. 62–63.

35. Monroy, *Strangers*, p. 138.

36. Smith, *Adobe Days*, p. 59.

37. Rawls and Bean, *California*, p. 51.

38. Ibid., pp. 69–71.

39. Ibid., pp. 47–52, 71–72; Monroy, *Strangers*, pp. 173–176.

40. Wright, *Yankee*, pp. 121–134.

41. Rawls and Bean, *California*, p. 79; Wright, *Yankee*, pp. 136–144.

42. C. Alan Hutchinson, "The Mexican Government and the Mission Indians of Upper California, 1821–1835," pp. 335–362.

43. Haas, *Conquests*, pp. 56–57.

44. Claudia Jurmain and William McCawley, *O, My Ancestor: Recognition and Renewal for the Gabrielino-Tongva People of the Los Angeles Area*, p. 30.

45. Haas, *Conquests*, p. 57.

46. Ibid.

47. Rawls and Bean, *California*, p. 98.

48. Ibid., p. 102.

49. Jurmain and McCawley, *O, My Ancestor*, p. 29.

50. Ibid., p. 121.

51. Rawls and Bean, *California*, p. 127

52. Jurmain and McCawley, *O, My Ancestor*, p. 48 FN.

53. Ibid., p. 118.

54. George Harwood Phillips, *Chiefs and Challengers*, pp. 76–85.

55. Jurmain and McCawley, *O, My Ancestor*, p. 122.

56. Cleland, *Cattle*, p. 57.

57. Monroy, *Strangers*, p. 180.

58. Berner, "Dos Ranchos," p. 86; Cleland, *Cattle*, pp. 193–194.

59. Kevin Starr, *Americans and the California Dream*, pp. 369–370.

60. Leonard Pitt, *The Decline of the Californios, A Social History of the Spanish-Speaking Californians, 1846–1890*, p. 113.

61. As quoted in Cleland, *Cattle*, p. 58.

62. Jurmain and McCawley, *O, My Ancestor*, p. 29.

63. Phillips, "Indians in Los Angeles," p. 445.

64. As quoted in Cleland, *Cattle*, pp. 59–60.

65. Phillips, "Indians in Los Angeles," p. 449.

66. Jeffrey Altschul Jeffrey, comp. "Puvunga: A Review of the Ethnohistoric, Archaeological, and Ethnographic Issues Surrounding a Gabrielino Rancheria Near Alamitos Bay, Los Angeles County, California," pp. 4–13.

67. Ibid., pp. 4–14.

68. Ibid.

69. Jurmain and McCawley, *O, My Ancestor*, p. 27.

70. Ibid., pp. 20–21.

71. Haas, *Conquests*, p. 64.

72. Ibid., p. 60.

73. Rawls and Bean, *California*, p. 122.

74. Monroy, *Strangers*, p. 203.

75. Starr, *Inventing the Dream*, p. 17.

76. Monroy, *Strangers*, p. 204.

77. Berner, "Dos Ranchos," pp. 75–79.

78. Ibid., pp. 91–94.

79. Cleland, *Cattle*, pp. 102–116.

80. Ibid., p. 119.

81. Ibid., pp. 117–120.

82. Ibid., pp. 125–130.

83. Pitt, *Decline*, p. 247.

84. Wright, *Yankee*, p. 90.

85. As quoted in Cleland, *Cattle*, p. 130

86. Ibid., pp. 130–131.

87. Ibid., p. 131.

88. Ibid.

89. Pitt, *Decline*, p. 247.

90. Cleland, *Cattle*, p. 133.

91. Ibid., pp. 135–136; Pitt, *Decline*, p. 247.

92. Walter H. Case, *History of Long Beach and Vicinity*, p. 62.

93. Berner, "Dos Ranchos," p. 94; Cleland, *Cattle*, p. 202.

94. Cleland, *Cattle*, p. 202; Frances Dinkelspiel, *Towers of Gold: How One Jewish Immigrant Named Isaias Hellman Created California*, p. 37.

95. Dinkelspiel, *Towers*, p. 37.

96. Cleland, *Cattle*, p. 202.

97. Ibid.

98. Ibid.

99. Ibid., p. 203.

100. Ibid., p. 207.

101. Pitt, *Decline*, p.247

102. Smith, *Adobe Days*, p. 55

103. Starr, *Inventing the Dream*, p. 26.

FOUR: PIONEERS ON THE MOVE

1. Sarah Bixby Smith, *Adobe Days*, p. 4.

2. James J. Rawls and Walton Bean, *California: An Interpretive History*, 8th ed., p. 92.

3. Kevin Starr, *Inventing the Dream: California through the Progressive Era*, p. 12.

4. Walton Bean and James J. Rawls, *California: An Interpretive History*, 4th ed., p. 92.

5. Douglas Monroy, *Thrown Among Strangers*, pp. 201–202.

6. William Deverell, *Whitewashed Adobe: The Rise of Los Angeles and the Remaking of its Mexican Past*, p. 13

7. Monroy, *Strangers*, pp. 201–203.

8. Dr. Thomas Flint, "California to Maine and Return," p. 54.

9. Ibid., p. 58.

10. Smith, *Adobe Days*, p. 55

11. Rawls and Bean, *California*, p. 105.

12. Starr, *Inventing the Dream*, p. 19.

13. Rawls and Bean, *California*, p. 105.

14. Smith, *Adobe Days*, p. 27.

15. Ibid., p. 38.

16. David Lavender, *The Southwest*.

17. Frances Dinkelspiel, *Towers of Gold: How One Jewish Immigrant Named Isaias Hellman Created California*, pp. 42–43.

18. Flint, "California to Maine," p. 63

19. Ibid.

20. Ibid., p. 64.

21. Ibid., pp. 72–73.

22. Ibid., pp. 74–75.

23. Ibid., p. 82.

24. Ibid., p. 72.

25. Ibid., pp. 75, 79–81, 85, 90.

26. Ibid., pp. 105–106, 109, 118–119, 122–123.

27. Ibid., pp. 100–101.

28. Ibid., p. 125.

29. Ibid., pp. 125–127.

30. Robert Glass Cleland, *The Cattle on a Thousand Hills*, p. 319, N8.3.

31. Smith, *Adobe Days*, p. 55.

32. Dinkelspiel, *Towers*, pp. 25–26.

33. Deverell, *Whitewashed Adobe*, p. 14

34. Quoted in Monroy, *Strangers*, p. 208.

35. Starr, *Inventing the Dream*, p. 13.

36. Deverell, *Whitewashed Adobe*, p. 26.

37. Ibid., p. 15

38. Monroy, *Strangers*, p. 204.

39. Ibid., p. 205.

40. Ibid.

41. Deverell, *Whitewashed Adobe*, p. 16.

42. Ibid., p. 18.

43. Starr, *Inventing the Dream*, p. 21.

44. Monroy, *Strangers*, pp. 222–223.

45. Howard R. Lamar, ed., "William Welles Hollister."

46. Smith, *Adobe Days*, p. 44.

47. Ibid., p. 45

48. Ibid., p. 46.

49. Ibid.

50. Ibid., pp. 51, 95.

51. Ibid., p. 51.

52. Ibid., p. 95.

53. Ibid., p. 45.

54. Ibid.

55. Ibid., pp. 47, 55.

56. Cleland, *Cattle*, p. 141.

57. Ibid., p. 139

58. Monroy, *Strangers*, p. 231.

59. Ibid.

60. Deverell, *Whitewashed Adobe*, p. 12.

61. Monroy, *Strangers*, p. 225.

62. Dinkelspiel, *Towers*, pp. 41–42.

63. Ibid., pp. 41–42, 47.

64. Ibid., pp. 49–50.

65. Monroy, *Strangers*, p. 235.

66. Dinkelspiel, *Towers*, pp. 49–50, pp. 108–111.

67. Starr, *Inventing the Dream*, p. 39.

68. Cleland, *The Irvine Ranch of Orange County*, pp. 43, 45, 58, 68, 72.

69. Walter H. Case, *History of Long Beach and Vicinity*, vol. 1, p. 63.

70. Cleland, *Irvine Ranch*, pp. 58–72.

71. Cleland, *Cattle*, p. 141.

72. Stephen Dudley, "The Bixby Family Quick Reference Guide," p. 15.

73. Larry Meyer and Patricia L. Kalayjian, *Long Beach: Fortune's Harbor*, p. 34.

74. W. W. Robinson, *Land in California*, p. 209.

75. Starr, *Inventing the Dream*, pp. 38–39.

76. Cleland, *Cattle*, pp. 152–153, 224; Starr, *Inventing the Dream*, pp. 52–53.

77. Mary A. Helmich, "Butterfield Overland Mail."

78. Charles Outland, *Stagecoaching on El Camino Real: Los Angeles to San Francisco, 1861–1901*, p. 983.

79. Cleland, *Cattle*, pp. 202–207.

80. Dinkelspiel, *Towers*, pp. 77–78.

FIVE: A PLACE TO SETTLE, A TIME TO BUILD

1. Carey McWilliams, *Southern California: An Island on the Land*, p. 14.

2. Ibid., 113.

3. Stephanie S. Pincetl, *Transforming California: A Political History of Land Use and Development*, p. 2

4. Kevin Starr, *Inventing the Dream: California through the Progressive Era*, p. 164.

5. Ibid., p. 27.

6. Claudia Jurmain and William McCawley, *O, My Ancestor: Recognition and Renewal for the Gabrielino-Tongva People of the Los Angeles Area,* p. 122.

7. Kevin Starr, *Endangered Dreams: The Great Depression in California,* p. 6.

8. David Lavender, *California: Land of New Beginnings,* p. 302.

9. Sarah Bixby Smith, *Adobe Days,* pp. 83–87.

10. Walter H. Case, *History of Long Beach and Vicinity,* p. 63; Smith, *Adobe Days,* pp. 84–85.

11. William McCawley, "Povuu'ngna: The Village at the Center of the World," p. 12.

12. Smith, *Adobe Days,* pp. 84–86; Case, *Long Beach,* p. 63.

13. Smith, *Adobe Days,* p. 55.

14. Lavender, *California,* p. 301.

15. Smith, *Adobe Days,* p. 48; Robert Glass Cleland, *The Irvine Ranch of Orange County,* p. 77.

16. Smith, *Adobe Days,* p. 57.

17. Cleland, *Irvine Ranch,* p. 87.

18. Smith, *Adobe Days,* p. 60.

19. Starr, *Inventing the Dream,* p. 132.

20. Smith, *Adobe Days,* p. 79.

21. Ibid., pp. 59–61; "Alamitos Ranch in the Year of the Grace, 1888," local newspaper account, 1888 (Rancho Los Alamitos Foundation Archives).

22. Smith, *Adobe Days,* pp. 58–60.

23. Ibid., pp. 59–61.

24. Ibid., p. 61.

25. Ibid.

26. Letter from John W. Bixby to his son Fred, January 11, 1885 (Rancho Los Alamitos Foundation Archives).

27. Smith, *Adobe Days* (foreword by Gloria Ricci Lothrop), pp. ix–xii.

28. Smith, *Adobe Days,* p. 77.

29. Ibid., p. 60; Case, *Long Beach,* p. 63; Deed to Rancho Los Alamitos from Michael Reese Estate to John W. Bixby, June 11, 1881 (Rancho Los Alamitos Foundation Archives).

30. Starr, *Inventing the Dream,* p. 132; "Alamitos Ranch...1888."

31. Lavender, *California,* p. 291.

32. Starr, *Inventing the Dream,* p. 131.

33. Ibid., p. 128.

34. Ibid., p. 172.

35. Starr, *Endangered Dreams,* p. 62.

36. Starr, *Inventing the Dream,* p. 165.

37. Local newspaper account, 1888 (Rancho Los Alamitos Foundation Archives).

38. Smith, *Adobe Days,* pp. 77, 116; Susan Lavia, "John W. Bixby, Sheep Rancher, Farmer, Dairyman," pp. 1–3.

39. Smith, *Adobe Days,* p. 77.

40. Deed to Rancho Los Alamitos...June 11, 1881.

41. David C. Streatfield, *California Gardens: Creating a New Eden,* p. 47

42. Ibid., p. 43.

43. William David Estrada, *The Los Angeles Plaza: Sacred and Contested Space,* pp. 98–99.

44. Judith K. Polanich, "Ramona's Baskets: Romance and Reality," p. 153.

45. Ibid., p. 151.

46. Smith, *Adobe Days,* pp. 3, 73; Martha Hathaway, "Reminiscences of My Father."

47. Smith, *Adobe Days,* p. 76.

48. Starr, *Inventing the Dream,* p. 141.

49. McWilliams, *Southern California,* p. 118.

50. Ibid., p. 113.

51. Kaye Briegel, "A Centennial History of the Alamitos Land Company," p. 1.

52. Ibid., pp. 6–9.

53. Ibid.

54. Ibid., p. 5.

55. Ibid., pp. 10–11.

SIX: HOME ON THE RANGE

1. Susanna Bryant Dakin, *The Scent of Violets,* pp. 14–15.

2. Ibid.

3. Memo from Chase Morgan to Joan Hotchkis, January 10, 1977, pp. 9–10 (Rancho Los Alamitos Foundation Archives).

4. Ibid.

5. Fred H. Bixby Cojo Diary, Thursday, May 28, 1896 (Rancho Los Alamitos Foundation Archives).

6. Ann Lage, "The Peaks and the Professors," pp. 1–2.

7. Philip Shabecoff, *A Fierce Green Fire: The American Environmental Movement*, pp. 64–67.

8. Speech given by Fred H. Bixby to the American National Livestock Association, February 1947 (Rancho Los Alamitos Foundation Archives).

9. Dakin, *Scent of Violets*, p. 22.

10. Larry L. Meyer and Patricia Kalayjian, *Long Beach: Fortune's Harbor*, p. 49; Kaye Briegel, "A Centennial History of the Alamitos Land Company," pp. 17–18.

11. *San Francisco Pacific Underwriter and Banker,* June 10, 1923 (Rancho Los Alamitos Foundation Archives).

12. Dakin, *Scent of Violets*, p. 16.

13. Los Angeles Superior Court Case No. 32,958, *Susan P. H. Bixby et al. vs. Los Alamitos Sugar Co.,* April 17, 1901 (Rancho Los Alamitos Foundation Archives).

14. Oral History with Walter Vlasschaert, May 30, 1902 (Rancho Los Alamitos Foundation Archives).

15. Oral History with George Watte, Frank Watte, and Eme Otte, April 12, 1990 (Rancho Los Alamitos Foundation Archives).

16. Oral History with Albert Cosyns, May 16, 1991 (Rancho Los Alamitos Foundation Archives).

17. Kevin Starr, *Inventing the Dream: California through the Progressive Era,* p. 165.

18. *Bixby vs. Los Alamitos Sugar.*

19. Ibid.

20. Morgan-Hotchkis memo.

21. Joan Hotchkis Collection, *Enchanted Ranch* (Hotchkis Collection, California State University Long Beach).

22. Oral History with Florence Elizabeth ("Sister") Bixby and Katharine Bixby Hotchkis by Joan Hotchkis, 1975 (Rancho Los Alamitos Foundation Archives).

23. Carey McWilliams, *Southern California: An Island on the Land*, p. 133.

24. Ibid., p. 130.

25. David Lavender, *Los Angeles, Two Hundred*, p. 57.

26. McWilliams, *Southern California*, p. 134.

27. Dakin, *Scent of Violets*, p. 23.

28. Morgan-Hotchkis memo.

29. Dakin, *Scent of Violets*, p. 48.

30. Janet L. Abu-Lughod, *New York, Chicago, Los Angeles: America's Global Cities*, p. 66.

31. Starr, *Inventing the Dream*, p. 136.

32. Details about ranch procedures from Joan Hotchkis, "Old Timers," consisting of interviews with her mother and aunt, Katharine and "Sister" (Rancho Los Alamitos Foundation Archives).

33. Oral History, F. E. Bixby and K. B. Hotchkis.

34. Katharine Bixby Hotchkis Diary, Tuesday, May 2, 1922 (Rancho Los Alamitos Foundation Archives).

35. Joan Hotchkis, "Old-Timers."

36. Katharine Bixby Hotchkis, *Trip with Father*, p. 1, 3–4, 20.

37. Katharine Bixby Hotchkis, *Trip with Father*.

38. Kenny A. Franks and Paul F. Lambert, *Early California Oil: A Photographic History, 1865–1940*, p. 109.

39. Kevin Starr, *Material Dreams: Southern California through the 1920s*, p. 85.

40. *Oil* by Upton Sinclair, as quoted in Starr, *Material Dreams*, p. 87.

41. Starr, *Material Dreams*, p. 87.

42. Oral History with Lindsay Jewett (former manager of Fred H. Bixby Ranches), May 1986 (Rancho Los Alamitos Foundation Archives).

43. Maurice Telleen, "The First Hundred Years of the American Shire Horse Association," *The Draft Horse Journal* 23, No. 1 (Spring 1986), pp. 12–13.

44. Kevin Starr, *The Dream Endures: California Enters the 1940s*, p. 9.

45. Letter from Fred Bixby to Mr. Truman, The American Shire Horse Association, Des Moines, Iowa, May 8, 1940.

46. Ibid.

47. Kevin Starr, *Endangered Dreams: The Great Depression in California*, p. 64.

48. Oral History with Mike Hernandez, October 3, 1979 (Rancho Los Alamitos Foundation Archives).

49. Oral History with Ray Rodriguez, May 31, 2000 (Rancho Los Alamitos Foundation Archives).

50. Oral History with Antonia Machuco Castillo, August 14, 1998 (Rancho Los Alamitos Foundation Archives).

51. Starr, *Endangered Dreams,* pp. 66–67.

52. William Deverell, *Whitewashed Adobe: The Rise of Los Angeles and the Remaking of its Mexican Past,* p. 38.

53. Starr, *The Dream Endures,* p. 171.

54. Oral History with José Vasquez, February 6, 1988 (Rancho Los Alamitos Foundation Archives).

55. McWilliams, *Southern California,* p. 14.

56. *New York Times,* January 22, 1922.

57. Katharine Bixby Hotchkis Diary, Jan. 16, 1922.

58. Starr, *Material Dreams,* p. 69.

59. Jeremiah B. C. Axelrod, *Inventing Autopia: Dreams and Vision of the Modern Metropolis in Jazz Age Los Angeles,* pp. 49–61.

60. Starr, *Material Dreams,* p. 107.

61. David Lavender, *California: Land of New Beginnings,* p. 372.

62. Katharine Bixby Hotchkis Diary, 1922.

63. *Pacific Underwriter and Banker.*

64. Starr, *Material Dreams,* p. 135

65. Meyer and Kalayjian, *Long Beach,* p. 99.

66. Walton Bean and James J. Rawls, *California: An Interpretive History,* p. 342.

67. Letter from Fred Bixby to I. W. (Warren) Hellman, May 24, 1934 (Rancho Los Alamitos Foundation Archives).

68. Baker, Robert D., et al., *Timeless Heritage: A History of the Forest Service in the Southwest,"* Ch. 7, p. 70.

69. Ibid., p. 71.

70. Shabecoff, *Fierce Green Fire,* pp. 89, 90.

71. "History of Public Land Livestock Grazing," U.S. Dept. of the Interior, Bureau of Land Management, Nevada Field Office, p. 2.

72. Letter from Fred H. Bixby to Del Neal, Three Bar Ranch, Roosevelt, Arizona, February 2, 1934 (Rancho Los Alamitos Foundation Archives).

73. Letter from Fred H. Bixby to Del Neal, Yucca, Arizona, January 24, 1944 (Rancho Los Alamitos Foundation Archives).

74. Letter from Steve Bixby, Secretary of the Tonto Forest Grazing Advisory Board to Mr. Preston Hotchkis, Fred H. Bixby Ranch, CO, 1944 (Rancho Los Alamitos Foundation Archives).

75. Interview with Jeffrey Green by David Lavender, February 17, 1987.

76. Oral History with Elizabeth Florence "Sister" Janeway, November 10, 1984 (Rancho Los Alamitos Foundation Archives).

77. Florence Green Bixby, *Is There a Thing Called Spring.*

78. Oral History with Angie Sisneros Mariscal, August 25, 1988 (Rancho Los Alamitos Foundation Archives).

79. Katharine Bixby Hotchkis Diary, April 22, 1922.

80. Katherine Bixby Hotchkis. *Christmas Eve at Los Alamitos,* 1971.

81. Oral History with Elizabeth Florence "Sister" Bixby Janeway, April 21, 1982 (Rancho Los Alamitos Foundation Archives).

82. Oral History with Eme Otte, May 14, 1987 (Rancho Los Alamitos Foundation Archives).

83. Katharine Bixby Hotchkis Diary, Dec. 8, Dec. 22, 1922.

84. Ibid., June 28, 1922.

85. June Party Invitation, 1920 (Rancho Los Alamitos Foundation Archives).

86. Starr, *The Dream Endures,* pp. 17–18.

87. Katharine Bixby Hotchkis Diary, Feb. 10, 1923.

88. Starr, *Inventing the Dream,* p. 339.

89. Katharine Bixby Hotchkis Diary, Sept. 5, Nov. 3, Nov. 11, 1921.

90. Letter from Florence Elizabeth "Sister" Bixby to her young brother "Icky" (Frederick), May 5, 1926.

91. Starr, *Material Dreams,* p. 131.

92. Florence Green Bixby, *Is There a Thing Called Spring,* "The Old Room."

93. Fred H. Bixby Family, "Declaration of Trust," July 7, 1930; "Rancho Los Alamitos Chronology, 22" (Rancho Los Alamitos Foundation Archives).

94. Pamela Young Lee, "Native American Artifacts in the Ranch House," in "Rancho Los Alamitos Volunteer Service Council Newsletter," August 2009, pp. 4–5.

95. Ibid.

96. Father Geronimo Boscana, *Chinigchinich*, p. 149.

97. Edward D. Castillo, "Description of the Mission Indian Federation," p. 1.

98. Santa Barbara Indian Center and Dwight Dutschke, "A History of American Indians in California: 1905–1933," pp. 1, 3.

99. Claudia Jurmain and William McCawley, *O, My Ancestor: Recognition and Renewal for the Gabrielino-Tongva People of the Los Angeles Area,* pp. 32–33.

100. Ibid., p. 70.

101. Letter from J. Frederick Dawes, Olmsted Brothers Landscape Architects, to Florence Bixby, August 11, 1927.

102. Boscana, *Chinigchinich,* p. 149.

103. Stephanie S. Pincetl, *Transforming California: A Political History of Land Use and Development,* p. 46.

104. Interview with Fred Bixby, *Long Beach Evening Express,* September 23, 1914.

105. Starr, *Material Dreams,* p. 45.

106. Briegel, "A Centennial History," p. 25.

107. Starr, *Material Dreams,* p. 161.

108. Oral History with Angie Sisneros Mariscal.

109. Fred H. Bixby Company Annual Reports, 1931–1961, Bixby Ranch Company, Long Beach.

110. Bixby Cojo Diary, Sept. 6, 7, 8, 1942.

111. Bean and Rawls, *California,* p. 278.

112. Starr, *Inventing the Dream,* p. 172.

113. Pincetl, *Transforming California,* p. 34.

114. McWilliams, *Southern California,* p. 321.

115. Fred H. Bixby interview in Long Beach newspaper, February 10, 1905.

116. Starr, *Endangered Dreams,* p. 62.

117. Bean and Rawls, *California,* p. 280.

118. Kevin Starr, *Golden Dreams: California in an Age of Abundance,* p. 440.

119. Oral History with Ray Rodriguez.

120. Written recollection of Mrs. Chiyo Kawanami Ohira, May 1998 (Rancho Los Alamitos Foundation Archives).

121. Philip L. Martin, *Promise Unfulfilled: Unions, Immigration, and the Farm Workers,* p. 47.

122. Bean and Rawls, *California,* p. 401.

123. Martin, *Promise Unfulfilled,* p. 46.

124. Ibid., p. 47.

125. Letter from Fred H. Bixby to Frank P. Doherty, President, Los Angeles Chamber of Commerce, March 22, 1943 (Ranch Los Alamitos Foundation Archives).

126. Letter from Fred H. Bixby to Governor Earl Warren, March 22, 1943 (Rancho Los Alamitos Foundation Archives).

127. Letter from Fred H. Bixby to Samuel Vickers, Long Beach City Manager, March 27, 1951 (Rancho Los Alamitos Foundation Archives).

128. Katharine Bixby Hotchkis, "Notes" (Rancho Los Alamitos Foundation Archives).

129. Oral History with Florence Elizabeth ("Sister") Bixby Janeway, Nov. 10, 1984.

130. Talk given by Katharine Bixby Hotchkis to the Pasadena Twilight Club at Rancho Los Alamitos, May 28, 1968; Talk given at the Ninth Annual Southern Symposium Conference of the California Historical Societies, Feb. 11, 1967 (Rancho Los Alamitos Foundation Archives).

BIBLIOGRAPHY

Abu-Lughod, Janet L. *New York, Chicago, Los Angeles: America's Global Cities.* Minneapolis: Univ. of Minnesota Press, 1999.

Altschul, Jeffrey, comp. "Puvunga: A Review of the Ethnohistoric, Archaeological, and Ethnographic Issues Surrounding a Gabrielino Rancheria near Alamitos Bay, Los Angeles County, California." Draft Report. Tucson: Statistical Research Technical Series, 1994.

Arizona Cattle Growers Association. "Proceedings of the Sixth Annual Meeting, November 8, 9, and 10, 1911." Accessed Sept. 10, 2009. http://uair.arizona.edu/item/293425.

Axelrod, Jeremiah B. C. *Inventing Autopia: Dreams and Visions of the Modern Metropolis in Jazz Age Los Angeles.* Berkeley: Univ. of California Press, 2009.

Baker, Robert D., et al. "The Pooler Era: 1920–45." In *Timeless Heritage: A History of the Forest Service in the Southwest.* U.S. Forest Service, August 1988. http://www.fs.fed.us/r3/about/history/timeless/index.shtml.

Barclay, Thomas S. "Reapportionment in California." *Pacific Historical Review* 5, No. 2 (June, 1936): 93–129.

Bean, Walton, and James J. Rawls. *California, An Interpretive History.* New York: McGraw-Hill, 1983.

"Beadwork Masterpieces: Native American Bandolier Bags of the Prairies and Lakes." Nevada State Historical Society, Feb. 4, 2005. http://www.nebraskahistory.org/sites/mnh/bandolier_bags/index.htm.

Berner, Loretta. "Dos Ranchos: Rancho Los Alamitos and Rancho Los Cerritos." Unpublished manuscript, 1990 (Rancho Los Alamitos Archives).

Bixby, Florence Green. *Is There a Thing Called Spring.* Pasadena, Calif.: Ward Ritchie Press, 1936 (Rancho Los Alamitos Foundation Archives).

Boscana, Father Gerónimo. *Chinigchinich: A Revised and Annotated Version of Alfred Robinson's Translation of Father Gerónimo Boscana's Historical Account of the Belief, Usages, Customs and Extravagencies of the Indians of this Mission of San Juan Capistrano, Called the Acagchemem Tribe.* Santa Ana, Calif.: Fine Arts Press, 1933.

Briegel, Kaye. "A Centennial History of the Alamitos Land Company." *Southern California Quarterly,* Summer 1988.

Carrico, Richard L. "San Diego Indians and the Federal Government: Years of Neglect, 1850–1865." *Journal of San Diego History* 26, No. 3 (Summer 1980).

Case, Walter H. *History of Long Beach and Vicinity.* Vol. 1. Chicago: S. J. Clarke, 1927.

Castillo, Edward D. "Description of the Mission Indian Federation." University of California, Irvine, School of Humanities. Accessed Dec. 4, 2009. www.hnet.uci.edu/IDP/nativeam/mif.html.

Caughey, John Walton, ed. *The Indians of Southern California in 1852: The B. D. Wilson Report and a Selection of Contemporary Comment.* Lincoln: Univ. of Nebraska Press, 1995.

Cleland, Robert Glass. *The Cattle on a Thousand Hills: Southern California, 1850–1880.* San Marino, Calif.: The Huntington Library, 1969.

———. *The Irvine Ranch of Orange County.* San Marino, Calif.: The Huntington Library, 1966.

Dakin, Susanna Bryant. *The Scent of Violets.* San Francisco, 1968.

———. *A Scotch Paisano in Old Los Angeles: Hugo Reid's Life in California, 1832–1852.* Berkeley: Univ. of California Press, 1978.

Deverell, William. *Whitewashed Adobe: The Rise of Los Angeles and the Remaking of Its Mexican Past.* Berkeley: Univ. of California Press, 2005.

Dinkelspiel, Frances. *Towers of Gold: How One Jewish Immigrant Named Isaías Hellman Created California.* New York: St. Martin's Press, 2008.

Dudley, Stephen. "The Bixby Family Quick Reference Guide." Long Beach: The Alamitos Land Company and Bixby Land Company, 1979.

Estrada, William David. *The Los Angeles Plaza: Sacred and Contested Space.* Austin: Univ. of Texas Press, 2008.

"Fact Sheet on the BLM's Management of Livestock Grazing." U.S. Dept. of the Interior, Bureau of Land Management, National, Aug. 19, 2010. http://www.blm.gov/wo/st/en/prog/grazing.1.html.

Flint, Richard, and Shirley Cushing Flint. "Fred Harvey and the Fred Harvey Company." New Mexico Office of the State Historian. Accessed Sept. 10, 2010. http://www.newmexicohistory.org/filedetails.php?fileID=21238.

Flint, Dr. Thomas. "California to Maine and Return." *Historical Society of California Annual Publications* 12, part 3:53–127.

Franks, Kenny A., and Paul F. Lambert. *Early California Oil: A Photographic History, 1865–1940.* College Station: Texas A&M Univ. Press, 1985.

Haas, Lisbeth. *Conquests and Historical Identities in California 1769–1936.* Berkeley: Univ. of California Press, 1996.

Hackel, Steven W. *Children of Coyote, Missionaries of Saint Francis: Indian-Spanish Relations in Colonial California, 1769–1850.* Chapel Hill: Univ. of North Carolina Press, 2005.

Harrington, John P. "Annotations." In *Chinigchinich: A Revised and Annotated Version of Alfred Robinson's Translation of Father Gerónimo Boscana's Historical Account...* Banning, Calif.: Malki Museum Press, 1978.

Hart, James D. *A Companion to California.* New York: Oxford University Press, 1978.

Hathaway, Martha. "Reminiscences of My Father." no date (Rancho Los Alamitos Foundation Archives).

Heizer, Robert F., ed. *The Indians of Los Angeles County: Hugo Reid's Letters of 1852.* Los Angeles: Southwest Museum, 1968.

Helmich, Mary A. "Butterfield Overland Mail." California State Parks, 2008. Accessed Sept. 10, 2010. http://www.parks.ca.gov/?page_id=25444.

Hise, Greg, and William Deverell. *Eden by Design: The 1930 Olmsted-Bartholomew Plan for the Los Angeles Region.* Berkeley: Univ. of California Press, 2000.

"History of Public Land Livestock Grazing." U.S. Dept. of the Interior, Bureau of Land Management, Nevada Field Office, July 17, 2009. http://www.blm.gov/nv/st/en/prog/grazing/history_of_public.html.

"History: Sierra Club Timeline." Sierra Club. Accessed Sept. 10, 2010. http://www.sierraclub.org/history/timeline.asp.

Hoag, Maury. *Stagecoaching on the California Coast: The Coast Line Stage from Los Angeles to San Juan.* Santa Barbara: Fithian Press, 2001.

Hotchkis, Katharine Bixby. *Christmas Eve at Los Alamitos.* San Francisco: California Historical Society, 1971.

———. *Trip with Father.* San Francisco: California Historical Society, 1971.

Hutchinson, C. Alan. "The Mexican Government and the Mission Indians of Upper California, 1821–1835." *The Americas* 21: 335–362.

Hutchinson, W. H. *Two Centuries of Man, Land, and Growth in the Golden State.* Palo Alto, Calif.: American West, 1969.

Jurmain, Claudia, and William McCawley. *O, My Ancestor: Recognition and Renewal for the Gabrielino-Tongva People of the Los Angeles Area.* Berkeley: Heyday Books and Rancho Los Alamitos Foundation, 2009.

"Key Concepts." Resilience Alliance. Accessed Jan. 19, 2009. http://www.resalliance.org564.php.

Kirsch, Robert R., and William S. Murphy. *West of the West: Witnesses to the California Experience, 1542–1906.* New York: Dutton, 1967.

Lage, Ann. "The Peaks and the Professors: University Names in the High Sierra." *Chronicle of the University of California* 3 (Spring 2000): 91–98.

Lamar, Howard R., ed. "William Welles Hollister." In *The Reader's Encyclopedia of the American West.* New York: Harper and Row, 1977.

"The Landscape Architects." The Athenaeum, California Institute of Technology. Accessed Sept. 8, 2010. http://athenaeum.caltech.edu/Yoch.html.

Lavender, David. *California: Land of New Beginnings.* Lincoln: Univ. of Nebraska Press, 1987.

———. *Los Angeles, Two Hundred.* Tulsa: Continental Heritage Press, 1980.

———. *The Southwest.* New York: Harper and Row, 1980.

Lavia, Susan. "John W. Bixby, Sheep Rancher, Farmer, Dairyman." *The Branded Word* (Winter 1987): 1–3.

Lee, Pamela Young. "Native American Artifacts in the Ranch House." *Rancho Los Alamitos Volunteer Service Council Newsletter* (August 2009).

Marinacci, Barbara. "Doña Arcadia, Santa Monica's Godmother." *Previews* 6, No. 1 (January 1985): 13.

Martin, Philip L. *Promise Unfulfilled: Unions, Immigration, and the Farm Workers.* Ithaca: Cornell Univ. Press, 2003.

McCawley, William. "Continuity within Change: Cultural Memory and Survival." Unpublished manuscript, 2007 (Rancho Los Alamitos Foundation).

———. "An Ethnographic-Ethnohistoric Survey of Povuu'nga–Rancho Los Alamitos." California State University, Los Angeles: Cultural Resources Management Report 80, 1994.

———. *The First Angelinos: The Gabrielino Indians of Los Angeles.* Banning, Calif.: Malki Museum/Ballena Press, 1996.

———. "From Village to City: Identity in a Changing World." Unpublished manuscript, 2007 (Rancho Los Alamitos Foundation).

———. "Povuu'ngna: The Village at the Center of the World." Unpublished manuscript, 2007 (Rancho Los Alamitos Foundation).

McWilliams, Carey. *Southern California: An Island on the Land.* Salt Lake City: Peregrine Smith Books, 1973.

Meyer, Larry L., and Patricia Kalayjian. *Long Beach: Fortune's Harbor.* Tulsa: Continental Heritage Press, 1983.

Milliken, Randall, and William R. Hildebrandt. "Assessment of Archaeological Resources at the Rancho Los Alamitos Historic Ranch and Gardens." Davis, Calif.: Far Western Anthropological Research Group, October 1997.

Monroy, Douglas. *Thrown Among Strangers: The Making of Mexican Culture in Frontier California.* Berkeley: Univ. of California Press, 1990.

Montenegro, Maywa, and Terry Glavin. "In Defense of Difference." *Seed* (October 2008): 73–82.

Nadeau, Remi A. *City Makers: The Story of Southern California's First Boom, 1868–76.* Los Angeles: Trans-Anglo Books, 1965.

Newmark, Harris. *Sixty Years in Southern California, 1853–1913.* New York: Knickerbocker Press, 1916.

Orange County Genealogical Society. *Saddleback Ancestors: Rancho Families of Orange County, California.* Orange, Calif.: Orange County Genealogical Society, 1969.

Outland, Charles. *Stagecoaching on El Camino Real: Los Angeles to San Francisco, 1861–1901.* Glendale, Calif.: Arthur H. Clark Co., 1907.

Phillips, George Harwood. *Chiefs and Challengers: Indian Resistance and Cooperation in Southern California.* Berkeley: Univ. of California Press, 1975.

———. "Indians in Los Angeles, 1781–1875: Economic Integration, Social Disintegration." *Pacific Historical Review* 49, no. 3 (August 1980): 427–451.

Pincetl, Stephanie S. *Transforming California: A Political History of Land Use and Development.* Baltimore: Johns Hopkins Univ. Press, 1999.

Pitt, Leonard. *The Decline of the Californios: A Social History of the Spanish-Speaking Californians, 1846–1890.* Berkeley: Univ. of California Press, 1998.

Polanich, Judith K. "Ramona's Baskets: Romance and Reality." *American Indian Culture and Research Journal* 21 (1997): 145–162.

"Rancho Los Alamitos Historic Structures Report." Rancho Los Alamitos Foundation, Feb. 1989.

Rawls, James J. *Indians of California: The Changing Image.* Norman: Univ. of Oklahoma Press, 1984.

Rawls, James J., and Walton Bean. *California: An Interpretive History.* New York: McGraw-Hill, 2002.

Reisler, Mark. "Always the Laborer, Never the Citizen: Anglo Perceptions of the Mexican Immigrant during the 1920s." *Pacific Historical Review* 45, no. 2 (May 1976): 231–254.

Robinson, W. W. *Land in California.* Berkeley: Univ. of California Press, 1948.

———. *Ranchos Become Cities.* Pasadena, Calif.: San Pasqual Press, 1939.

San Diego History Center. *San Diego Biographies.* "Juan Bandini (1800–1859)." Accessed Dec. 2009. https://www.sandiegohistory.org/bio/bandini/bandini.htm.

Santa Barbara Indian Center and Dwight Dutschke. *Five Views: An Ethnic Historic Site Survey for California,* "A History of American Indians in California: 1905–1933." National Park Service. Sacramento: California Dept. of

Parks and Recreation, 1988. http://www.nps.gov/history/history/online_books/5views/5views1e.htm.

Shabecoff, Philip. *A Fierce Green Fire: The American Environmental Movement.* New York: Hill and Wang, 1993.

Smith, Sarah Bixby. *Adobe Days.* Lincoln: Univ. of Nebraska Press, 1987.

Starr, Kevin. *Americans and the California Dream, 1850–1915.* New York: Oxford Univ. Press, 1973.

———. *The Dream Endures: California Enters the 1940s.* New York: Oxford Univ. Press, 1997.

———. *Endangered Dreams: The Great Depression in California.* New York: Oxford Univ Press, 1996.

———. *Golden Dreams: California in an Age of Abundance, 1950–1963.* New York: Oxford Univ. Press, 2009.

———. *Inventing the Dream: California through the Progressive Era.* New York: Oxford Univ. Press, 1985.

———. *Material Dreams: Southern California through the 1920s.* New York: Oxford Univ. Press, 1990.

"A State Park System Is Born." California State Parks. Accessed Sept. 10, 2010. http://www.parks.ca.gov/?page_id=940.

Streatfield, David C. *California Gardens: Creating a New Eden.* New York: Abbeville Press, 1994.

"The Taylor Grazing Act." U.S. Dept. of the Interior Bureau of Land Management, Wyoming, Casper Field Office, May 29, 2008. http://www.blm.gov/wy/st/en/field_offices/Casper/range/taylor.1.html.

Tompkins, Walker A. *Little Giant of Signal Hill: An Adventure in American Enterprise.* Englewood Cliffs, N.J.: Prentice-Hall, 1964.

Wright, Doris Marion. *A Yankee in California: Abel Stearns, 1798–1848.* Santa Barbara, Calif.: Wallace Hebberd, 1977.

Zakian, Michael. "The Art Collection of Fred and Florence Bixby." Unpublished manuscript, 1992 (Rancho Los Alamitos Foundation).

The espedientes and U.S. Land Commission Case 404 documents that appear in Chapters 2 and 3 are from the National Archives, Los Angeles Branch at Laguna Niguel; California State Archives; and The Bancroft Library, University of California, except as noted. Copies of these and the unpublished work "Los Dos Ranchos" can be found in the Rancho Los Alamitos Archives, as can the remaining primary source material.

INDEX

ABOUT THE AUTHORS

CLAUDIA JURMAIN is Director of Special Projects and Publications at Rancho Los Alamitos Historic Ranch and Gardens in Long Beach, California. She began her work at the Smithsonian Institution as a research historian in the National Portrait Gallery and since then has developed and produced award-winning projects for museums, sites, and educational institutions across the country. She is coeditor of *California: A Place, A People, A Dream* (1986), author of *Planting Perspectives: The Landscape at Rancho Los Alamitos* (2000), and coauthor of *O, My Ancestor: Recognition and Renewal for the Gabrielino-Tongva People of the Los Angeles Area* (2009).

DAVID LAVENDER, the renowned author of over forty books on the American West, was nominated for the Pulitzer Prize for his *Bent's Fort* and *Land of the Giants*. Born in Telluride, Colorado, he worked in a silver mine early on, was a cowboy on his stepfather's ranch before the Depression, climbed the peaks of Colorado, and rafted rivers. He graduated from Princeton University and for many years taught English at Thacher School in Ojai, California, where he lived most of his adult life. Admired for their scholarship and verve, David Lavender's books echo his ready familiarity with the places and people he wrote about, and they are an enduring contribution to western history.

LARRY L. MEYER has written seven previous books, including *Shadow of a Continent: The Prize That Lay to the West in 1776; California Quake; Long Beach: Fortune's Harbor;* and *My Summer with Molly: The Journal of a Second Generation Father*—winner of the 1990 Benjamin Franklin Award for Autobiography. Meyer is a professor emeritus in journalism at California State University, Long Beach, where he headed the department's Magazine Option for fifteen years. Prior to that he held the position of editor-in-chief at *Westways* and *Colorado* magazines.

HEYDAY
into California

About Heyday

Heyday is an independent, nonprofit publisher and unique cultural institution. We promote widespread awareness and celebration of California's many cultures, landscapes, and boundary-breaking ideas. Through our well-crafted books, public events, and innovative outreach programs we are building a vibrant community of readers, writers, and thinkers.

Thank You

It takes the collective effort of many to create a thriving literary culture. We are thankful to all the thoughtful people we have the privilege to engage with. Cheers to our writers, artists, editors, storytellers, designers, printers, bookstores, critics, cultural organizations, readers, and book lovers everywhere! We are especially grateful for the generous funding we've received for our publications and programs during the past year from foundations and hundreds of individual donors. Major supporters include:

Anonymous; Audubon California; Barona Band of Mission Indians; B.C.W. Trust III; S. D. Bechtel, Jr. Foundation; Barbara and Fred Berensmeier; Berkeley Civic Arts Program and Civic Arts Commission; Joan Berman; Peter and Mimi Buckley; Lewis and Sheana Butler; Butler Koshland Fund; California Council for the Humanities; California Indian Heritage Center Foundation; California State Coastal Conservancy; California State Library; California Wildlife Foundation / California Oak Foundation; Keith Campbell Foundation; John and Nancy Cassidy Family Foundation, through Silicon Valley Community Foundation; Christensen Fund; Compton Foundation; Creative Work Fund; Lawrence Crooks; Nik Dehejia; Donald and Janice Elliott, in honor of David Elliott, through Silicon Valley Community Foundation; Evergreen Foundation; Federated Indians of Graton Rancheria; Mark and Tracy Ferron; Furthur Foundation; George Gamble; The Fred Gellert Family Foundation; Wallace Alexander Gerbode Foundation; Richard & Rhoda Goldman Fund; Wanda Lee Graves and Stephen Duscha; Evelyn & Walter Haas, Jr. Fund; Walter & Elise Haas Fund; James and Coke Hallowell; Sandra and Chuck Hobson; James Irvine Foundation; JiJi Foundation; Marty and Pamela Krasney; Robert and Karen Kustel, in honor of Bruce Kelley; Guy Lampard and Suzanne Badenhoop; LEF Foundation; Michael McCone; Moore Family Foundation; National Endowment for the Arts; National Park Service; David and Lucile Packard Foundation; Pease Family Fund, in honor of Bruce Kelley; PhotoWings; Resources Legacy Fund; Alan Rosenus; Rosie the Riveter/ WWII Home Front NHP; The San Francisco Foundation; San Manuel Band of Mission Indians; Deborah Sanchez; Savory Thymes; Hans Schoepflin; Contee and Maggie Seely; James B. Swinerton; Swinerton Family Fund; Taproot Foundation; TomKat Charitable Trust; Lisa Van Cleef and Mark Gunson; Marion Weber; John Wiley & Sons; Peter Booth Wiley; and Yocha Dehe Wintun Nation.

Board of Directors

Michael McCone (Chairman), Barbara Boucke, Steve Costa, Nik Dehejia, Peter Dunckel, Karyn Y. Flynn, Theresa Harlan, Nancy Hom, Susan Ives, Bruce Kelley, Marty Krasney, Guy Lampard, Katharine Livingston, R. Jeffrey Lustig, Lee Swenson, Jim Swinerton, Lisa Van Cleef, and Lynne Withey.

Getting Involved

To learn more about our publications, events, membership club, and other ways you can participate, please visit www.heydaybooks.com.